T0178332

Lecture Notes of the Institute for Computer Sciences, Social Informatics and Telecommunications Engineering 473

The LNICST series publishes ICST's conferences, symposia and workshops. It reports state-of-the-art results in areas related to the scope of the Institute.

LNICST reports state-of-the-art results in areas related to the scope of the Institute. The type of material published includes

- Proceedings (published in time for the respective event)
- Other edited monographs (such as project reports or invited volumes)

LNICST topics span the following areas:

- General Computer Science
- E-Economy
- E-Medicine
- Knowledge Management
- Multimedia
- Operations, Management and Policy
- Social Informatics
- Systems

Cong Vinh Phan · Thanh Dung Nguyen
Editors

Nature of Computation and Communication

8th EAI International Conference, ICTCC 2022
Vinh Long, Vietnam, October 27–28, 2022
Proceedings

Editors
Cong Vinh Phan 🆔
Nguyen Tat Thanh University
Ho Chi Minh City, Vietnam

Thanh Dung Nguyen
Mekong University
Vinh Long Province, Vietnam

ISSN 1867-8211 ISSN 1867-822X (electronic)
Lecture Notes of the Institute for Computer Sciences, Social Informatics
and Telecommunications Engineering
ISBN 978-3-031-28789-3 ISBN 978-3-031-28790-9 (eBook)
https://doi.org/10.1007/978-3-031-28790-9

Preface

ICTCC 2022 (the 8th EAI International Conference on Nature of Computation and Communication), was held during October 27–28, 2022 at Mekong University in Vinh Long province, Vietnam, in hybrid style, due to the travel restrictions caused by the worldwide COVID-19 pandemic. The aim of the conference is to provide an internationally respected forum for scientific research in the technologies and applications of natural computing and communication. ICTCC provides an excellent opportunity for researchers to discuss modern approaches and techniques for natural computing systems and their applications.

For this eighth edition of ICTCC, and repeating the success of the previous year, the Program Committee received submissions from authors in six countries and each paper was reviewed by at least three expert reviewers. We chose 11 papers after intensive discussions held among the Program Committee members. We really appreciate the excellent reviews and lively discussions of the Program Committee members and external reviewers in the review process. This year we had three prominent invited speakers, Giacomo Cabri from the University of Modena and Reggio Emilia in Italy, Hafiz Mahfooz Ul Haque from the University of Central Punjab in Pakistan and Dang Thanh Tin from Ho Chi Minh City University of Technology, HCM-VNU in Vietnam. ICTCC 2022 was jointly organized by the European Alliance for Innovation (EAI), Mekong University (MKU), and Nguyen Tat Thanh University (NTTU). This conference could not have been organized without the strong support of the staff members of the three organizations. We would especially like to thank Imrich Chlamtac (University of Trento), Patricia Gabajova (EAI), and Martin Vojtek (EAI) for their great help in organizing the conference. We also appreciate the gentle guidance and help of Luong Minh Cu, Rector of MKU.

October 2022

Cong Vinh Phan
Thanh Dung Nguyen

Organization

Steering Committee

Imrich Chlamtac	Bruno Kessler Professor, University of Trento, Italy
Phan Cong Vinh	Nguyen Tat Thanh University, Vietnam

Organizing Committee

General Chair

Phan Cong Vinh   Nguyen Tat Thanh University, Vietnam

Honorary General Chair

Luong Minh Cu   Mekong University, Vietnam

Technical Program Committee Chairs

Nguyen Thanh Dung	Mekong University, Vietnam
Nguyen Thanh Binh	Ho Chi Minh City University of Technology, HCM-VNU, Vietnam

Web Chairs

Nguyen Van Han	Nguyen Tat Thanh University, Vietnam
Nguyen Thanh Trung	Mekong University, Vietnam

Publicity and Social Media Chairs

Nguyen Kim Quoc	Nguyen Tat Thanh University, Vietnam
Nguyen Thanh Tam	Mekong University, Vietnam

Workshops Chair

Hafiz Mahfooz Ul Haque   University of Central Punjab, Pakistan

Sponsorship & Exhibits Chair

Bach Long Giang   Nguyen Tat Thanh University, Vietnam

Publications Chair

Phan Cong Vinh   Nguyen Tat Thanh University, Vietnam

Local Chairs

Nguyen Thanh Dung   Mekong University, Vietnam
Tran Thi Hong Lan   State Agency of Technology Innovation, Ministry
                                   of Science and Technology, Vietnam

Technical Program Committee

Technical Program Committee Chairs

Abdur Rakib   Coventry University, UK
Nguyen Thanh Dung   Mekong University, Vietnam

Technical Program Committee Members

Anh Dinh   University of Saskatchewan, Canada
Ashish Khare   University of Allahabad, India
Bui Cong Giao   Saigon University, Vietnam
Cao Van Kien   Nguyen Tat Thanh University, Vietnam
Chernyi Sergei   Admiral Makarov State University of Maritime
                                   and Inland Shipping, Russia
Chien-Chih Yu   National ChengChi University, Taiwan
Dang Thanh Tin   Ho Chi Minh City University of Technology,
                                   Vietnam
David Sundaram   University of Auckland, New Zealand
Gabrielle Peko   University of Auckland, New Zealand
Giacomo Cabri   University of Modena and Reggio Emilia, Italy
Hafiz Mahfooz Ul Haque   University of Central Punjab, Pakistan
Harun Baraki   University of Kassel, Germany
Hiroshi Fujita   Gifu University, Japan
Huynh Xuan Hiep   Can Tho University, Vietnam
Hyungchul Yoon   Chungbuk National University, South Korea

Issam Damaj	Beirut Arab University, Lebanon
Kurt Geihs	University of Kassel, Germany
Le Hoang Thai	Ho Chi Minh City University of Science, Vietnam
Le Hong Anh	University of Mining and Geology, Vietnam
Le Xuan Truong	Ho Chi Minh City Open University, Vietnam
Manish Khare	Dhirubhai Ambani Institute of Information and Communication Technology, India
Muhammad Athar Javed Sethi	University of Engineering and Technology (UET) Peshawar, Pakistan
Ngo Ha Quang Thinh	Ho Chi Minh City University of Technology, Vietnam
Nguyen Ha Huy Cuong	Da Nang University, Vietnam
Nguyen Huu Nhan	Nguyen Tat Thanh University, Vietnam
Nguyen Manh Duc	University of Ulsan, South Korea
Nguyen Thanh Hai	Can Tho University, Vietnam
Om Prakash	Hemvati Nandan Bahuguna Garhwal University, India
Pham Quoc Cuong	Ho Chi Minh City University of Technology, Vietnam
Rajiv Tewari	University of Allahabad, India
Shahzad Ashraf	Hohai University, China
Tran Huu Tam	University of Kassel, Germany
Truong Cong Doan	International School, VNU, Vietnam
Vu Tuan Anh	Industrial University of Ho Chi Minh City, Vietnam
Waralak V. Siricharoen	Silpakorn University, Thailand

Contents

Fuzzy Logic, Quantum Logic, Data Virtualization, Automated Test

Modeling with Words: Steps Towards a Fuzzy Quantum Logic 3
 Nguyen Van Han and Phan Cong Vinh

Proposed Solution for Log Collection and Analysis in Kubernetes
Environment 9
 Josef Horalek, Patrik Urbanik, Vladimir Sobeslav, and Tomas Svoboda

Automated Tests Using Selenium Framework 23
 Josef Horalek, Patrik Urbanik, and Vladimir Sobeslav

Data Mining

The Performance of a Kernel-Based Variable Dimension Reduction Method ... 43
 Thanh Do Van and Hai Nguyen Minh

Detecting Major Extrema in Streaming Time Series 61
 Bui Cong Giao and Ho Van Cuu

Use of Raman Spectroscopy to Diagnose Diabetes with SVM 79
 Le Anh Duc and Nguyen Thanh Tung

A New Approach for Visual Analytics Applying to Multivariate Data
of Student Intakes in the University 88
 Dang Van Pham, Vinh Cong Phan, and Nam Hoang Do

Machine Learning, Deep Learning

Predicting Academic Performance of High School Students 123
 Nguyen Dinh-Thanh and Pham Thi-Ngoc-Diem

Gross Domestic Product Prediction in Various Countries with Classic
Machine Learning Techniques 136
 Chi Le Hoang Tran, Trang Huyen Phan, Pham Thi-Ngoc-Diem,
 and Hai Thanh Nguyen

Palmprint Recognition Using Learning Discriminant Line Direction
Descriptors 148
  Hoang Van Thien, Thong Dinh Duy Phan, and Thai Hoang Le

Layering Images with Convolution Neural Networks on Cloud Computing 160
  Tam Van Nguyen, Luan Khanh Tran, Tu Cam Thi Tran,
  and Hiep Xuan Huynh

Author Index 173

Fuzzy Logic, Quantum Logic, Data Virtualization, Automated Test

Modeling with Words: Steps Towards a Fuzzy Quantum Logic

Nguyen Van Han[ID] and Phan Cong Vinh[(✉)][ID]

Faculty of Information Technology, Nguyen Tat Thanh University,
300A Nguyen Tat Thanh Street, Ward 13, District 4,
Ho Chi Minh City, Vietnam
{nvhan,pcvinh}@ntt.edu.vn

Abstract. On 1936, Birkhoff and von Newmann proposed the introduction of a "quantum logic", as the lattice of quantum mechanical proposition which is not distributive and also not a Boolean. Seven years later, Mackey tried to provide a set of axioms for the propositional system to predict of the outcome set of experiments. He indicated that the system is an orthocomplemented partially ordered set. Physical complex systems can be modeled by using linguistic variables which are variables whose values may be expressed in terms of a specific natural or artificial language, for example $\mathbb{L}=\{$*very less young; less young; young; more young; very young; very very young* ...$\}$. In language of hedge algebra ($\mathbb{HA}$), $\mathbb{L}$ set which is generated from $\mathbb{HA}$ is the POSET (partial order set). In this paper, we introduce a quantum logic ℓ to assert that, let $\perp$ be the orthocomplementation map $\perp : \ell \rightarrow \ell$, all $\clubsuit, \spadesuit \in \perp$ must satisfy the following conditions:

- $(\clubsuit^{\perp})^{\perp} = \clubsuit$
- If $\spadesuit \leq \clubsuit$ then $\clubsuit^{\perp} \leq \spadesuit^{\perp}$
- The greatest lower bound $\clubsuit \vee \clubsuit^{\perp} \in \ell$ and the least upper bound $\clubsuit \wedge \clubsuit^{\perp} \in \ell$

Keywords: Linguiatic variable · Fuzzy quantum logic · Quantum bit

1 Introduction

Fuzzy set, linguistic fuzzy logic and fuzzy dynamic system have been studied and applied in artificial intelligence such as neural network as well as machine learning. Fuzzy set or "computing with words" (CWW) was introduced by Lotfi A. Zadeh in 1965 as an extension of the classical notion of set [15, 22, 23] and was just a tool to knowledge represent and reasoning in intelligent system [16]. As Zadeh indicated in [16], human acknowledgment is nothing different from words. In daily activity, we see the real world through words. Many smart devices established based on CWW such as fuzzy neural network, fuzzy querying, fuzzy data mining, and so on have been studied [2, 6, 7, 13, 14, 20] In Quantum information

© ICST Institute for Computer Sciences, Social Informatics and Telecommunications Engineering 2023
Published by Springer Nature Switzerland AG 2023. All Rights Reserved
C. V. Phan and T. D. Nguyen (Eds.): ICTCC 2022, LNICST 473, pp. 3–8, 2023.
https://doi.org/10.1007/978-3-031-28790-9_1

science [1, 5, 17], fuzzy logic holds important roles in modeling and verifying quantum computing and has been developed for decades [21]. Together with fuzzy logic, fuzzy set and fuzzy Z-number have also widely been applied in quantum fuzzy set [18] and quantum Z-number [3]. The rest of the paper is organized as follows: Sect. 2 recalls some of the main foundation concepts of quantum fuzzy logic and linguistic variables that are set up on hedge algebra $\mathbb{HA}$ [8–10, 12–14]. Section 3 proposes a quantum linguistic fuzzy logic. Section 4 outlines summaries and forthcoming work.

2 Preliminary: Linguistic Variables and Quantum Fuzzy Logic

This section revises relational knowledgement in both fuzzy quantum logic ($\mathbb{FQL}$) and linguistic fuzzy quantum logic ($\mathbb{LQL}$) that associate with our study paper.

2.1 Quantum Fuzzy Logic

Element of quantum logic ($\mathbb{QL}$) is orthomodular partial order set (poset), which is defined in [21].

Definition 1. *In [21], a non-empty set L together with a binary relation $\leq$ on it is said to be a poset if for $\forall a, b, c \in L$, we have:*

1. $a \leq a$ *(reflexive property)*
2. *if $a \leq b$ and $b \leq a$, then $a = b$ (antisymmetric property).*
3. *if $a \leq b$ and $b \leq c$, then $a = c$ (transitive property).*

For estimating $\mathbb{QL}$, it is based on distributive and modular lattices

Definition 2. *In [21], for any a, b, $c \in L$, a distributive lattice is a lattice, which satisfies the following two conditions:*

$$a \wedge (b \vee c) = (a \wedge b) \vee (a \wedge c), \tag{1}$$
$$a \vee (b \vee c) = (a \vee b) \wedge (a \vee c), \tag{2}$$

In which, the meet $\wedge$ operation has a higher priority than the join $\vee$ operation.

Definition 3. *In [21], a mapping $\perp : L \to L$ is said to be an orthocomplementation on a poset L with 1 and 0 if for all a, $b \in L$:*

1. $(a^\perp)^\perp) = a$
2. *if $a \leq b$ then $b^\perp \leq a^\perp$*
3. $a \vee a^\perp = 1$

Definition 4. *[21] A lattice L is called modular if for any $a, b, c \in L$, the following condition holds:*

$$a \vee (b \wedge c) = (a \vee b) \wedge c \quad if \quad a \leq c. \tag{3}$$

Let $\perp$ be the orthocomplementation on poset L, two elements $a, b \in L$ are called orthogonal, denote $a \perp b$ if $a \le b^{\perp}$

Definition 5. *An orthocomplemented poset L is said to be an orthomodular poset (OMP for short) if $a, b \in L$ then:*

1. if $a \perp b$ then $a \vee b \in L$.
2. if $a \le b$ then

$$b = a \vee (b \wedge a^{\perp}) \tag{4}$$

In general, for $a_i \perp a_j$, $i \ne j$ and $a_i, a_j \in L$, an OMP L meets fully expression:

$$\bigvee_{i=1}^{\infty} a_i \in L \tag{5}$$

L is called a quantum logic.

Example 1. In [4], an OMP $A = \{0 = min, x, y, z, x^{\perp}, y^{\perp}, z^{\perp}, 1 = max\}$ whose Hasse diagram is presented in Fig. 1 is a $\mathbb{QL}$.

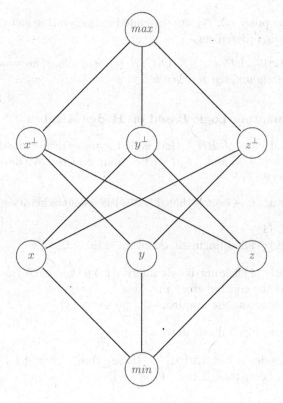

Fig. 1. Hasse diagram for OMP $A = \{min, x, y, z, x^{\perp}, y^{\perp}, z^{\perp}, max\}$

2.2 Hedge Algebra and Linguistic Variables

Linguistic variables used in the paper are based on 3-Tuple $\langle X, G, H, \leq \rangle$, see in [13,14]:

- X is the name of linguistic variable
- G is the generating elements
- H is the linguistic hedges.

Example 2. In [11], consider an $\mathsf{HA} = \langle Temperature, \{high, \ low\}, \{0, W, 1\}, \{less, \ more, \ very\} \leq \rangle$ Fuzzy set X *is Temperature*, $G = \{c^+ = high; \ c^- = low\}$, $H = \{more or less; more; very\}$ so term-set which is generated by the linguistic variable *Temperature* X is $\mathfrak{L}(X)$ or $\mathfrak{L}$ for short:

$$\mathfrak{L} = \{very \ low, \ very \ less \ low; \ more \ or \ less \ low; \ low; \ more \ or \ less \ high; \ more \ high; \ very \ young; \ very \ very \ high \ldots \}.$$

3 Steps Towards Linguistic Fuzzy Quantum Logic

3.1 Hedge Algebra and Orthomodular Lattice (OML)

Properties of the poset $\langle \mathfrak{L}, \leq \rangle$ are depended on generating element G which is totally or partially ordered set.

Theorem 1. *In* [19]*, let* $\mathsf{HA} = \langle X, G, C, H, \leq \rangle$ *be a refined hedge algebra (RHA) where G is a totally ordered set then* HA *is a distributive lattice.*

3.2 Fuzzy Quantum Logic Based on Hedge Algebra

In [19], a special case of RHA that called symmetrical refined HA ($\mathcal{SH}$ for short). On $\mathcal{SH}$, let $\ell \subset \mathfrak{L}$ and $\perp \subseteq \ell \times \ell$ be a map on ℓ set. We have the following important property:

Property 1. Let $\perp : \ell \to \ell$ such that $\perp(x \in \ell)$ is a contradictory element in ℓ

1. ℓ is the OML (1)
2. ℓ is a $\mathbb{QL}$ and is called linguistic quantum logic ($\mathbb{LQL}$) (2)

Proof. 1. property (1) is immediately inferred from theorem 5.1 in [19] by setting $\perp \leftarrow$ which is the contradictory mapping.
2. property (2) is a consequence from the property (1)

Example 3 and Fig. 2 illustrate the Property 1.

Example 3. Consider a $\mathcal{SH}$ with $G = \{false, true\}$, $H = \{\mathcal{V}\}$. Subset OML $\ell^q = \{0, \mathcal{V}false, false, true, \mathcal{V}true, 1\}$ is a $\mathbb{LQL}$

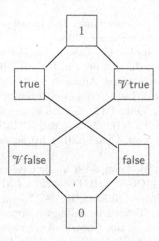

Fig. 2. Hasse diagram for OML $\ell^q = \{0, \mathcal{V}\text{false}, \text{false}, \text{true}, \mathcal{V}\text{true}, 1\}$

4   Conclusions and Forthcoming Study

The paper recommends a method to represent the fuzzy FQL using linguistic variables which is developed from HA. HA is a particular abstract algebra whose properties $fm(c^+) + fm(c^-) = 1$ [13], a quantum bit can be written as

$$|qu\rangle = fm(x)^{\frac{1}{2}}|0\rangle + (1 - fm(x))^{\frac{1}{2}}|1\rangle \tag{6}$$

In the future, two forthcoming studies will be:

– Calculating a quantum state $|\Psi\rangle$ from N quantum $|qu\rangle$ bits is based on equation (6)

$$|\Psi\rangle = \bigotimes_{i=1}^{N}[fm(x_i)^{\frac{1}{2}}|0\rangle + (1 - fm(x_i))^{\frac{1}{2}}|1\rangle] \tag{7}$$

– Designing quantum gates and tensor product for fuzzy quantum bits that use linguistic variables.

References

1. Birkhoff, G., von Neumann, J.: The logic of quantum mechanics. Ann. Math. **37**(4), 823–843 (1936)
2. Caarvalho, J.: On the semantics and the use of fuzzy cognitive maps and dynamic cognitive maps in social sciences. Fuzzy Sets Syst. **214**, 6–19 (2013)
3. Deng, J., Deng, Y.: QZNs: quantum z-numbers. arXiv:2104.05190 (2021)
4. Dvurečenskij, A.: Gleason's Theorem and Its Applications. Mathematics and its Applications. Springer, Heidelberg (1993). https://doi.org/10.1007/978-94-015-8222-3

5. Engesser, K., Gabbay, D.M., Lehmann, D.: Handbook of Quantum Logic and Quantum Structures. Elsevier Science (2009)
6. Frias, M., Filiberto Y., Nápoles, G., Vahoof, K., Bello, R.: Fuzzy cognitive maps reasoning with words: an ordinal approach. In: ISFUROS (2017)
7. Glykas, M.: Fuzzy Cognitive Maps, Advances in Theory, Tools and Applications. Springer, Heidelberg (2010). https://doi.org/10.1007/978-3-642-03220-2
8. Van Han, N., Hao, N.C., Vinh, P.C.: Toward aggregating fuzzy graphs a model theory approach. In: Vinh, P.C., Rakib, A. (eds.) ICCASA/ICTCC -2019. LNICST, vol. 298, pp. 215–222. Springer, Cham (2019). https://doi.org/10.1007/978-3-030-34365-1_17
9. Van Han, N., Vinh, P.C.: Modeling with words based on hedge algebra. In: Cong Vinh, P., Alagar, V. (eds.) ICCASA/ICTCC -2018. LNICST, vol. 266, pp. 211–217. Springer, Cham (2019). https://doi.org/10.1007/978-3-030-06152-4_18
10. Van Han, N., Vinh, P.C.: Toward modeling and reasoning with words based on hedge algebra. EAI Endors. Trans. Context-Aware Syst. Appl. 5(15), e5 (2018)
11. Han, N.V., Vinh, P.C., Phung, B.M., Dan, T.N.: Hidden pattern: toward decision support fuzzy systems. In: Cong Vinh, P., Rakib, A. (eds.) ICCASA 2021. LNICST, vol. 409, pp. 71–76. Springer, Cham (2021). https://doi.org/10.1007/978-3-030-93179-7_6
12. Ho, N.C., Long, N.V.: Fuzziness measure on complete hedge algebras and quantifying semantics of terms in linear hedge algebras. Fuzzy Sets Syst. 158(4), 452–471 (2007)
13. Ho, N.C., Son, T.T., Khang, T.D., Viet, L.X.: Fuzziness measure, quantified semantic mapping and interpolative method of approximate reasoning in medical expert systems. J. Comput. Sci. Cybern. 18(3), 237–252 (2002)
14. Ho, N.C., Wechler, W.: Hedge algebras: an algebraic approach to structure of sets of linguistic truth values. Fuzzy Sets Syst. 35(3), 281–293 (1990)
15. Zadeh, L.A.: The concept of a linguistic variable and its applications to approximate reasoning. Inf. Sci. 8(3), 199–249 (1975)
16. Zadeh, L.A.: Computing with Words - Principal Concepts and Ideas. Studies in Fuzziness and Soft Computing, Springer, Heidelberg (2012). https://doi.org/10.1007/978-3-642-27473-2
17. Mackey, G.W.: Mathematical Foundations of Quantum Mechanics. W.A Benjamin (1963)
18. Mannucci, M.A.: Quantum fuzzy sets: blending fuzzy set theory and quantum computation. arXiv:cs/0604064 (2006)
19. Nguyen, C.-H., Huynh, V.-N.: An algebraic approach to linguistic hedges in Zadeh's fuzzy logic. Fuzzy Sets Syst. 129(2), 229–254 (2002)
20. Papageorgiou, E.I.: Fuzzy Cognitive Maps for Applied Science and Engineering From Fundamentals to Extensions and Learning Algorithms. Springer, Heidelberg (2014). https://doi.org/10.1007/978-3-642-39739-4
21. Pykacz, J.: Quantum Physics, Fuzzy Sets and Logic: Steps Towards a Many-Valued Interpretation of Quantum Mechanics. SpringerBriefs in Physics, Springer, Heidelberg (2015). https://doi.org/10.1007/978-3-319-19384-7
22. Zadeh, L.A.: Outline of a new approach to the analysis of complex systems and decision processes. IEEE Trans. Syst. Man Cybern. 3(1), 28–44 (1973)
23. Zadeh, L.A., Kacprzyk, J.: Computing with Word in Information Intelligent System 1. Springer, Heidelberg (1999). https://doi.org/10.1007/978-3-7908-1873-4

Proposed Solution for Log Collection and Analysis in Kubernetes Environment

Josef Horalek[ID], Patrik Urbanik[ID], Vladimir Sobeslav[✉][ID], and Tomas Svoboda[ID]

Faculty of Management and Informatics, University of Hradec Kralove, Hradec Kralove, Czech Republic
{josef.horalek,patrik.urbanik,vladimir.sobeslav, tomas.svoboda}@uhk.cz

Abstract. The aim of the paper is to design and verify a solution for collecting and analysing logs of a distributed application, which is operated as Software as a Service (SaaS) in the cloud environment in Kubernetes technology. Applications running in cloud environment are not monolithic in most cases, but consist of a large number of co-operating microservices. Providing logging for such distributed applications presents a complex issue, where to provide a comprehensive view of the application state, it is necessary to provide logging across all microservices representing the application. This paper first introduces modern approaches for application development using the technical means of virtualization, containerization and orchestration with an emphasis on Kubernetes technology. Next, approaches and analysis of application logging options are presented with the emphasis on the use of ELK and PLG stack technologies. Based on the analysis, a technical solution for logging applications in Kubernetes environment, operated in the form of SaaS, is proposed and verified.

Keywords: Kubernetes · container · virtualization · orchestrator · log · cloud · SaaS · PLG Stack · ELK stack

1 Introduction

Modern times place ever greater demands on applications in terms of computing power and the use of HW resources. This is mainly due to the increase in the number of users accessing these applications [1, 2] and using their services. A secondary reason, according to [3], is mainly the massive expansion of the Internet whose impact is the increasing number of users and connected devices. The above problem is solved by horizontal scaling, where the performance of HW resources is increased to run the application. Another solution is to use vertical scaling, where the application is run in multiple instances. These two approaches and especially the associated high financial and operation and maintenance costs are the main reasons for moving the applications in question to cloud solutions [4]. This is because cloud services make it very easy to scale, typically using GUI interfaces [5], and also the financial costs, since the application operator only pays

© ICST Institute for Computer Sciences, Social Informatics and Telecommunications Engineering 2023
Published by Springer Nature Switzerland AG 2023. All Rights Reserved
C. V. Phan and T. D. Nguyen (Eds.): ICTCC 2022, LNICST 473, pp. 9–22, 2023.
https://doi.org/10.1007/978-3-031-28790-9_2

for the resources it actually uses, without the need to purchase its own HW, including the provision of its management [6]. A major challenge in cloud-based application development nowadays is to ensure fast delivery of the target functionality. This requirement increases the demands on the human resources that develop the application. At the same time, with new functionalities, the amount of source code and thus the overall complexity of the application increases [7]. The need for frequent and fast delivery of the functionalities of a given application is the primary purpose of DevOps [8, 9]. Virtualization, containerization, and orchestrators are key technologies whose advent has been a catalyst for DevOps [10]. Despite the undeniable changes in the approach to software development, it remains a fact that developed applications have bugs in them whose manifestations and occurrences are random and unpredictable. It is imperative to monitor every application using logging, and at the level of application metrics and logs [11], where it must be taken into account that applications running in a cloud environment consist of a large number of cooperating microservices [12], but where logs are decentralized, as each microservice stores its logs separately. In order to provide a comprehensive view of the application behaviour, or a comprehensive view of the application logging, it is necessary to aggregate these logs from the individual microservices in one central location [13]. The above problem is addressed in several areas, influenced by sub-technologies, and mainly covers the use of ElasticSearch technology with subsequent provision of data for real-time analytics [14]. Logstash technology is often used for indexing and data normalization purposes [15]. Research in the area of downstream log analysis and the use of technical means for visualization is currently mainly focused on the use of Kibana [16]. All of these components allow communication with each other through APIs. Thanks to this architecture, any component can be replaced by another component provided that the new component supports the same interface [17]. At the same time, a major problem is the volatility of log information, e.g., due to restarts of compute nodes. A different view of cloud application monitoring concerns the architecture of a monitoring framework that is able to collect metrics not only from applications but also from system services. Metrics can be pushed from all types of services to the aggregator, where they are then streamed by processors [18].

1.1 Microservices, Containerisation and Orchestrators

Container virtualization is one of the main catalysts for designing applications using microservices. Microservices are built on two main pillars [19], the first is that a microservice addresses just one responsibility for a specific functionality and the second defines a microservice as a small application that can be deployed independently including independent scaling. The concept of leveraging microservices is key in the proper implementation of a DevOps approach. Distributed applications that are run in the cloud on a SaaS platform consist of many cooperating microservices [20]. In order to access microservices as packages of functionality, it is necessary to have a way to encapsulate the application and its configuration so that it can be migrated anywhere else. Container technologies or containerization are suitable candidates.

The principle of containerization is to encapsulate the application logic along with the configuration of the application into a minimized runtime environment that can then be easily deployed and operated [21].

Containers then do not need their own operating system, which results in lower hardware requirements and does not create memory and computational overhead. It is therefore possible to run more of them on hardware, and at the same time, they boot and restart much faster than traditional virtual machines. When using containers, the boot speed is $50\times$ to $70\times$ faster compared to standard operating systems [22]. Orchestrators are used to manage, deploy containers and support these processes [23].

Orchestrator is a system that provides an enterprise-level framework for container integration and management that simultaneously manages containers while allowing containers to be aggregated into a single entity, scaled, and comprehensively managed through their lifecycle. The Kubernetes orchestrator was developed by Google as an open source successor to an internal project called Borg and its successor project Omega [24, 25]. Several research teams are currently analysing the development of Kubernetes, including its features and deployment issues [26, 27]. To run the Kubernetes technology itself, it is necessary to have servers, their initial setup and subsequent management. The necessity of providing initial setup and subsequent management places great demands on the provision of hardware and especially human resources, to which end cloud providers offer managed Kubernetes cluster solutions that the customer uses as a cloud service. Currently, research in this area further focuses mainly on analysing the performance results of clusters [28], running applications in Kubernetes clusters [29], and ensuring high availability of applications [30].

1.2 Logging in Kubernetes

In order to provide logging in the Kubernetes environment, ELK stack and PLG stack technologies are mainly used nowadays [31]. ELK stack technology is a combination of Elasticsearch, Logstash and Kibana [32]. All these projects are backed by the main Elastic project. Elasticsearch is a database of data over which query-based search is implemented. Data is stored in indexes that are persisted to disk, over which queries are then executed. Elastic search then performs sorting and aggregation of the data. When data normalization and indexing is needed, the Logstash component is used. The normalized and indexed data is stored from Logstash to the Elasticsearch database. To visualize the data in the form of dashboards, the Kibana component in the ELK stack is used as a tool to support data manipulation [33].

PLG stack technology represents a combination of Promtail, Loki and Grafana projects. Currently, there is no research on the use of PLG stack for logging in Kubernetes. Loki technology represents the main component for dealing with persistence and querying log data. Compared to ELK stack, the approach to the problem of persistence and logging is different. The log data in Loki's submission is divided into two channels (index and blob). The indexes are used to store metadata about the log data. Blobs are pure logs, stored in their original format While in ELK stack the indexing of log files is done using Logstash technology, PLG stack provides the above functionalities through a single Loki technology. Promtail is a project primarily used for collecting data from servers. This collection is divided into three phases. The first phase is discovery, or discovering the targets from which data will be taken. The second phase involves the description of the collected information using labels. This extracted information is sent to the Loki technology for further processing. Compared to Kibana, Grafana is a generic visualisation tool.

2 Problem Analysis

The examined solution used dedicated virtual servers of the cloud provider Microsoft Azure. In view of the increasing demands on CPU and memory, as well as the requirements for automatic scaling and dynamic creation of new services, it was decided to transfer the existing solution from virtual servers to Kubernetes based on a business analysis. In the context of the aforementioned migration of the runtime environment, there are also change requirements for the logging solution, which in the original solution relied on the stability of virtual machines and especially in the area of high availability.

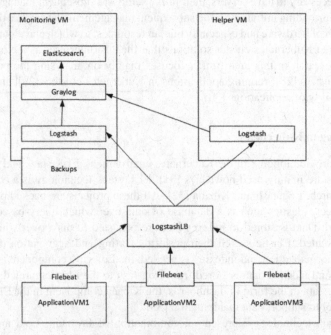

Fig. 1. Legacy logging solution

Figure 1 shows that only the Logstash component was optimized for high availability. The data on the virtual machine named monitoring was backed up once a day, and in case of failure of this virtual machine, a new one is started from this backup, and in the worst case scenario, one day of logs is lost. The original solution, ran on a single dedicated virtual server running all the necessary applications, including Elasticsearch, Logstah, Graylog. These components determined a minimum requirement of 64 GB RAM, 8 CPU cores and a 2 TB SSD drive for sufficient capacity to store the indexes. Logstash receives around 2,000 log lines per second, mediated by Filebeat, which collects this information from the output of docker containers running on all virtual machines. Thus, high availability is out of the question in this solution. Minor failures of the Graylog tool to process incoming information are picked up by Logstash's retry mechanism. However, a failure of the entire monitoring server means an automatic loss of data.

2.1 Definition of Requirements

The requirements for a new solution can be divided into functional and non-functional requirements. From the analysis of the existing solution, the first functional requirement is the minimum number of processed log lines, set to 2 000. The second functional requirement is the possibility of alerting based on the information obtained from the logs. In the area of non-functional requirements, the main criteria for the new solution are stability and high availability. Outages of computing machines can be caused on the Azure side, for example, when moving a virtual machine running a Kubernetes worker node. Last but not least, the logging system must also provide decision support and support for easy issue tracking. This means that there must be the ability to perform event-specific queries over the data stored in the central repository, as well as statistical queries. Testing of the proposed will be carried out on an AKS cluster comprising three computing machines of type Standard_DS3_v2, i.e. machines having 4 CPUs and 14 GB of memory. The cost of the whole solution will be calculated on a running production cluster. The requirement for the **managed log volume** is defined with regard to the sustainability and development of the user base and the provided application portfolio specifies a threshold of 25,000 lines per second as a sufficient volume of processed logs. The system must be able to persist this volume of data and also be able to search over it. In the area of **high availability**, the requirements take into account the situation where a Kubernetes cluster is much more unstable than virtual machines. The system must therefore be prepared for virtual machine failure and must not lose data. At the same time, the system must be able to serve requests even if a node is unavailable, i.e. it must always appear to be fully functional externally. Requirements in the area of **Forensic Analysis and Statistical Queries**, the system must be able to provide support to developers as well as management. The developers will be particularly useful when they are looking for bugs in the application. Thus, the system must be able to provide the developer with data over which the developer will then be able to perform filtering and other refinements to the data they need. The system should also be able to perform statistical queries over the collected data for possible decision support. A typical example that will be tested is a query on the number of queries to an endpoint. In the area of **alerting**, given the number of running services in the Kubernetes cluster, the system must be able to provide support to the operations team for monitoring these services. This support should be represented by a message to some community channel if an error occurs in a service. Last but not least, the **cost** of the whole solution must be taken into account, which must be at most as expensive as the original solution was. The cost evaluation will be done on a long running Kubernetes cluster.

2.2 High Available PLG Stack Solution

Highly available Loki (used in version 2.1) solution represents for each part of the log processing and working process its own component always running in multiple replicas, i.e. not only in one instance. At the highest level of abstraction, two log paths are addressed. The first is the write path that a log must travel from the moment it is recorded by the application until it is stored in some format. The second path is the reading path, which takes the log from the stored form to the visualized and filtered form required by the user. At a lower level of abstraction, these paths can then be broken down into the individual components that figure in these paths. A complete diagram of the cooperating components can be seen in Fig. 2. The individual components communicate with each other for maximum efficiency using an RPC implementation in the form of GRPC, an opensource RPC framework from Google.

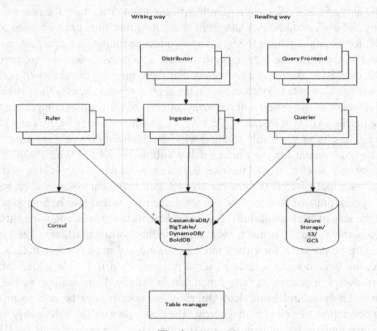

Fig. 2. HA Loki

2.3 Azure Kubernetes Services (AKS)

Azure Kubernetes Services is a managed service provided by Microsoft Azure cloud provider that takes care of the management of the running Kubernetes cluster, i.e. the operation and maintenance of the highly available master nodes on which the Kubernetes control plane runs. To make the logging ecosystem as resilient as possible to compute machine failures, it is necessary to ensure that there is always one pod of a given type running on a compute node, i.e., for example, each ingester runs on a different machine. This can be achieved using so-called anti-affinity. Anti-affinity places restrictions on Kubernet for scheduling individual pods.

For applications running in AKS as pods, logs will be collected from standard output. Thus, nothing special is needed in terms of application-level logging configuration. The only major requirement for an application in terms of logging is to think about the correct labelling of the pod it is running in, so it is necessary to choose a mandatory set of labels for uniform search queries for all applications monitored by Loki. It is also advisable to consider the possibility that data from multiple Kubernetes clusters will be sent to a single Loki and possibly adapt the mandatory labels to this, i.e. introduce for example a label cluster that will describe the source cluster log information. A significant problem is where to store the chunks (logs in their textual, compressed form). AKS has two options, the first being mount storage, which in terms of Loki pods running inside a Kubernetes cluster, pretends to be a local disk. In terms of speed and cost, the optimal solution is to use Azure Files as local disks, even though there are real problems associated with Ingester component reboots, which in Kubernetes means that this disk is unmounted, and then remounted into a rebooted pod, which in extreme cases took up to an hour in tests. Another downside to this solution is that in the case of performance optimization, it is advisable to reach for the premium tier of Azure Files, which offers $5\times$ the number of I/O operations, $4\times$ the incoming traffic, and roughly the same outgoing traffic capability.

2.4 Alerting Solution

To support alerting, Loki comes with the Ruler component, which is able to analyse log information and trigger actions based on defined queries. To execute actions, a component that is familiar from the ecosystem around Prometheus is used. Specifically, it is the AlertManager component. This component takes care of deduplication, grouping and forwarding to the correct channel. The code sample shows a rule that will execute when the proportion of errors against all logs in a time-interval is greater than 5% and will execute once every 10 min. The handler is typically executed in a single replica and its theoretical unavailability does not matter. In the event that a large number of logs are expected to be evaluated over and alerting is a critical functionality, it is also possible to run Ruler in HA mode. In this mode, the Ruler needs information to access the hash ring through which individual Ruler instances exchange information.

```
1  groups:
2      - name: should_fire
3        rules:
4        - alert: HighPercentageError
5        expr: |
6        sum(rate({app="foo", env="production"} |= "error"[5m])) by (job)
7        /
8        sum(rate({app="foo", env="production"}[5m])) by (job)
9            > 0.05
10       for: 10m
11       labels:
12           severity: page
13           annotations:
14       summary: High request latency
```

3 Discussion and Results

The results were verified at the level of metrics collected by the Prometheus tool, for their visualization the Grafana tool was used, which also displays and visualizes logs.

3.1 Volume Test

In order to verify that the logging system can handle a relatively high load, a test was carried out in which 30 services were run in parallel, each of which will write approximately 900 records per second to its standard output, i.e. 27,000 processed lines per second in total, which is approximately 13 times more than the set lower limit. The service that takes care of writing the logs is a simple Node.js that outputs a sequence of numbers in an infinite loop, complete with the id of the running pod. During this test, Prometheus metrics of the components involved in the write path were monitored, from which it is possible to track how the system handles the load.

```
1 const process = require("process");
3 const ClientId = process.env["CLIENT_ID"];
4 (async function run() {
5 for await (let num of generateSequence()) {
6 console.log('${ClientId} - ${num}'); }})();
7 async function* generateSequence() {
8 let counter = 0;
9 while (true) {
10 await tick();
11 yield counter++;16 }}
12 async function tick() {
23 return new Promise((res) => setTimeout(res, 1)); }
```

The Promtail component responded to the increase by increasing processor activity. It consumes about 2.5 CPU more to handle this amount of logs. The memory increase was essentially negligible compared to the CPU load. A substantial increase in network load can also be observed. As the number of processed rows increases, the amount of data required to be forwarded to the Distributor component also increases. This component reacted with a slight increase (0.1 CPU) in processor activity. The memory load remains constant. The increase in network load was significant. This was calculated as the result of the sum of the amount of data received and sent. Finally, a marked difference in memory usage can be observed on the Ingester component. This memory is used to temporarily store the logs so that queries can be processed in the shortest possible time. Based on the settings of the component, the data stored is 20 min old.

3.2 High Availability Test

In this test, a simulation of a machine failure was performed. This should verify the readiness of the system for problems of this type. The simulated outage was achieved by downscaling the nodepool by one machine, i.e. removing one node. Throughout the test, writes were performed at a rate of approximately 15,000 lines per second. To achieve this number of lines, the same program as in the previous test was used, only it will be run in fewer instances. The stability of the write was measured by a post-power promtail metric that tells how many log lines were discarded. First, the system will be put into an uncorrupted state, i.e., the number of replicas of the ingester com- ponents will be reduced to 1. Figure 3 captures this state will show the lost lines. Then the whole system will be restored to its original state followed by a simulated node failure. These two states will be compared against each other. In the first part of the graph, the lost log lines should be visible, while in the second part of the graph, no losses should occur. It was observed that a stable write of about 18,000 logs per second was in progress. At around 9:38 the system was put into a non-valid state by reducing the number of ingesters to 1. This resulted in a loss of logs and an increased number of Grafana query errors. At 9:45 the system was returned to a valid state and the graph shows that the error messages stopped appearing and the number of lost logs also dropped to 0. Around this time a local outlier can be observed on the graph showing the number of lines read. This reaches a threshold of 110,000 processed lines per second, which is successfully managed to clear. At about 9:49, the downscale of the number of worker nodes to 2 followed. This was reflected by reducing the number of Ingester instances and Distributor instances to 2, logically removing instances that were running on the removed compute node. This number is still valid for the system. Thus, there is no loss and Grafana can handle all queries, which implies that the log read path is fully functional. At approximately 10:01 the test was terminated.

Based on this test, we can say that the logging system is ready to run in the unstable Kubernetes environment due to its distributed nature and proper anti-affinity settings. This is a substantial improvement over the original solution, in which a failure would have meant momentary non-functionality and loss of logs. Furthermore, the power of Kubernetes in automating the whole process was shown here. After removing the com- pute machine from the cluster, Loki component instances that could not be deployed to the two remaining worker nodes disappeared, as deploying them to these machines would have violated the anti-affinity rules. However, the moment a newly started worker node appears in the cluster, Kubernetes automatically switches on all the missing components and everything runs again as it was originally.

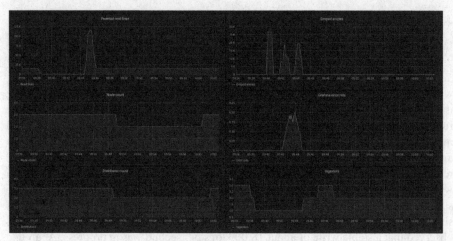

Fig. 3. Logging in case of single node failure

3.3 Decision Support and Forensic Analysis

This test contained two parts. The first part focused on the ability of the system to provide relevant information, which is understandable and visualised, for the management of the company, on the basis of which the management must be able to decide where the application is able to go from here. The second part tested the ability of the system to provide relevant information to the developer, who should be able to trace the error based on this information. For the test, a REST service was used, which has three endpoints exposed, named for illustration Feature1, Feature2, Feature3. This service will then be called using a BASH script in a 5:3:1 ratio. At the same time, the application will log an error every 15th call to the Feature3 endpoint. From the results obtained, it can be seen that the primary functionality is Feature1, which represents 56% of all calls, which de-emphasizes the ratio in which the functionalities were called. Furthermore, a relatively high frequency of error logs can be observed from this dashboard, namely 0.062 errors per second. This value should be 0. Therefore, its elevated value could be a stimulus for further analysis of what is happening in the application. When the Feature3 endpoint is called, the current application state is 15, which triggers an error in the application. This test, by successfully verifying the distribution of calls to individual endpoints, proved that it is possible to extract useful information from the logs using LogQL for management, which can then be nicely visualized in graphs using Grafana. This visualization greatly helps to understand the data presented.

3.4 Alerting

In this test, the ability of the system, or rather the Ruler component, to alert when defined triggers occur in the application was verified. The same services as in the previous test were used for this test. For this service, it is known that every 15th call to the Feature3 endpoint an error is reported. This error was followed by an alert that is reflected by a message in the Microsoft Teams communication tool. Ruler itself only serves as a tool that analyses the defined LogQL queries. If a query is evaluated as true, a notification is sent to the Alert Manager component. It is used to accumulate these notifications and then forward them to the selected communication channel. Alert Manager does not have a direct connector to Microsoft Teams. For this test, it is therefore necessary to choose an alternative solution and send the notification using the Webhook functionality. For this option, a target HTTP end-point is selected, to which a POST request is sent that contains the alert information in its body. Based on this information, Alert Manager then groups the alerts and sends them on if necessary. Microsoft Teams can receive messages using the Webhook mechanism. However, the exposed endpoint requires quite specific data, the structure of which can be seen in the Microsoft Webhook documentation.1 However, Alert Manager component cannot structure the data in this way. Therefore, it is necessary to use a proxy server that will receive data from Alert Manager and transform it into Microsoft Teams-compatible data. This component will be the open source project Prometheus-Msteams available from Github. 2 This setup is capable of sending alerts on errors from the application for the previous test. Even though the integration between Ruler component and Microsoft Teams was not straightforward, this test proved that alerting can work in a solution built on Loki project. By using the open source pro-projects AlertManager and Prometheus-Msteams, integration between the mentioned components was achieved. A big advantage is the definition of rules in a form that is similar to Prometheus rules. This greatly simplifies the operations team that already operates Prometheus to create these rules and use this functionality.

4 Conclusion

The proposed solution was rigorously tested and passed all tests successfully. Based on the test results, the solution can process more than 10 times the required lower bound and in one of the tests 110,000 lines were processed at one point. This solution is ready for future application growth and increasing number of processed lines. In terms of high availability, the solution passed a test in which a computing machine failure was simulated. Due to its distributed nature, the solution remained functional despite this outage and was able to handle 18,000 log lines per second without losing a single one. The moment the Kubernetes node in the cluster went down again, the system automatically returned to its original state without a single human intervention. The LogQL language is suitable for forensic and statistical log queries. The test was successful in demonstrating the capabilities of the system, how it will serve developers for log analysis as well as managerial positions as a possible sub-task for decision making. The data obtained by querying could be easily filtered or transformed into metrics. The response to bugs will be very fast thanks to the alerting support that was presented by one of the tests. Moreover, the rules for alerting are also written in LogQL and the user does not have to learn a new language or procedure to set up the alert. Furthermore, their definition is similar to Prometheus rule definition, making them easier for the operations team to write and maintain. Despite the fact that the solution could not be configured to write data directly to Blob Storage, but had to use the option of writing to Azure Files, the solution managed to beat the targets on the price test. Specifically, there was a 26% price reduction.

Acknowledgment. The research has been supported by the Faculty of Informatics and Management UHK specific research project 2107 Integration of Departmental Research Activities and Students' Research Activities Support II. We would like to thank Mr. P. Kratochvil, a graduate of Faculty of management and informatics, University of Hradec Kralove, for the practical verification of the proposed solutions and close cooperation in the solution.

References

1. Morley, J., Widdicks, K., Hazas, M.: Digitalisation, energy and data demand: the impact of Internet traffic on overall and peak electricity consumption. Energy Res. Soc. Sci. **38**, 128–137 (2018). ISSN 22146296
2. Abbasi, A.A., Abbasi, A., Shamshirband, S., Chronopoulos, A.T., Persico V., Pescape, A.: Software-defined cloud computing: a systematic review on latest trends and developments (2019). ISSN 2169-3536
3. Tranos, E., Stich, Ch.: Individual internet usage and the availability of online content of local interest: a multilevel approach. Comput. Environ. Urban Syst. **79**, 101371 (2020). ISSN 01989715
4. Villamizar, M., Garces, O., Castro, H., et al.: Evaluating the monolithic and the microservice architecture pattern to deploy web applications in the cloud. In: Sanchez, M., Gonzalez, O. (eds.) 2015 10th Computing Colombian Conference (10ccc). IEEE, New York (2015). ISBN 978-1-4673-9464-2, iSSN 2378-8216
5. El Kafhali, S., El Mir, I., Salah, K., Hanini, M.: Dynamic scalability model for containerized cloud services. Arab. J. Sci. Eng. **45**(12), 10693–10708 (2020). https://doi.org/10.1007/s13 369-020-04847-2. SSN 2193-567X
6. Piraghaj, S.F., Vahid Dastjerdi, A., Calheiros R.N., Buyya, R.: A survey and taxonomy of energy efficient resource management techniques in platform as a service cloud. In: Handbook of Research on End-to-End Cloud Computing Architecture Design. Advances in Systems Analysis, Software Engineering, and High Performance Computing (2017). ISBN 9781522507598
7. Senapathi, M., Buchan, J., Osman, H.: DevOps capabilities, practices, and challenges. In: Proceedings of the 22nd International Conference on Evaluation and Assessment in Software Engineering (2018). ISBN 9781450364034
8. Maroukian, K., Gulliver, S.R.: Leading DevOps practice and principle adoption. In: 9th International Conference on Information Technology Convergence and Services (ITCSE 2020) (2020)
9. Balalaie, A., Heydarnoori, A., Jamshidi, P.: Microservices architecture enables DevOps migration to a cloud-native architecture. IEEE Computer, Los Alamitos (2016). ISSN 0740-7459
10. Elbert, C., Gallardo, E., Hernantes, J.; DevOps. IEEE Computer Society, Los Alamitos (2016). ISSN 0740-7459
11. Pi, A., Chen, W., Zhou, X., Ji, M.: Profiling distributed systems in lightweight virtualized environments with logs and resource metrics. In: Proceedings of the 27th International Symposium on High-Performance Parallel and Distributed Computing (2018). ISBN 9781450357852
12. Jash, S., Ganesh, R., Rachhadia, T.D., Shah, P.K.: A hierarchical approach to extract application logs with visualization in a containerized environment. In: 2019 International Conference on Computing, Power and Communication Technologies (GUCON) (2019)
13. Solomon, F.I.: Securing websites web applications using data analytics. In: 2019 International Conference on Computational Intelligence in Data Science (ICCIDS) (2019)

14. Li, Y., Jiang, Y., Gu, J., et al.: A cloud-based framework for large-scale log mining through apache spark and elasticsearch. Appl. Sci. **9**(6) (2019. https://doi.org/10.3390/app9061114). ISSN 2076-3417. Accessed 09 Nov 2021

15. Lee, B.-H., Yang, D.-M.: A security log analysis system using Logstash based on apache elasticsearch. J. Korea Inst. Inf. Commun. Eng. **22**(2), 382–389 (2018)

16. Shonia, O., Topuria, N., & Kulijanovi, K. Collection and analysis of log data with cloud services. Bull. Georg. Natl. Acad. Sci. (2021)

17. Mfula, H., Nurminen, J.K.: Self-healing cloud services in private multi-clouds. In: 2018 International Conference on High Performance Computing & Simulation (HPCS), pp. 165–170. IEEE (2018)

18. Ramos, F., Viegas, E., Santin, A., Horchulhack, P., Dos Santos, R., Espindola, A.: A machine learning model for detection of Docker-based APP overbooking on kubernetes. In: ICC 2021 - IEEE International Conference on Communications (2021). ISBN 978-1-7281-7122-7

19. Pradhan, R., Dash, A.K.: An Overview of Microservices. Lecture Notes in Electrical Engineering, vol. 601. Springer, Singapore (2020)

20. Pahl, C., Jamshidi, P., Zimmermann, O.: Microservices and containers. Softw. Eng. **2020** (2020)

21. Srirama, S.N., Adhikari, M., Paul, S.: Application deployment using containers with auto-scaling for microservices in cloud environment. J. Netw. Comput. Appl. **160**, 102629 (2020). ISSN 10848045

22. Abdullah, M., Iqbal, W., Bukhari, F.: Containers vs virtual machines for auto-scaling multi-tier applications under dynamically increasing workloads. In: Bajwa, I.S., Kamareddine, F., Costa, A. (eds.) INTAP 2018. CCIS, vol. 932, pp. 153–167. Springer, Singapore (2019). https://doi.org/10.1007/978-981-13-6052-7_14 ISBN 9789811360527, ISSN 1865-0929

23. Zhang, Q., Liu, L., Pu, C., et al.: A comparative study of containers and virtual machines in big data environment. New York (2018). ISBN 978-1-5386-7235-8

24. Khan, A.: Key characteristics of a container orchestration platform to enable a modern application. IEEE Cloud Computing (2017). ISSN 2325-6095

25. Muddinagiri, R., Ambavane, S., Bayas, S.: Self-hosted kubernetes: deploying docker containers locally with minikube. In: 2019 International Conference on Innovative Trends and Advances in Engineering and Technology (ICITAET) (2019)

26. Dewi, L.P., Noertjahyana, A., Palit, H.N., Yedutun, K.: Server scalability using kubernetes. In: 2019 4th Technology Innovation Management and Engineering Science International Conference (TIMES-iCON) (2019). ISBN 978-1-7281-3755-1

27. Ferreira, A.P., Sinnott, R.: A performance evaluation of containers running on managed kubernetes services. In 2019 IEEE International Conference on Cloud Computing Technology and Science (CloudCom) (2019). ISSN 2330-2186

28. Vayghan, L.A., Saied, M.A., Toeroe, M., et al.: Deploying microservice based applications with kubernetes: experiments and lessons learned. In: 2018 IEEE 11th International Conference on Cloud Computing (CLOUD) (2018). ISSN 2159-6190

29. Vayghan, L.A., Saied, M.A., Toeroe, M., et al.: Microservice based architecture: towards high-availability for stateful applications with kubernetes. In: 2019 IEEE 19th International Conference on Software Quality, Reliability and Security (QRS) (2019)

30. Pichan, A., Lazarescu, M., Soh, S.T.: Towards a practical cloud forensics logging framework. J. Inf. Secur. Appl. **42**, 18–28 (2019). ISSN 22142126

31. Jayathilaka, H., Krintz, C., Wolski, R.: Performance monitoring and root cause analysis for cloud-hosted web applications. Association for Computing Machinery, New York (2017). ISBN 978-1-4503-4913-0

32. Lamouchi, N.: Flying All Over the Sky with Quarkus and Kubernetes. In: Lamouchi, N. (ed.) Pro Java Microservices with Quarkus and Kubernetes, pp. 363–395. Apress, Berkeley, (2021). https://doi.org/10.1007/978-1-4842-7170-4_14 ISBN 978-1-4842-7169-8

33. Dooley, R., Brandt, S., Liang, K., Tanner, E. Experiences migrating the agave platform to a kubernetes native system on the jetstream cloud. In: Practice and Experience in Advanced Research Computing, 17 July 2021, pp. 1–4. ACM, New York (2021). https://doi.org/10. 1145/3437359.346559. ISBN 9781450382922. Accessed 09 Nov 2021

Automated Tests Using Selenium Framework

Josef Horalek[ID], Patrik Urbanik[ID], and Vladimir Sobeslav[✉][ID]

Faculty of Informatics and Management, University of Hradec Kralove, Hradec Kralove, Czech Republic
{josef.horalek,patrik.urbanik,vladimir.sobeslav}@uhk.cz

Abstract. Today, software testing is already an integral part of every software development cycle. However, even this does not guarantee that the final product will be free of software bugs. Testing needs to be implemented from the lowest possible stage of development so that the bugs can be detected as early as possible to reduce the cost of fixing them at later stages. However, this is hampered by the ever-increasing demands for software from customers, increasing testing requirements to the point where it is impossible to meet them all. This is why automated software testing is becoming increasingly popular. Automated test scripts can partially replace manual user testing and help significantly improve the quality of the software. Automated testing using the Selenium framework is the focus of this paper. The functionality and process of testing in Selenium are demonstrated with five testing scripts in a sample scenario.

Keywords: Automation · Automated testing · Selenium framework · Software quality

1 Introduction

The increasingly modern technologies and practices involved in the application development cycle are no guarantee that the software being developed will be bug-free. Therefore, it is very important to implement a testing process early in the development cycle to prevent bugs from being transferred to later phases or even to the final deployment. The very meaning of testing is often distorted. According to [1], testing aims not to prove that the software works correctly, but to increase its value by improving its quality by removing bugs. As a suitable definition, the author states: Testing is the process of executing a program with the intent of finding errors. Thus, the goal of software testing is to find bugs as early as possible, or in other words, to ensure a certain level of quality of the application in development. It is the so-called Quality Assurance (QA) that is of great importance in the corporate competitive environment [2]. According to [3], the meaning of quality, or software quality, can be expressed as: The degree to which the system, process, or component meets the specified requirements.

Software bugs can take many forms. They range from grammatical errors that do not affect the functionality of the software, to logical errors in the code that can result in crashes. It is not always true that an error leads to failure. Therefore, the terms software

© ICST Institute for Computer Sciences, Social Informatics and Telecommunications Engineering 2023
Published by Springer Nature Switzerland AG 2023. All Rights Reserved
C. V. Phan and T. D. Nguyen (Eds.): ICTCC 2022, LNICST 473, pp. 23–40, 2023.
https://doi.org/10.1007/978-3-031-28790-9_3

bug and software failure need to be distinguished. Failure only occurs when certain conditions (and/or errors) are activated. Thus, a failure never has to occur because the errors are never activated [4].

The cost to fix bugs increases in proportion to the stage of development at which the bug is discovered. Examples of well-known and very costly incidents related to development errors are the failed launch of the civilian rocket called Ariane 5 in 1996 [5], and the so-called Y2K Bug [6], which nowadays looks quite ridiculous. Among the more recent ones, the Log4j bug from December 2021, which affects millions of web servers and is described as one of the biggest bugs of recent years, is definitely worth mentioning [7].

The testing process itself can be divided into several categories depending on the focus. For example, based on the layer of the application into frontend and backend testing, then based on the knowledge level of the code into black-box, white-box, and grey-box, and last but not least based on the type of the execution into manual and automated testing [8].

The principle of automated testing is the creation of test scripts that run without human intervention. The tester in this case is responsible for creating and maintaining these scripts and for checking the test results [9]. The main advantages of automated tests are considered to be:

- Reusability of test scripts,
- higher coverage in the application under test,
- increased software quality,
- faster compared to manual testing,
- reduced cost and time of testing,
- much better error detection.

On the other hand, users see disadvantages such as:

- The actual scripting and maintenance,
- the need for even more skilled personnel,
- cannot fully replace manual testing,
- initial high cost of implementation [10].

A large number of aspects influence the effectiveness and sustainability of automated testing. These include the choice of appropriate test automation tools, the test framework used, the planning of automation activities, integration into DevOps at the organizational and technical level, and more.

The growing popularity of automated tests is mainly due to the fact that customers are placing ever greater demands on systems, thus increasing the complexity of the programs being developed. This increases the requirements for testing to the point where it cannot be done manually in terms of human resources, time, and money.

2   Methods and Technologies

The capabilities and effectiveness of automated tests depend on the technologies and methods that are used to run automated tests of the GUI of a corporate web application.

Test development tools can be divided into two categories according to their focus - complex development environments, so-called IDEs (Integrated development environments), and simpler editors. The main differences are in price, system requirements, performance, and the options offered by each environment. As part of the solution, the Visual Studio development environment was used as the main tool for creating automated tests, which has the advantage of a wide range of available extensions and tools. It is possible to download so-called NuGet packages into the project in Visual Studio, where these are basically files that contain compiled code created by another developer and in this way made available for use by other users, which were also used in the development of automatic Selenium tests. Specifically, the following have been used:

- `DotNetSeleniumExtras.WaitHelpers,`
- `Selenium.Support,`
- `Selenium.WebDriver,`
- `Selenium.WebDriver.ChromeDriver,`
- `Xunit,`
- `Xunit.assert,`
- `Xunit.runner.visualstudio,`
- `XunitXml.TestLogger.`

The automated tests use the *XUnit* tool [11], which is an open-source testing framework created by Jim Newkirk, the creator of another testing framework. At the time of the pilot design, the current XUnit version was 2.4.1. This framework tries to take a minimalist approach by scanning all public classes when running tests for methods with the [Fact] or [Theory] attribute. These attributes identify the method as a test. The [Fact] attribute denotes a method that has no arguments on the input. This is a classical test where everything must be specified in the method. In contrast, the [Theory] attribute is used for methods when we want to insert specific data into the test. This attribute alone is not enough and another attribute [InlineData] must be used with it. This is used to specify the subset of data on which the parameterized tests will be executed.

GitLab was chosen as the pilot testbed for automated tests. Unit tests were run in GitLab pipelines to separate the testing and production environments. All automated tests were run here, both for the frontend and the backend. In total, four environments are used in the development of the application:

1. *Develop* - An environment used mainly for programmers to develop new functionality. Sometimes manual testing is also done here.
2. *Test* - Here automatic tests are run for frontend and backend.
3. *Stag* - This environment is used for user acceptance testing.
4. *Prod* - The environment in which the application runs for live use. This environment, thanks to all the previous tests, should not get any bugs, or as few as possible.

Which environment to run the tests on is set using the `.gitlab-ci.yml` file. This file is used to set up individual pipelines within GitLab. An example of this particular file, for setting up Selenium tests to run automatically, is shown below.

```
stage: qa-test
  image: mcr.microsoft.com/dotnet/sdk
rules:
  - if: $CI_COMMIT_REF_NAME == "master"
      when: on_success
  - when: never
script:
  - dotnet test tests/uitest/Selenium_tests.csproj
  --logger html
artifacts:
  when: always
  paths:
    - ./tests/uitest/TestResults
  expire_in: 1 week
```

This file guarantees to run automatic tests if the name of the branch on which the new version of the application is being deployed is the master. The test environment is located in this branch. For other branches, this job will not run at all. It is also possible to see the artifact settings from this job. An artifact is a file that is created from the output of a job. In this case, it is the HTML report of the test result shown at the end of the article (Fig. 3).

A general flowchart of the solution (Fig. 1), where automated UI tests are run, is shown below. As mentioned, the tests are run automatically when a new version is deployed to the master branch, where the test environment is also set up. If the tests reveal a bug, a hotfix is created by the developer and then the tests are run again. If all is well, a new tag is created to ensure automatic deployment to the stag environment for customer testing. Customers have a certain amount of time, on the order of a few days, to test it. If they confirm that everything works, the version is manually deployed to the production environment for official use.

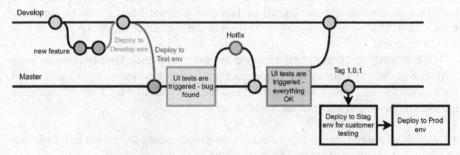

Fig. 1. Running automated UI Tests in GitLab

The *DevTool* [12] is also essential for developing automated tests. It is a set of tools integrated directly into Google Chrome. The most important tab, when creating automated UI tests, is the Elements tab, which displays all the elements of the web page. Here all the needed locators for the elements are retrieved, which are then included in the test script. The other tabs that the DevTool interface offers are:

- *Elements* - displays CSS and page elements,
- *Console* - displays JavaScript messages,
- *Network* - displays network activity,
- *Performance* - displays the loading speed of the web page,
- *Application* - displays all loaded resources, local storage, session storage, cookies, and application cache.

2.1 Selenium Tools

Selenium does not refer to only one particular tool but refers to three different tools, namely *Selenium IDE*, *Selenium WebDriver*, and *Selenium Grid* [13].

Selenium IDE
It is a tool or development environment that is primarily used to develop test scenarios for Selenium tests. It is a simple web browser extension, so it does not require any complex configuration. The Selenium IDE is a graphical environment that records the user's actions in the browser, using pre-existing Selenium commands with the parameters of the web elements that the user clicked on while recording the test. This makes it ideal for users with no experience in developing test cases for web applications [14].

Selenium WebDriver
Using the APIs provided by individual browsers, allows you to automate the functioning of the browser. For web browsers, it defines behavior control interfaces to simulate the behavior as if controlled by a real user [15].

Selenium Grid
The main purpose of Selenium Grid is to run tests in parallel on multiple machines. The grid allows you to run tests created in WebDriver remotely. It can run tests on both physical and virtual machines, and even in parallel for different browsers. So if a test suite contains, for example, fifty tests, using Grid it is possible to reduce the testing time by running a set of ten tests on five different machines in parallel [16].

3   Test Design and Implementation

Now the implementation of specific test cases will be shown. The case scenario is to make sure that the application for ordering and managing physical material for production is working properly and safely. For the purpose of this paper, the arguments of each test case are anonymized with more general variants. Some web elements are also changed in the same way. All modified data is shown in italics in the code samples, and specific values need to be entered instead for the tests to work properly.

3.1 Defining the Test Case

At the beginning of each test, it is absolutely necessary to think about what functionality of the web application we want to test and then design which steps the test will contain to achieve the desired level of testing. For this purpose, it is possible to use the already mentioned Selenium IDE tool or rely on the tester's knowledge of the tested application and let him develop the test case independently. For the needs of the implemented testing, the Selenium IDE tool was used to create a test case, which was comprehensively converted into executable code for use in the automated test. The main points of the test scenario are shown in Table 1.

Table 1. The test case/scenario

Step#	Step detail	Expected results	Test data
1	Open the login page	Display the login form	–
2	Enter a valid username and password	Relevant data entered	*username, password*
3	Click on the "Sign in" button	Successful login of a user	–
4	Search for desired materials	Display details of the entered material	*material*
5	Click on the "Order material" button	View the material order form	–
6	Enter the quantity of material in the "qty" field	The field contains the required data	*quantity*
7	Enter the order identifier in the "Order ID" field	The field contains the required data	*identifier*
8	Enter the desired replenishment date in the "Delivery Date" field	The field contains the required data	*deliveryDate*
9	Click on the "Create Order" button	The field contains the required data	–

3.2 Test Script

The test case project contains three separate classes – `SeleniumConfig.cs`, `Steps.cs`, and `Tests.cs`, which are available at https://github.com/horalekjos/Selenium_test. The `Tests.cs` class contains all the tests that will be run. These tests are composed using individual steps contained in the `Steps.cs` class. This makes it easier to manage the tests in smaller chunks and to make changes. It should always be sufficient to change only part of the code in a single step and not the entire test. Changes in individual steps do not affect other steps of the test.

The SeleniumConfig class is described below. All tests are closed in a try/finally block. The try block contains the test itself. The finally block calls the Quit() method which closes the browser window and ends the test session. This ensures that the container is always free for the next test and not blocked by the previous one. Each test consists of several smaller steps. The most important parts of the tests are shown below. Configuration file for test job setup in GitLab pipeline is available at \gitlab\job-config-file\.gitlab-ci.yml.

Basic Test Configuration

The basic class that is needed for the tests is SeleniumConfig.cs. This class is where all the basic settings related to the browser used for testing are made. This is done by creating an instance of the ChromeOptions class, which contains the appropriate methods for Chrome-specific settings. For these settings to take effect, a ChromeOptions object needs to be added to the WebDriver constructor.

In the code below you can see the two parameters for the settings. The first is the headless parameter. This makes the web browser run without a graphical interface. It is useful to use it if the tests are run on a server where this GUI is not visible, so it is not needed. This also saves limited server resources such as RAM or disk space. If new tests are being developed locally, it is preferable not to use this setting, as no video of the test run is available. This can make it difficult to find a possible reason why the test is broken, and the test developer has to go by the logs only.

The next parameter is the start maximized, where it is clear from the name that the browser will automatically start in the maximum window size, not just in a reduced form. In total, there are around 140 of these parameters/settings [17]. There is also a variable hubAddress in the script that contains the address to which the tests should connect. For local development and testing, they are redirected to port 4444, which exposes a running local docker container containing the Selenium grid. To run tests on a server, for example in Kubernetes clusters, this address must be changed to a specific corresponding IP address.

```
public class SeleniumConfig
{
    String hubAdress = "http://localhost:4444";
    ChromeOptions options = new ChromeOptions();
    public Zalenium()
    {}
    public void PrepareDriver(string name ="SeleniumTest")
    {
        options.AddArguments("--headless");
        options.AddArguments("--start-maximized");
        remoteDriver = new RemoteWebDriver(new Uri
        (hubAdress),options);
    }
}
```

User Login

In the `Steps.cs` class, the `Login` method is created to test the successful login. It is also used in all other tests since each instance of the web browser requires a new login to the application. For this reason, the login name and password are not provided as parameters, as it is not expected that different values will be used in each test.

```
public void Login(RemoteWebDriver driver)
{
   var wait = new WebDriverWait(driver, new TimeSpan(0, 0, 10));
   wait.Until(SeleniumExtras.WaitHelpers.ExpectedConditions.
   ElementToBeClickableBy.XPath("//button/span[text()=
   'SignIn']"))).Click();
   driver.FindElement(By.XPath("//span[text()=
   'CompanyUsers']")).Click();
driver.FindElement(By.Id("userNameInput")).SendKeys("username");
driver.FindElement(By.Id("passwordInput")).SendKeys("password");
driver.FindElement(By.Id("submitButton")).Click();
}
```

If we would like to verify that the user login was successful, we can add, for example, the code below, which checks the condition that the correct username is displayed in the required element. This element is only displayed after a successful login.

```
wait.Until(SeleniumExtras.WaitHelpers.ExpectedConditions.TextTo
BePresentInElementLocated(By.XPath("//button[3]/span[1]"),
"username"));
```

Ordering Materials for Production

The *"MaterialOrder_RequiredFields"* test checks the correct entry of data into the individual fields of the form for ordering physical material that is used in production after delivery. The form contains multiple fields. This test checks only the required fields to order the material. The test accepts the parameters `material`, `supplier`, `numberOfWeeks`, `view`, `quantity`, `identifier`, `deliveryDate`. The XUnit testing framework provides an InlineData attribute that passes specific values, provided by us, to our test. The order of values in this attribute corresponds to the order in which the parameters are declared in the function or test.

Next, the instance from the `Steps.cs` class is declared. This allows to access the methods of this class that make up the steps of the test. As you can see from the sample below, there are a total of five steps (the name of the steps should make it clear at a glance what each one does):

1. Login,
2. Dashboard_SearchMaterial,
3. EnterMaterialOrder_RequiredFields,
4. SearchForMaterialOrder,
5. DeleteMaterialOrder.

```
[Theory(DisplayName = "Material order (Required fields)")]
[InlineData("material", "supplier", "numberOfWeeks", "view",
"quantity", "identifier", "deliveryDate")]

public void MaterialOrder_RequiredFields(string partNumber,
string vendorCode, string numberOfWeeks, string viewName, string
quantity, string invoiceNO, string ETAdate){
  try
  {
    Steps step = new Steps();
    fix.remoteDriver.Navigate().GoToUrl(url);
    step.Login(fix.remoteDriver);
    step.Dashboard_SearchMaterial(fix.remoteDriver,
    material, supplier, numberOfWeeks, view);
    step.EnterMaterialOrder_RequiredFields
    (fix.remoteDriver, quantity, identifier, deliveryDate);
    step.SearchForMaterialOrder(fix.remoteDriver, identifier);
    step.DeleteMaterialOrder(fix.remoteDriver);
  }
finally{
    fix.remoteDriver.Quit();
  }
}
```

The example below shows an example of one step of the test, namely the step *EnterMaterialOrder_RequiredFields*. In the first stage of the test, an instance of the WebDriverWait class is declared. The constructor of this class requires two parameters - which driver to wait for and how long to wait for each element. In this case, the wait will be a maximum of 10 s. If a specific condition is not met by this time, the test will exit with an error. Here, the condition must be met to be able to click on the selected element during this time. Successively, values are sent to each element of the form. After the values have been entered, the button to create the material order is clicked. At the end of this step, the successful creation of the order is checked by the displayed text, which must be "Material order created".

```
public void EnterMaterialOrder_RequiredFields
(RemoteWebDriver driver, string quantity, string identifier,
string deliveryDate){
(RemoteWebDriver driver, string quantity, string identifier,
string deliveryDate)
{
var wait = new WebDriverWait(driver, newTimeSpan(0, 0, 10));
wait.Until(SeleniumExtras.WaitHelpers.ExpectedConditions.Element
ToBeClickable(By.CssSelector("mat-icon[aria-label='Open new
order form']"))).Click();
wait.Until(SeleniumExtras.WaitHelpers.ExpectedConditions.Element
ToBeClickable(By.XPath("//input[@placeholder='Qty']"))).Click();
wait.Until(SeleniumExtras.WaitHelpers.ExpectedConditions.Element
ToBeClickable(By.XPath("//input[@placeholder='Qty']"))).SendKeys
(quantity);
wait.Until(SeleniumExtras.WaitHelpers.ExpectedConditions.Element
ToBeClickable(By.XPath("//input[@placeholder=OrderId']"))).
SendKeys(identifier);
wait.Until(SeleniumExtras.WaitHelpers.ExpectedConditions.Element
ToBeClickable(By.XPath("//input[@placeholder='DeliveryDate']")))
.Click();
Actions action = new Actions(driver);
action.SendKeys(Keys.Escape).Perform();
wait.Until(SeleniumExtras.WaitHelpers.ExpectedConditions.Element
ToBeClickable(By.XPath("//input[@placeholder='DeliveryDate']")))
.SendKeys(deliveryDate);
wait.Until(SeleniumExtras.WaitHelpers.ExpectedConditions.Element
ToBeClickable(By.Id("submit"))).Click();
// checking the displayed message after creating a new order
wait.Until(SeleniumExtras.WaitHelpers.ExpectedConditions.Element
IsVisible(By.XPath("//span[contains(text(),'Material order
created.')]")));
}
```

The Formula for Calculating the Number of Pieces of Material
The "*CreateCalculationFormula*" test verifies the correctness of the formula for calculating the number of pieces of material in stock in each week. This formula is then used in multiple places in the application. However, this is not the focus of this test, only its basic creation and subsequent deletion are tested here.

```
[Theory(DisplayName = "Calculation formula - Create, Search, De-
lete")]
[InlineData("view", "Selenium - Calculation formula")]
public void CreateCalculationFormula(string view, string
nameOfCalculationFormula){
  try{
    Steps step = new Steps();
    fix.remoteDriver.Navigate().GoToUrl(url);
    step.Login(fix.remoteDriver);
    step.Dashboard_SelectViewModule(fix.remoteDriver);
    step.OpenConcreteView(fix.remoteDriver,viewName);
    step.View_CreateCalculationFormula
      (fix.remoteDriver, nameOfCalculationLine);
    step.View_SearchForSpecificCalculationFormula
      (fix.remoteDriver, nameOfCalculationLine);
    step.View_DeleteCalculationFormula
      (fix.remoteDriver, nameOfCalculationLine);
  }finally{
    fix.remoteDriver.Quit();
  }
}
```

This test consists of six steps. The first is the "Login" step, which is the same for all tests. It ensures that the user logs in to the application. The second step "Dashboard_SelectViewModule" ensures that the appropriate application module is selected, which is used to set up the formulas. The third step "OpenConcreteView" opens the desired view. It needs to be specified which view to open by entering its name into the function parameter. The fourth step establishes the specific formula for the calculation. The fifth step searches the based record by the specified name, this step is given as an example below. The last step deletes this record and checks for successful deletion.

```
public void View_SearchForSpecificCalculationFormula
(RemoteWebDriver driver, string name)
{
  var wait = new WebDriverWait(driver, newTimeSpan(0, 0, 10));

  // search
  wait.Until(SeleniumExtras.WaitHelpers.ExpectedConditions.
  ElementToBeClickable(By.Id("Grid_searchbar"))).SendKeys(name);

  // solves the problem with the occasional disappearance of
  inserted text in the search bar

  for (int i = 0; i < 10; i++)
  {
    var enteredTextSearch=wait.Until(SeleniumExtras.WaitHelpers.
    ExpectedConditions.ElementIsVisible
    (By.Id("Grid_searchbar"))).GetAttribute("value");

    if (enteredTextSearch != name)
    {
      wait.Until(SeleniumExtras.WaitHelpers.ExpectedConditions.
      ElementToBeClickable(By.Id("Grid_searchbar"))).Clear();

      wait.Until(SeleniumExtras.WaitHelpers.ExpectedConditions.
      ElementToBeClickable
      (By.Id("Grid_searchbar"))).SendKeys(name);
      continue;
    }
      else{break;}
  }

  wait.Until(SeleniumExtras.WaitHelpers.ExpectedConditions.
  ElementIsVisible(By.CssSelector("td[aria-label= Selenium
  Calculation formula]")));
}
```

This loop solves the occasional problem with the text disappearing into the search box, caused by the test script inserting the text too quickly. The `GetAttribute()` function gets the text that is inserted into the search bar. If this text does not match the name, that is being searched for, the script sends the text to the search box again and rechecks if the texts now match. If it does, it continues the test, if not, it tries to send the text to the array again. If the search text fails to be inserted within ten attempts, the test ends with an error. The last line checks whether the formula has indeed been searched for by name. If the name matches, the next step deletes it.

Virtual Material Group

The "*VirtualGroup*" test is designed to verify the correct creation and deletion of the so-called virtual group. This group can then be used to add other individual specific materials. The first step is to log in to the application, the second is to select the appropriate module to create the virtual group, the third is to create this group and the last step is to delete it.

```
[Theory(DisplayName = "Virtual group - Create,Delete")]
[InlineData("Selenium Virtual Group")]
public void VirtualGroup(string VirtualGroupName)
{
  try{
    Steps step = new Steps();
    fix.remoteDriver.Navigate().GoToUrl(url);
    step.Login(fix.remoteDriver);
    step.Dashboard_SelectVirtualGroupModule(fix.remoteDriver);
    step.CreateVirtualGroup(fix.remoteDriver,
    VirtualPNGroupName);
    step.DeleteVirtualGroup(fix.remoteDriver)
  }

  finally{
    fix.remoteDriver.Quit();
  }
}
```

Below is an example of the "*CreateVirtualGroup*" step. Firstly, the script clicks the button to add a virtual group and then enters the name of the group in the appropriate field. Secondly, it will compare whether the group name matches the one that was entered during creation. If it does, the test continues with the next step.

```
public void CreateVirtualGroup(RemoteWebDriver driver, string
nameOfGroup){
  var wait = new WebDriverWait(driver, new TimeSpan(0, 0, 10));

  // clicks the add button
  wait.Until(SeleniumExtras.WaitHelpers.ExpectedConditions.
  ElementToBeClickable(By.XPath("//mat-icon[text()='add']"))).
  Click();

  // virtual group name
  wait.Until(SeleniumExtras.WaitHelpers.ExpectedConditions.
  ElementToBeClickable(By.XPath("//input[@placeholder='Virtual
  Group add']"))).Click();

  wait.Until(SeleniumExtras.WaitHelpers.ExpectedConditions.
  ElementToBeClickable(By.XPath("//input[@placeholder='Insert
  Name']"))).SendKeys(nameOfGroup);

  wait.Until(SeleniumExtras.WaitHelpers.ExpectedConditions.
  ElementToBeClickable(By.XPath("/html/body/div[2]/div[2]/div/
  mat-dialog-container/app-platform-add-group/form/mat-dialog
  -actions/button[2]"))).Click();

  // Compare
  wait.Until(SeleniumExtras.WaitHelpers.ExpectedConditions.
  TextToBePresentInElementLocated(By.XPath("//div[contains
  (text(),'Selenium Virtual Group')]"), nameOfGroup));
}
```

Assigning User Rights

The last test "*UserMaterialsRights*" verifies the correct assignment of user rights. A user can be assigned rights to what material they have access to. A special module is used for this purpose, which is tested here. The test consists of four steps. As with the other tests, the first step is "Login", i.e., logging the user into the application. The second step is to select the module for assigning rights. The third step is to set rights for the user on the corresponding material and the last, fourth step, is to delete them.

```
[Theory(DisplayName = "User material rights - Create, Delete")]
[InlineData("userEmail", "material")]
public void UserMaterialsRights(string userEmail, string
material)
{
  try
  {
    Steps step = new Steps();
    fix.remoteDriver.Navigate().GoToUrl(url);
    step.Login(fix.remoteDriver);
    step.Dashboard_SelectUserMaterialRightsModule
    (fix.remoteDriver);
    step.UserMaterialRights_AddRights(fix.remoteDriver,
    userEmail, material);
    step.UserMaterialRights_DeleteRights(fix.remoteDriver);
  }finally{
    fix.remoteDriver.Quit();
}
```

The "*UserMaterialRights_AddRights*" step adds rights between the user and the required material. First, the script clicks the button to add the record. When the window opens, it enters the user's required email and the designation of the material they have rights to. It then presses the save button and proceeds to the next step of the test.

```
public void UserMaterialRights_AddRights(RemoteWebDriver driver,
string UserEmail, string VendorCodes)
{
  var wait = new WebDriverWait(driver, new TimeSpan(0, 0, 10));
  // clicks the add button
  wait.Until(SeleniumExtras.WaitHelpers.ExpectedConditions.
  ElementToBeClickable(By.XPath("//maticon[text()='add']"))).
  Click();

  // entering email and allowed records to view
  wait.Until(SeleniumExtras.WaitHelpers.ExpectedConditions.
  ElementToBeClickable(By.XPath("//input[@placeholder='User
  Email']"))).Click();
  wait.Until(SeleniumExtras.WaitHelpers.ExpectedConditions.

  ElementToBeClickable(By.XPath("//input[@placeholder=
  'User Email']"))).SendKeys(UserEmail);
  wait.Until(SeleniumExtras.WaitHelpers.ExpectedConditions.
  ElementToBeClickable(By.XPath("//textarea[@placeholder=
  'Material']"))).Click();
  wait.Until(SeleniumExtras.WaitHelpers.ExpectedConditions.
  ElementToBeClickable(By.XPath("//textarea[@placeholder=
  'Material']"))).SendKeys(material);
  // save button
  wait.Until(SeleniumExtras.WaitHelpers.ExpectedConditions.
  ElementToBeClickable(By.Id("submit"))).Click();
}
```

4 Assessment

Displaying the results is also important for the tests themselves. Here it depends on whether we want to see the results for locally running tests or for tests running only on the server.

For local development, it is advisable to use Text Explorer directly inside Visual Studio (Fig. 2). This will provide a clear summary of all the tests and additional information about them, such as the length of each test run, or the arguments used. If an error occurs during the test, the program will show the specific exception that caused the test to fail and, if possible, will also show the exact line in the code where the validation or error occurs.

If the automated tests are then run on the server, you must use other means to display the results. The `logger` tool provided by the `dotnet test` driver is used for this purpose. This command is used to execute tests in a given project. The tests are executed using the selected test framework, in this case, XUnit. Use the – `logger` parameter to specify the logging tool for the test results. It can be seen that in our case the resulting file should be in HTML format. Figure 3 below shows the generated report after the completion of five tests. In the upper left corner, there is basic information such as the total number of tests taken, the number of passes, failures, and skips. Also, the percentage of success rate and the total running time of all tests. In addition, the tests that failed are described in more detail. Thanks to this description, in which part of the code the error occurred, it is possible to check the tests manually, run them again or report the discovered error in the application for correction.

Fig. 2. Microsoft Visual Studio – Test Explorer

Test run details

Total tests	Passed : 4	Pass percentage	Run duration
5	Failed : 1	80 %	2m 7s
	Skipped : 0		

Failed Results

/tests/ui-tests/bin/Debug/net6.0/UHK-Selenium-Adam-Kucera.dll

X Virtual group - Create, Delete(VirtualPNGroupName: "Selenium Virtual PN")
  Error:

OpenQA.Selenium.WebDriverTimeoutException : Timed out after 10 seconds
---- OpenQA.Selenium.NoSuchElementException : no such element: Unable to locate element: {"method":"xpath","selector":"//input[@placeholder='VirtalGroup_add']"}
  (Session info: headless chrome=98.0.4758.102)

Stack trace:
     at OpenQA.Selenium.Support.UI.DefaultWait`1.ThrowTimeoutException(String exceptionMessage, Exception lastException)
     at OpenQA.Selenium.Support.UI.DefaultWait`1.Until[TResult](Func`2 condition, CancellationToken token)
     at OpenQA.Selenium.Support.UI.DefaultWait`1.Until[TResult](Func`2 condition)
     at UHK_Selenium_Adam_Kucera.Steps.CreateVirtualGroup(RemoteWebDriver driver, String nameOfPNGroup)
     at UHK_Selenium_Adam_Kucera.Tests.VirtualGroup(String VirtualPNGroupName) in
----- Inner Stack Trace -----
     at OpenQA.Selenium.WebDriver.UnpackAndThrowOnError(Response errorResponse)
     at OpenQA.Selenium.WebDriver.Execute(String driverCommandToExecute, Dictionary`2 parameters)
     at OpenQA.Selenium.WebDriver.FindElement(String mechanism, String value)
     at OpenQA.Selenium.By.<.ctor>b__11_0(ISearchContext context)
     at OpenQA.Selenium.By.FindElement(ISearchContext context)
     at OpenQA.Selenium.WebDriver.FindElement(By by)
     at SeleniumExtras.WaitHelpers.ExpectedConditions.<>c__DisplayClass19_0.<ElementToBeClickable>b__0(IWebDriver driver)
     at OpenQA.Selenium.Support.UI.DefaultWait`1.Until[TResult](Func`2 condition, CancellationToken token)

Fig. 3. HTML logger

5   Conclusion

The aim of the paper was to present the possibilities of creating tests for automatic testing of the graphical user interface of an application in a manufacturing company. The article shows a specific sample test suite written in C# using Selenium WebDriver. The tests cover the basic functionality of the application, such as logging in to the application, ordering material, creating a formula for calculation, a virtual material group, and assigning rights to the user as to what material they can see. In addition, two possible report types for the results of these tests were shown. The first used Visual Studio's tool directly, which is very useful for local test creation. The second is an HTML report that is generated after the tests have finished running in the GitLab environment. The tests were created for the current version of the company application.

From the results of the pilot deployment of the presented automated tests, it is not possible to tell, whether it is more advantageous to use automated or manual testing for software development. Each type has its pros and cons, especially in its reliability and finding covered bugs. Thus, the optimal solution seems to be to use mainly automatic testing, suitably supplemented by manual testing, especially in the case of specific projects. However, automated testing has undoubtedly brought, in the pilot deployment, a great time saving, especially in regression testing, when its need is practically eliminated and gradually fully implemented into the company's processes.

Acknowledgment. The research has been supported by the Faculty of Informatics and Management UHK specific research project 2107 Integration of Departmental Research Activities and Students' Research Activities Support II. Special thanks to our colleague Adam Kučera for his significant help in the practical verification of the tests.

References

1. Myers, G.J., Badgett, T., Sandler, C.: The Art of Software Testing: Now Covers Testing for Usability, Smartphone Apps, and Agile Development Environments, 3rd edn. Wiley, Hoboken (2012)
2. Jamil, M.A., Arif, M., Abubakar, N.S.A., Ahmad, A.: Software testing techniques: a literature review. In: 2016 6th International Conference on Information and Communication Technology for The Muslim World (ICT4M), Jakarta, Indonesia, pp. 177–182, November 2016. https://doi.org/10.1109/ICT4M.2016.045
3. IEEE Standard Glossary of Software Engineering Terminology. IEEE. https://doi.org/10.1109/IEEESTD.1990.101064
4. Galin, D.: Software Quality Assurance. Pearson Education Limited, Harlow; New York (2004)
5. Lynch, J.: The Worst Computer Bugs in History: The Ariane 5 Disaster. BugSnag, 07 September 2017. https://www.bugsnag.com/blog/bug-day-ariane-5-disaster
6. The Editors of Encyclopedia Britannica: "Y2K Bug," Britannica Encyclopedia, 21 April 2021. https://www.britannica.com/technology/Y2K-bug
7. Stojmanovska, M.: 10 Biggest Software Bugs and Tech Fails of 2021. TestDevLab, 27 December 2021. https://www.testdevlab.com/blog/2021/12/27/10-biggest-software-bugs-and-tech-fails-of-2021/
8. Patton, R.: Software Testing, 2nd edn. Sams Pub, Indianapolis (2006)
9. Henry, P.: The Testing Network: An Integral Approach to Test Activities in Large Software Projects. Springer, Heidelberg (2008). https://doi.org/10.1007/978-3-540-78504-0
10. Rafi, D.M., Moses, K.R.K., Petersen, K., Mantyla, M.V.: Benefits and limitations of automated software testing: systematic literature review and practitioner survey. In: 2012 7th International Workshop on Automation of Software Test (AST), Zurich, Switzerland, pp. 36–42, June 2012. https://doi.org/10.1109/IWAST.2012.6228988
11. Xunit. In: NuGet [online]. [cit. 2022-05-05]. https://www.nuget.org/packages/xunit

12. ChromeDevTools: Overview. In: Chrome Developers [online]. [cit. 2022-05-05]. https://developer.chrome.com/docs/devtools/overview/List of
13. Selenium Overview: Selenium (2021). https://www.selenium.dev/documentation/overview/
14. Selenium IDE: Getting Started: Selenium IDE (2019). https://www.selenium.dev/selenium-ide/docs/en/introduction/getting-started
15. Selenium WebDriver: Selenium (2021). https://www.selenium.dev/documentation/webdriver/
16. When to Use a Grid: Selenium (2021). https://www.selenium.dev/documentation/grid/applicability/
17. Chromium Command Line Switches. In: Peter Beverloo [online]. [cit. 2022-05-05]. https://peter.sh/experiments/chromium-command-line-switches/

Data Mining

The Performance of a Kernel-Based Variable Dimension Reduction Method

Thanh Do Van[1] and Hai Nguyen Minh[2]([✉])

[1] Nguyen Tat Thanh University, Ho Chi Minh, Vietnam
dvthanh@cmc-u.edu.vn
[2] Industrial University of Ho Chi Minh City, Ho Chi Minh, Vietnam
nguyenminhhaidhcn@iuh.edu.vn

Abstract. Building forecast models, especially nowcast models, on large data sets of time series variables is a topic of great interest. The most popular method used to build such models is the dynamic factor model, in which factors are extracted from input data sets using the principal component analysis (PCA) or sparse PCA (SPCA) methods. Many studies have shown that the forecast accuracy of models built under such an approach is higher than that of other benchmark models. But the PCA and SPCA methods are only effective when input data sets approximate a hyperplane, while real-world data sets are not always so.

The purpose of this article is to briefly introduce a kernel-based variable dimension reduction method called the KTPCA, and a process of trial and error of this method called the KTPCA#. Experimenting on real-world data sets at the same sampling frequency as well as mixed sampling frequencies shows that the KTPCA# method is superior to the PCA, SPCA, Randomized SPCA (RSPCA), and robust SPCA (ROBSPCA) methods.

Keywords: Time series · Big data · Nowcast · Dimensional reduction · Kernel trick · Factor model

1 Introduction

Forecasting on data sets of a large number of time series variables is a long-standing challenge. There are many approaches to solving the "high dimension curse" in forecasting exercises. First, several regression methods have been proposed to narrow down the coefficient values of some predictors that have a small contribution to the variability of the target variable so that those values are close to zero or zero.

Then the predictors with a coefficient close to zero or zero will be removed from the forecast model of the target variable on input predictors. The RIDGE regression method [1, 2] is intended to narrow the coefficient value of predictors that are less related to the target variable to close to zero, while the LASSO [3, 4], Adaptive LASSO [5], and Elastic Net regression [6] regression methods narrow down the coefficient of less relevant predictors to be zero, and thus the interpretation of forecasts is easier.

C. V. Phan and T. D. Nguyen (Eds.): ICTCC 2022, LNICST 473, pp. 43–60, 2023.
https://doi.org/10.1007/978-3-031-28790-9_4

Thus, the above-mentioned regression methods are all variable selection (or feature selection) ones according to the embedded approach. Bayesian regression methods are also considered variable selection techniques in the same way. One of the commonly used Bayesian regression methods for variable selection is the Bayesian Averaging model [7]. Bayesian regression models are closely related to RIDGE Regression and sparse LASSO regression models [8].

However, when the set of predictors is very large, it is clear that reducing the variable dimension by using the above regression models is not feasible because we still have to perform regression (which is essentially solving optimal exercises) on all predictors to select a subset of suitable predictors. Different from the variable selection approach, the feature learning (or variable transformation) approach transforms the original predictors into new variables with a much smaller number but still retain crucial information in the original predictors.

At present, there have been many feature learning techniques for reducing the variable dimension under different approaches. In scalar time series forecasting exercises, the PCA and SPCA methods are most commonly used [8]. Different from many previous beliefs that the variable dimension reduction performance of the SPCA methods is superior to that of the PCA method, the study [9] has shown experimentally that the dimensional reduction performances of the PCA method and the SPCA methods, including the RSPCA and ROBSPCA methods are competitive.

Van Der Maaten and Postma [10] conducted experiments on real-world data sets and artificial data sets to compare the dimensionality reduction performance of the PCA method with the top 12 nonlinear dimensionality reduction methods such as the kernel principal component analysis (KPCA), Isomap, Maximum Variance Unfolding, Locally Linear Embedding, Laplacian Eigenmap, Hessian LLE, Multilayer Autoencoders, Diffusion Maps, Multidimensional Scaling, Local Tangent Space Analysis, Locally Linear Coordination, and Charting a Manifold. The authors have shown that although the 12 nonlinear dimensionality reduction methods mentioned above can all reduce dimensionality well on artificial data sets, with real-world data sets, none of them reduces the dimensionality better than the PCA method. The article [11] also compares the dimensionality reduction performance of the PCA method and 02 other nonlinear PCA methods, including the robust fuzzy PCA (RFPCA) and KPCA methods, and uses an artificial neural network (ANN) technique for classification. That article has shown that PCA + ANN gives better classification results than RFPCA + ANN and KPCA + ANN.

The PCA method is a typical unsupervised linear learning technique to transform data sets in a high dimensional space to a much lower dimensional space while preserving the maximal variance and covariance structures of the original data set [12]. This method is only effective when data points of the data set of input predictors are approximately a hyperplane. But real-world datasets are not always like that.

The KPCA method is a natural extension of the PCA method [13, 14] and a dimensionality reduction technique for any large data set that may or may not approximate a manifold, whereas the 11 remaining methods are only manifold learning techniques, i.e., they are only suitable for data sets where their data points are approximately a manifold. In another study, we have shown that as a natural extension of the PCA method, the KPCA method is the observation dimension reduction technique, not the variable dimension reduction technique. This method can be the variable dimension reduction technique, but then it is not a natural extension of the PCA method.

On the other hand, the works [8, 15–19] showed that the effective modeling method on macroeconomic large data sets is the dynamic factor model and Kalman filter, in which the dynamic factor model including the factor bridge equation (BE model for short) and the factor mixed data sampling (MIDAS for short) models are the most applied [20, 21]. In the dynamic factor model, factors are extracted from data sets of input predictors using the PCA method. The presentations above suggest that it is necessary to propose a new variable dimension reduction method that is a natural extension of the PCA method. It can be used to reducet the variable dimension of large data sets where their data points do not approximate a hyperplane and its variable dimension reduction performance must be superior to that of the PCA method.

This article briefly introduces the KTPCA# method and experiments showing that the variable dimension reduction performance of the KTPCA# method is superior to that of the PCA, SPCA, RSPCA, and ROBSPCA methods in forecasting exercises on large data sets of predictors at the same sampling frequency as well as mixed sampling frequency.

The structure of this article is as follows: following this section, Sect. 2 introduces the dynamic factor model as a necessary preparatory for further sections. Section 3 presents briefly the KTPCA# method. Section 4 introduces experimental results comparing the variable dimension reduction performance of the KTPCA# method with the PCA, SPCA, RSPCA, and ROBSPCA methods in forecasting as well as nowcasting exercises. Section 5 finally presents some conclusions and directions for further research in near future.

2 Dynamic Factor Model

2.1 Dynamic Factor Model

Suppose $y = (y_1, \ldots, y_m) \in \mathbb{R}^m$ and $X_t = [x_{1,t}, x_{2,t}, \ldots, x_{N,t}]$, where $x_{i,t} = (x_{i,1}, x_{i,2}, \ldots, x_{i,m}) \in \mathbb{R}^m$ are a target variable and a set of predictors, respectively; m and N are the number of observations and predictors, respectively. The model to forecast the target variable according to the predictors has the form:

$$y_t = F(y_{t-k}, X_t) + u_t \tag{1}$$

here u_t is white noise, y_{t-k} the target variable y_t lagged at the order k ($k \geq 1$); F() is a linear or nonlinear function. In practice application, F() is estimated from m observations of the target variable and predictors. When N is very large, we can use the dynamic factor model to build a forecast model. This model assumes that p dynamic factors not observed can capture information in the set of N predictors X_t and p < < N. In general form, the model is defined as follows [22, 23]:

$$X_t = \Lambda f_t + \varepsilon_t \tag{2}$$

$$f_t = \psi(L)f_{t-1} + \eta_t \tag{3}$$

here L is the lag operator, f_t is the matrix of p hidden factors (not be observed) as columns; Λ is the N x p weight matrix of the p factors; ε_t is a vector of idiosyncratic errors, which may be weakly correlated [24]. Stock and Watson [25] showed that the principal component vectors of a data set can consistently estimate hidden factors under the assumptions of the dynamic factor model. If W is the N $\times$ p matrix of the principal component vectors as the columns of the covariance matrix $S_X = \frac{1}{m} X_t^T X_t$ then the hidden factors at time t are estimated by:

$$\hat{f}_t = W^T . X_t \tag{4}$$

Then, the out-of-sample forecast of h periods of the target variable y_t is determined by regressing the variable y_{t+h} on $\hat{f}_t, \hat{f}_{t-1}, \ldots, \hat{f}_{t-q+1}$. In other words:

$$\hat{y}_{t+h} = \hat{f}_t^T \hat{\delta}_1 + \hat{f}_{t-1}^T \hat{\delta}_2 + \ldots + \hat{f}_{t-q-1}^T \hat{\delta}_q \tag{5}$$

where $\hat{\delta}_i \in \mathbb{R}^p$ is the vector of the coefficients estimated by the least-squares method. When the predictors are at frequencies differing from the frequency of the target variable and the number of factors is small, to regress the variable y_{t+h} on $\hat{f}_t, \hat{f}_{t-1}, \ldots, \hat{f}_{t-q+1}$ one has to represent the dynamic factor model as a factor state-space model. Details can be found in [26]. Although forecasting the target variable y_t using the dynamic factor model is done according to the two-step procedure, this forecast is still a linear function of predictors in X_t. By replacing (4) in (5), and putting $\hat{\theta}_t = \widehat{W}.\hat{\delta}_t$, then Eq. (5) can be written as:

$$\hat{y}_{t+h} = X_t^T \hat{\theta}_1 + X_{t-1}^T \hat{\theta}_2 + \ldots + X_{t-q+1}^T \hat{\theta}_q \tag{6}$$

As such in case the number of factors extracted from X_t is not large, we can estimate the coefficients $\hat{\theta}_i$ in another way, that is by using the RIDGE, LASSO, and Elastic Net regression models. But if the number of factors extracted from X_t is still too large, one only chooses k principal component vectors to include in Eq. (6) so that these k vectors still carry a lot of critical information in these hidden factors.

The build of nowcast models on large mixed-frequency data sets is usually based on the factor BE and MIDAS models.

2.2 The Factor BE Model

It is a linear regression model that links variables at higher frequencies with variables at lower frequencies [21]. The BE model is proposed very naturally and is defined as follows

$$y_t = \sum_{k=1}^{P} b_k y_{t-k} + \sum_{i=1}^{N} \sum_{j=0}^{r_i} \beta_{ij} x_{i,t-j} + \sum_{j=1}^{M} \sum_{h=0}^{p_j} \gamma_{jh} F_{j,t-h} + c + u_t \tag{7}$$

where y_t is a low-frequency target variable at date t; $x_{i,t}$ are predictors at the same low-frequency as y_t; $F_{j,t}$ are factors at the same frequency as y_t and are aggregated from $F_{j,t/S}^H$ factors at a higher frequency. $F_{j,t/S}^H$ are extracted using a feature learning method from a large set of original predictors $z^H_{j,t/s}$ sampled at the higher frequency with S values for each low-frequency value. $F^H_{j,t/S}$ as well as $z^H_{j,t/S}$ are called high-frequency components in a mixed frequency model; u_t is residuals; r_i (i = 1,..., N), p_j (j = 1,..., M) and p, are optimal lags of the variables $x_{i,t}$, $F_{j,t}$ and y_t, respectively. The optimal lags can be determined using the Akaike information criterion (AIC) or Bayesian information criterion (BIC).

If the predictors $x_{i,t}$, $z^H_{j,t/S}$, and the target variable are at the same frequency, i.e., S = 1, then $F_{j,t}=F^H_{j,t/S}$, , and model (7) becomes an autoregressive distributed lag model.

Model (7) can be rewritten as:

$$\psi(L)y_t = \sum_{i=1}^{N} \beta_i(L)x_{i,t} + \sum_{j=1}^{M} \gamma_j(L)F_{j,t} + c + u_t \tag{8}$$

where L denotes usual lag operator, $\psi(L) = 1 - \sum_{k=1}^{P} b_k L^k$, $\beta_i(L) = \sum_{j=0}^{r_i} \beta_{ij}L^j$, and $\gamma_j(L) = \sum_{h=0}^{p_j} \gamma_{jh}L^h$.

2.3 Factor MIDAS Model

The general factor MIDAS model is defined as follows [17, 27]:

$$\psi(L)y_t = \sum_{i=1}^{N} \beta_i(L)x_{i,t} + f(\{F^H_{t/S}\}, \theta, \lambda) + u_t \tag{9}$$

where y_t is the target variable sampled at a low frequency, at date t; $x_{i,t}$ are the predictors at the same low frequency as y_t; $\{F^H_{t/S}\}$ is a set of the factors extracted from a large set of predictors sampled at a higher frequency with S values for each low-frequency value; $\psi(L) = 1 - \sum_{k=1}^{P} b_k L^k$; $\beta_i(L) = \sum_{j=0}^{r_i} \beta_{ij}L^j$; f is a function describing the effect of the higher frequency data in the low-frequency regression; b $= (b_k)$, $\beta_i = (\beta_{ij})$, θ, and λ are vectors of parameters to be estimated.

U-MIDAS Model

If we like only to include each of the higher frequency components as a predictor in the low-frequency regression, then the model (9) can be given by

$$\varphi(L)y_t = \sum_{i=1}^{N} \beta_i(L)x_{i,t} + \sum_{\tau=0}^{k-1} F^{H}_{(t-\tau)/s}{}^T \theta_\tau + u_t \tag{10}$$

where T stands transpose, $F^{H}_{(t-\tau)/S}{}^T$ is a factor at the τ high-frequency periods before t. Then, a distinct θ_τ is associated with each of the S high-frequency lag factors. The number of θ_τ coefficients may be large. If these coefficients are not constrained, then model (10) is called the unrestricted MIDAS model (U-MIDAS for short).

STEP Weighting MIDAS Model (STEP-MIDAS)

If we like only to add an equally weighted sum (or average) of high-frequency data as a predictor in the low-frequency regression, then the MIDAS model (10) can take the form:

$$\psi(L)y_t = \sum_{i=1}^{N} \beta_i(L)x_{i,t} + (\sum_{\tau=0}^{S-1} F^{H}_{(t-\tau)/S})^T \lambda + u_t \tag{11}$$

The parameter vector λ is associated with a new predictor, and at that time, model (11) is also essentially the factor BE model, and it is almost the same as the model defined by the formula (9). Model (11) is called the equally weighted aggregation model.

In the STEP-MIDAS model, the coefficients on high-frequency data are restricted using a STEP function. Specifically, this model is derived from the model (11) and has the form:

$$\psi(L)y_t = \sum_{i=1}^{N} \beta_i(L)x_{i,t} + \sum_{\tau=0}^{K-1}(F_{(t-\tau)/S}^{H})^T \varphi_\tau + u_t \qquad (12)$$

where K is a chosen number of lagged high-frequency periods to use (K may be less than or greater than S); δ is a step length; $\varphi_m = \theta_i$, for K = int(m/δ).

Polynomial Almon Weighting MIDAS Model (PAW-MIDAS model): for each high frequency up to k, the regression coefficients of high-frequency components in the model (14) are modeled as a p-dimensional lag polynomial in the MIDAS parameter θ, and the model is as follows:.

$$\psi(L)y_t = \sum_{i=1}^{N} \beta_i(L)x_{i,t} + \sum_{\tau=0}^{k-1}(F_{(t-\tau)/S}^{H})^T \left(\sum_{j=0}^{p} \tau^j \theta_j\right) + u_t \qquad (13)$$

where p is the Almon polynomial order, and the chosen number of lags k may be less than or greater than S. Then, the number of coefficients to be estimated depends on the polynomial order and not the number of high-frequency lags.

The model (13) is called the Polynomial Almon weighting MIDAS model.

The exponential almon weighting MIDAS model (or EAW-MIDAS model) is a type of non-polynomial distributed lag MIDAS model. This model uses exponential weights and a lag polynomial of degree 2. Specifically, the EAW-MIDAS model takes the form [27]:

$$\psi(L)y_t = \sum_{i=1}^{N} \beta_i(L)x_{i,t} + \sum_{\tau=0}^{k-1}(F_{(t-\tau)/S}^{H})^T \left(\frac{\exp(\tau\theta_1 + \tau^2\theta_2)}{\sum_{j=0}^{k}\exp(j\theta_1 + j^2\theta_2)}\right) + u_t \qquad (14)$$

where k is a chosen number of lags. Then the exponential weighting function and the lag polynomial depend on the two MIDAS coefficients θ_1 and θ_2.

It can be said that models (11) and (10) can be considered extreme polar ones of MIDAS models. Model (10) offers the greatest flexibility but requires a large number of coefficients. The models from (12) to (14) are considered to fall between these two models. By offering different restrictions on the effects of high-frequency variables at various lags, one can create the middle MIDAS models between the equally weighted aggregation model (11) and the U-MIDAS model (10). Such restrictions on the effects of high-frequency variables can be realized through MIDAS weighting functions.

3   Kernel-Based Factor Extraction Method

3.1   The KTPCA Method

Suppose $\mathbf{X} = [x_1, x_2, \ldots, x_N]$, here $x_i = (x_{i1}, x_{i2}, \ldots, x_{im})^T \in \mathbb{R}^m$; m, N are respectively the number of observations, the number of predictors (or the dimension number of the data set $\mathbf{X}$).

Dimensional reduction is a mapping $\mathcal{R} : \mathbb{R}^N \to \mathbb{R}^p$.

$(x_{1j}, x_{2j}, \ldots, x_{Nj}) \mapsto (z_{1j}, z_{2j}, \ldots, z_{pj})$, so that p $\ll$ N and the dataset of $\{z_1, z_2, \ldots, z_p\} = \mathcal{R}(\{x_1, x_2, \ldots, x_N\})$ still retains the critical information of the dataset **X**, here $z_j = (z_{j1}, z_{j2}, \ldots, z_{jm})^T, j = 1, 2, \ldots, p$; $(x_{1j}, x_{2j}, \ldots, x_{Nj})$ is called a data point of **X**. Without loss of generality, it can be assumed that **X** is mean-centered, i.e. $\sum_{j=1}^{m} x_{ij} = 0$ for all i = 1,..., N. The KTPCA method can be briefly presented as follows:

Suppose $\mathbf{K} = [\kappa(x_i, x_j)]$ is the kernel matrix of **X** corresponding to the kernel function κ. If the function κ is symmetric and positive definite (semi-deterministic), so is the matrix **K** [10]. Then the eigenvalues of **K** are positive (or non-negative) and **K** is diagonalized by an orthogonal matrix of **K**'s eigenvectors. Each factor of **X** is determined by linearly projecting the set **X** onto an eigenvector of the matrix **K** and the set of factors corresponding to the **K**'s eigenvectors is determined by:

$$\mathbf{PC}_{mxN} = \mathbf{X_{mxN}} \cdot \widetilde{\mathbf{E}}_{NxN} \tag{15}$$

here $\widetilde{\mathbf{E}}_{NxN}$ is the NxN matrix of N eigenvectors of the matrix **K**. In this matrix the columns are sorted in descending order of their respective eigenvalues.

Because N is very large, in the practical application one only needs to choose k vectors corresponding to the first k columns in the matrix $\mathbf{PC}_{mxN}$ for replacing the set of input predictors in forecast models on the data set **X**.

The question is, how is the number of chosen factors used to replace input predictors determined? With the note that when the kernel function $\kappa(x_i, x_j)$ is the dot product of two vectors, we see that the KTPCA method becomes the PCA method, and in this case, according to [28], the number of first principal components can be determined by the Cross-validation, Screening, or Use the Cumulative Percentage of Variance (or eigenvalues or mean eigenvalues), the Coded Error Function, the Akaike Information Criterion, the Minimum Description Length Criterion or the Variance of Reconstruction Error,... If the cumulative percentage of variance is used, it should be in the range (70% to 90%). If that percentage is <70%, then there is usually not enough information from the original data set in the chosen factors, and if this percentage is >90%, there may be a situation that is too suitable to make forecasts using the model. The selection of the number of factors in the KTPCA method can be done by selecting the number of principal component factors as in the PCA method.

3.2   The KTPCA# Method

Another problem is how to choose the suitable kernel function $\kappa(x_i, x_j)$ when implementing the KTPCA variable dimension reduction method due to kernels satisfying the requirements are very rich and varied. In the practical application, polynomial kernels $\kappa(x_i, x_j) = (c_1 \langle x_i, x_j \rangle + c_2)^d$ and Gaussian kernels $\kappa(x_i, x_j) = \exp(\frac{-\|x_i - x_j\|^2}{2\rho^2})$ are the most commonly used [14, 29]. In the case of Gaussian kernels the parameter ρ^2 needs to be taken around the value:

$$\frac{c}{N} \sum_{i=1}^{N} min_{i \neq j} \|\mathbf{x}_i - \mathbf{x_j}\|^2 \tag{16}$$

where c is a user-defined tuning parameter [30].

Thus, to choose the most suitable kernel κ, it is necessary to perform a trial and error process based on the criterion that the error of the forecast model is the smallest. The standard mean error of forecast models (Root Mean Squared Errors – RMSE forshot) is used in this article to evaluate the forecast accuracy of forecast and nowcast models. The KTPCA# method can be described in a general way in Fig. 1 below.

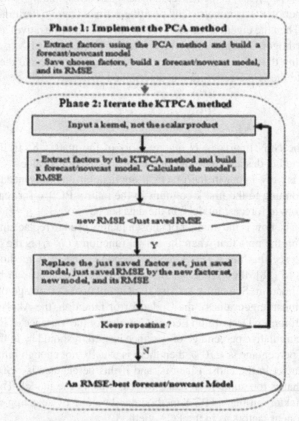

Fig. 1. Framework of the KTPCA # method

The KTPCA# method is an iterative process of kernels. That process depends on the user. The more iterative process with the more reasonable selection of kernels, the higher the probability of choosing the most suitable kernel with the forecast/nowcast model having the lowest forecast error. At the end of that iterative process, we get the result of variable dimension reduction and a forecast/nowcast model having the highest forecast accuracy among the models built according to the chosen kernels. Figure 1 also shows that the process of building a forecast/nowcast model on time series large data set using the KTPCA# method has integrated the variable dimension reduction phase and the phase using a forecast algorithm in one.

4   Dimensional Reduction Performance of KTPCA# Method

The variable dimension reduction performance of a method is measured by the RMSE of a forecast/nowcast model built based on a regression model on factors extracted from the data set of original predictors using this method. In this section, the variable dimension reduction performance of the KTPCA# method is compared with that of the PCA, SPCA, RSPCA, and ROBSPCA methods. Those are the methods commonly used and currently considered the most effective factor extraction methods for building forecast/nowcast models on scalar time series large data sets.

The extraction of factors by the SPCA, RSPCA, and ROBSPCA methods is performed using the 'Sparsepca' package [31], while this extraction by the KTPCA# method is performed by a self-developed tool based on the "Kernlab" package [32] and framework presented in Fig. 1 above.

Because the KTPCA# method can be used to reduce the variable dimension for data sets of predictors at the same sampling frequency as well as at mixed sampling frequencies, so the performance of this method is also compared and evaluated in the two types of these data sets.

4.1   For the Same Sampling Frequency Data Sets

Experimental Data Sets

Data sets used for the experiment include 04 real data sets of the Vietnam economy and 07 data sets in the UCI-Machine Learning Repository [33]. They are named EXP, VN30, CPI, VIP, Residential Building, S&P 500, DJI, and Nasdaq, Air Quality, Appliances energy, and Superconductivity. Table 1 below introduces some statistical characteristics of these data sets. In this table, the number of attributes is the number of predictors excluding the target variable. Missing data were processed by the weighted moving average method.

Table 1. The statistical characteristics of experimental data sets

Data sets	Type of data set	Type of Attribute	No. of Observs	No. of Attributes	Missing data	The target variable	Frequency
EXP	Time series	Real	60	63	No	Total exports	Monthly
VN30	Time series	Real	366	34	No	VN30 index	Daily
CPI	Time series	Real	72	102	No	CPI index	Monthly
VIP	Time Series	Real	60	265	No	Production value of industries	Monthly

(*continued*)

Table 1. (*continued*)

Data sets	Type of data set	Type of Attribute	No. of Observs	No. of Attributes	Missing data	The target variable	Frequency
Residential Building	Multivariate	Real	371	27^1	No	Sales prices	
S&P500	Time series	Real	1760	52	Yes	S&P 500 index	Daily
DJI	Time series	Real	1760	81	Yes	Dow Jones Index	Daily
NASDAQ	Time series	Real	1760	81	Yes	Nasdaq Index	Daily
Air Quality	Time series	Real	9348	12	Yes	CO of Air	Hourly
Appliances Energy	Time series	Real	19704	23	No	The energy use of Appliances (wh)	Every 10 min
SuperConduct	Multivariate	Real	21263	81	No	Critical temperature	

[1]: Remove the column V1: zip codes

Experimental Method

To compare the variable dimension reduction performance of the KTPCA# method with those of PCA, SPCA, RSPCA, and ROBSPCA methods, for the experimental 11 data sets, excepting the special polynomial kernel $PL_0(X_i, X_j) = \ <X_i, X_j>$ (then the KTPCA and PCA methods are the same), the article unanimously chooses only five other kernels to experiment with the KTPCA method, where two polynomial kernels and three Gaussian kernels. Specifically, they are as follows: for the EXP, VN30, CPI, Air quality, and Appliances Energy data sets, two chosen polynomial kernels are of the forms $PL_1(X_i, X_j) = \ <X_i, X_j> +0.5)^2$ and $PL_2(X_i, X_j) = \ <X_i, X_j> +0.5)^3$, while for the remaining data sets, two chosen polynomial kernels are $PL_1(X_i, X_j) = 0.5 <X_i, X_j> +0.5)^2$ and $PL_2(X_i, X_j) = 0.5 <X_i, X_j> +0.5)^3$. For Gaussian kernels with the parameter ρ^2, the three chosen kernels with this parameter value correspond to equal to, smaller than, and larger than the expected value, and they are denoted GA_3, GA_4, and GA_5, respectively. The level of smaller or larger than the expected value depends on each specific data set and is based on the analysis of the number of factors extracted by the KTPCA method with the Gaussian kernel's parameter ρ^2 to obtain the expected value. The autoregressive distributed lag model is used to build forecast models on data sets of predictors at the same sampling frequency.

According to the work [34], when building forecast models on data sets of economic and financial variables at the monthly frequency using the autoregressive distributed lag model, the optimal lag of all variables in the models, in general, is 6, 12, or even 24.

Except for the EXP data set, here the maximum lag of variables in a forecast model is determined according to the experience [34] and is 6, for the remaining 10 data sets, the maximum lag of all variables is precisely determined using a combination of the Akaike information criterion (AIC) and the seasonality of these time-series data sets. Thus, the maximum lag of the factors extracted using different variable dimension reduction methods for each data set is generally different.

All factors are tested for unit roots and transformed to stationary time series before performing model estimate, and in the estimated models, all variables are high statistical significance, at least below 10%. The conditions for the best, linear, and unbiased estimate (BLUE for short) are guaranteed.

Results

The average minimum distance between two data vectors of the 11 data sets used for the experiment is presented in Table 2. These values are the expected value of the parameter ρ^2 in the Gaussian kernel for corresponding data sets. Specifically, each expected value is an important guideline to choose suitable Gaussian kernels $\kappa(x_i, x_j) = \exp\left(-\frac{\|X_i - X_j\|^2}{2\rho^2}\right)$ when performing the KTPCA method on a given corresponding data set.

Table 2. The average minimum distance between two data vectors of data sets

Data sets	EXP	VN30	CPI	VIP	Res. Buil.	S&P500
The average minimum distance between two data vectors of predictors $(=\rho^2)$	$e^{-0.5639}$	$e^{7.046}$	$e^{1.461}$	$e^{34.906}$	$e^{26.919}$	$e^{15.426}$
	DJI	NASDAQ	AirQuality	App. Energy	SuperCond.	
	$e^{15.171}$	$e^{12.971}$	$e^{18.977}$	$e^{13.595}$	$e^{22.353}$	

With the cumulative eigenvalue percentage threshold of 75% for all the aforementioned variable dimension reduction methods and the experimental data sets, results of variable dimension reduction, the RMSE of built forecast models on the factors extracted by the PCA, SPCA, RSPCA, ROBSPCA methods as well as the KTPCA# method with the PL_0, PL_1, PL_2, GA_3, GA_4, and GA_5 kernels are shown in Table 3, where the values of the parameter ρ^2 in the kernels GA_4, and GA_5 are shown in Table 4, in which the codes from S1 to S11 are assigned to the 11 experimental data sets in Table 1 from top to bottom. Column 3 in Table 3 shows the most suitable kernel in the 06 experimented kernels, the number of chosen factors, and the RMSE of the forecast model built on these chosen factors.

Table 3 shows that for the EXP data set, with the maximum optimal lag determined as in [34] and to be 6, it is not possible to perform regressions for estimating forecast models based on Eq. (8) on factors extracted by the PCA, SPCA, RSPCA, and ROBSPCA methods because 60 data observations are not enough degrees of freedom to perform. However, if using the KTPCA# method to reduce the variable dimension of this data set, this limitation is overcome.

Table 3 also shows that for each of the 11 experimental data sets, it is always possible to find the most suitable kernel so that the RMSE of the forecast model of the target

Table 3. The dimension reduction performance of the KTPCA# method

Datasets	Methods	KTPCA#	PCA	SPCA	RSPCA	ROBSPCA
EXP	No. of factors & kernel	$GA_5, 6$	14	10	10	10
	RMSE	**0.0104**	NA	NA	NA	NA
VN30	No. of factors & kernel	$GA_3, 14$	14	14	14	15
	RMSE	**0.1819**	0.1895	0.1968	0.1968	0.2054
CPI	No. of factors & kernel	$GA_4, 6$	4	4	4	4
	RMSE	**0.4452**	1.4836	1.0659	1.0673	1.0659
VIP	No. of factors & kernel	$PL_1, 4$	4	4	4	4
	RMSE	**672.66**	715.96	826.28	1373.57	2642.83
Res. Building	No. of factors & kernel	$GA_4, 2$	1	1	1	1
	RMSE	**919.9**	1152.4	1152.5	1152.5	1151.2
S&P500	No. of factors & kernel	$GA_4, 2$	1	1	1	1
	RMSE	**61.60**	161.415	161.441	161.441	161.441
DJI	No. of factors & kernel	$PL_0, 1$	1	1	1	1
	RMSE	**91.82**	**91.82**	309.24	309.24	309.23
NASDAQ	No. of factors & kernel	$PL_1, 1$	1	1	1	1
	RMSE	**81.05**	365.97	85.47	85.47	85.46
Air Quality	No. of factors & kernel	$GA_4, 5$	1	1	1	1
	RMSE	**50.297**	71.459	71.499	71.499	71.427
App. Energy	No. of factors & kernel	$GA_4, 6$	3	3	3	3
	RMSE	**98.81**	101.74	101.76	101.76	101.75
SuperCon.	No. of factors & kernel	$GA_4, 2$	2	2	2	2
	RMSE	**26.094**	27.314	27.332	27.332	27.319

variable on factors extracted by the KTPCA method is equal to or less than the RMSE of forecast models built on factors extracted by the PCA, SPCA, RSPCA, and ROBSPCA methods.

Table 4. Values of the parameter ρ^2 in the GA_4 and GA_5 Gaussian kernels

Datasets	S1	S2	S3	S4	S5	S6	S7	S8	S9	S10	S11
GA_4	$e^{-0.693}$	$e^{6.9}$	$e^{0.7}$	$e^{34.1}$	e^{22}	e^{8}	e^{8}	e^{8}	e^{18}	$e^{12.8}$	$e^{18.5}$
GA_5	$e^{-0.183}$	$e^{7.5}$	e^{2}	$e^{35.3}$	$e^{27.2}$	$e^{15.7}$	$e^{15.5}$	$e^{13.5}$	e^{20}	$e^{24.5}$	$e^{22.8}$

4.2 For Data Sets of Predictors at Mixed Sampling Frequencies

In this section, the regression model used to build nowcast models is the factor BE model, the factor U-MIDAS model, and some other restricted MIDAS models, including the STEP-MIDAS, PAW-MIDAS, and EAW-MIDAS models.

Experimental Datasets

Datasets used for experiments are presented in Table 5. Specifically, they include 07 datasets in the UCI-Machine Learning Repository introduced in Table 1 and three real-world data sets of Vietnam's economy in which the CPI data set is in Table 1, and the RGDP and IIP data sets are new. With the data sets already in Table 1, the target variables in these datasets are aggregated at a lower frequency so that they are mixed sampling frequency data sets. The value of the aggregated target variable is determined in one of two ways: the first way is the arithmetic average of S values of this variable, and the second way is the sum of the S values, where S is the number of high-frequency values for each low-frequency value. It is different for different data sets, as shown in Table 5. Precisely, the value of the aggregated target variable of the Air Quality, Residential Building, S & P 500, DJI, Nasdaq, Super Conductivity, and CPI data sets is calculated according to the first way, while for the Appliances Energy data set, it is calculated according to the second way.

Furthermore, the article has assumed that the number of working days in the months is the same and equals 20 days per month. This assumption is close to the number of working days in the months. So, in Table 5, when S equals 20, we understand that the target variable is at the monthly frequency, while the predictors are at the daily frequency.

Table 5. The statistical characteristics of experimental datasets

Statistical Characteristics	RGDP	CPI	IIP	Air Quality	App. Energy
Characteristics of dataset	Time-series	Time-series	Time-series	Time-series	Time-series
Variable Characteristics	Real	Real	Real	Real	Real

(continued)

Table 5. (*continued*)

Statistical Characteristics	RGDP	CPI	IIP	Air Quality	App. Energy
Number of low-frequency variables	3	3	1	1	1
Number of high-frequency variables	87	102	42	12	27
Total number of observations	72	72	1840	9348	19704
Number of low-frequency observations	24	24	92	779	3284
S - the number of high-frequency values for a low-frequency value[2]	3	3	20	12	6
Missing data	No	No	Yes	Yes	No
The target variable	The growth rate of GDP	Consumer Price Inflation	Index of Industrial production	The Air CO	Energy use of Appliances
Statistical Characteristics	Res. Build	S&P 500	DJI	NASDAQ	SuperCond
Characteristics of dataset	cross data	Time-series	Time-series	Time-series	cross data
Variable Characteristics	Real	Real	Real	Real	Real
Number of low-frequency variables	1	1	1	1	1
Number of high-frequency variables	27	52	81	81	81
Total number of observations	366	1760	1760	1760	21260
Number of low-frequency observations	122	88	88	88	1063

(*continued*)

Table 5. (*continued*)

Statistical Characteristics	RGDP	CPI	IIP	Air Quality	App. Energy
S - the number of high-frequency values for each low-frequency value	3	20	20	20	20
Missing data	No	Yes	Yes	Yes	No
The target variable	Sales Prices	S&P500 Index	DJI index	NASDAQ Index	Critical temperature

[2]: The total number of observations (or the number of high-frequency observations) = S * the number of low-frequency observations.

In the RGDP and CPI datasets, there are several other predictors at the same frequency as the target variable, and they are at the quarterly frequency.

4.3 Experimental Method

To build nowcast models, first, the time series target variable at a low frequency, the predictors at the same frequency as the target variable, and the factors extracted from higher frequency predictors are transformed into stationary time series. The criterion for selecting the number of extracted high-frequency factors is also their cumulative eigenvalues percentage [28].

Nowcast models are estimated under ideal cases, namely: for nowcast models built based on the factor BE model, the optimal common lag of the target variable and predictors are determined precisely using the AIC and all variables in the built nowcast models are statistically significant, at least at the $< 10\%$ level. For nowcast models built based on the factor MIDAS models, the optimal common lag of the target variable and predictors at the same frequency as the target variable is determined as in the nowcast model built based on the BE model. In contrast, the optimal lags of different factors at higher frequencies are generally different and determined as follows: first, determine the optimal common lag based on the RMSE criterion, then determine the individual optimal lag for each factor using the RMSE criterion. This approach is always suitable for the STEP-MIDAS and PAW-MIDAS models but for the EAW-MIDAS and U-MIDAS models, it is only suitable if the number of the factors in nowcast models is pretty small. On the contrary, that is, the number of factors in the model is not small, the article determines a maximum optimal common lag for all high-frequency factors by using the RMSE criterion.

To compare the variable dimension reduction performance of the KTPCA# method with the PCA, SPCA, RSPCA, and ROBSPCA methods, for the KTPCA# method, the article also only experiments with the 06 kernels mentioned above. The article uses the packet "Midas-r" in R.CRAN [35] to build nowcast models on mixed sampling frequency data sets.

4.4 Results

The average minimum distance between two data vectors of the 08 experimental datasets in Table 1 is presented in Table 2, while for the RGDP and IIP data sets, this value corresponds to $\rho^2 = e^{1.464}$ and $\rho^2 = e^{8.978}$.

With the same cumulative eigenvalue minimum threshold of 75% for all the five variable dimension reduction methods, the experimental datasets, and the five regression models: BE, STEP-MIDAS, PAW-MIDAS, EAW-MIDAS, and U-MIDAS, the RMSE of built nowcast models on the chosen extracted factors is shown in Table 6. This table includes five subtables 6a, 6b, 6c, 6d, and 6e containing the RMSE of nowcast models built based on the factor BE, STEP-MIDAS, PAW-MIDAS, EAW-MIDAS, and U-MIDAS models, respectively. Here, factors are extracted from the ten aforementioned experimental datasets using the PCA, SPCA, RSPCA, ROBSPCA, and KTPCA[#] methods. Here SET1,..., SET10 is another writing way for the 10 data sets in Table 4 in order from left to right and from top to bottom.

Table 6 shows that for all the factor regression models and the all experimental datasets, it is always possible to choose a suitable kernel so that the RMSE of the nowcast model built on factors extracted by the KTPCA method corresponding to this

Table 6. Performance of the KTPCA# method for mixed sampling frequency data sets

6a. BE	PCA	SPCA	RSPCA	ROBSPCA	KTPCA*	6b.STEP	PCA	SPCA	RSPCA	ROBSPCA	KTPCA*
SET1	**0.000493**	0.000788	0.00079	0.000788	**0.000493**	SET1	**0.00744**	0.009727	0.009722	0.009727	**0.00744**
SET2	**0.000183**	0.000485	0.00051	0.000485	**0.000183**	SET2	0.008236	0.00439	0.004387	0.00439	**0.003948**
SET3	1.348981	1.203836	1.04437	1.545299	**0.56932**	SET3	26.52232	21.39361	28.86856	28.13315	**8.78805**
SET4	0.615228	0.611051	0.6104	0.61106	**0.592861**	SET4	**0.630038**	0.63004	0.63004	**0.630038**	**0.630038**
SET5	377.6252	377.2618	377.262	377.0618	**360.131**	SET5	**385.1972**	385.68	385.68	385.3454	**385.1972**
SET6	565.5147	565.523	565.523	565.516	**513.6189**	SET6	430.8412	430.8373	430.8373	430.8397	**421.709**
SET7	**4.3074**	4.3076	4.3076	4.3076	**4.3074**	SET7	259.8844	259.8083	257.6644	259.8065	**72.7871**
SET8	57.1033	56.4321	56.4321	56.4321	**56.2975**	SET8	4101.593	4101.958	4101.958	4102.275	**1024.708**
SET9	18.5945	18.5941	18.5941	18.5489	**18.3479**	SET9	1419.767	1419.807	1419.807	1419.756	**687.2987**
SET10	13.5381	13.5397	13.5425	13.5429	**13.3662**	SET10	14.3425	14.3462	14.3462	14.3431	**13.9649**
6c.PAW	PCA	SPCA	RSPCA	ROBSPCA	KTPCA*	6d.EAW	PCA	SPCA	RSPCA	ROBSPCA	KTPCA*
SET1	**0.000026**	0.000208	0.000197	0.000208	**0.000026**	SET1	0.005232	0.005274	0.005277	0.005274	**0.004544**
SET2	**0.001473**	0.001833	0.001819	0.001833	**0.001473**	SET2	0.006911	0.005465	0.007418	0.005465	**0.00509**
SET3	1.1268	0.7342	0.7508	0.6208	**0.0433**	SET3	4.4983	4.7174	4.3561	4.3146	**4.1810**
SET4	0.6298	0.6293	0.6402	0.6298	**0.6174**	SET4	0.4762	0.4765	0.4765	0.4761	**0.4392**
SET5	384.4007	384.4115	384.3218	384.3270	**384.0171**	SET5	385.4549	385.4515	385.4515	385.4597	**385.000**
SET6	404.3389	399.4798	399.4798	399.4800	**399.3498**	SET6	504.9074	504.9076	504.9076	504.9069	**379.0157**
SET7	40.7019	42.8444	42.8444	42.8444	**33.6159**	SET7	**2.806**	2.953	2.953	2.953	**2.8060**
SET8	337.8048	337.8025	337.8025	337.8026	**311.3913**	SET8	240.0	239.7	239.7	239.5	**118.900**
SET9	107.9667	107.9666	107.9666	107.9666	**107.0302**	SET9	82.2279	82.1254	82.1254	82.0357	**36.3656**
SET10	13.9580	13.9580	13.9580	13.9580	**13.9485**	SET10	13.9322	13.931	13.931	13.9322	**13.9302**
6e.U	PCA	SPCA	RSPCA	ROBSPCA	KTPCA*	6e.U	PCA	SPCA	RSPCA	ROBSPCA	KTPCA*
SET1	0.00204	0.000951	0.000919	0.000951	**0.000699**	SET6	430.1182	430.1732	430.1732	430.1286	**389.1229**
SET2	**0.000109**	0.002515	0.002955	0.002512	**0.000109**	SET7	0.000701	5.58E-05	0.0000558	0.0000587	**0.0000546**
SET3	**0.0283**	0.9860	0.3109	0.6632	**0.0283**	SET8	2.932	2.931	2.931	2.931	**2.9300**
SET4	0.4054	0.4058	0.4058	0.4055	**0.3330**	SET9	0.8993	0.8992	0.8992	0.8992	**0.8841**
SET5	376.9851	377.4016	377.4016	376.8008	**351.2000**	SET10	14.0231	14.0219	14.0219	14.0231	**13.9115**

kernel is less than or equal to the RMSE of nowcast models built on factors extracted by the PCA, SPCA, RSPCA, and ROBSPCA methods.

5 Conclusions

This article briefly introduced the variable dimension reduction method KTPCA#. Experimental results on real data sets of predictors at the same sampling frequency and mixed sampling frequencies show that the dimensional reduction performance of this method is higher than that of the PCA, SPCA, RSPCA, and ROBSPCA methods. Here the variable dimension reduction performance of a method is measured by the RMSE of forecast/nowcast models built based on the autoregressive distributed lag model/ the factor BE, U-MIDAS, and some other restricted MIDAS models such as STEP-MIDAS, PAW-MIDAS, and EAW-MIDAS, where factors are extracted from a data set of predictors using this method. The KTPCA# method is an iterative, trial-and-error process over the kernels. It is uncomplicated and can be used to reduce the variable dimension of large data sets.

Bagging and Boosting are currently emerging as prediction/classification methods on data sets of a large number of predictors. In the upcoming study, we will compare the forecast accuracy of models built based on the dynamic factor regression model where factors are extracted by the KTPCA# method with the forecast accuracy of models built based on these methods.

References

1. Hoerl, A.E., Kennard, R.W.: Ridge regression: Biased estimation for nonorthogonal problems. Technometrics **12**(1), 55–67 (1970)
2. Marquardt, D.W., Snee, R.D.: Ridge regression in practice. Am. Stat. **29**(1), 3–20 (1975)
3. Tibshirani, R.: Regression shrinkage and selection via the lasso. J. R. Stat. Soc. Ser. B **58**(1), 267–288 (1996)
4. Zou, H., Hastie, T., Tibshirani, R.: Sparse principal component analysis. J. Comput. Graph. Stat. **15**(2), 265–286 (2006)
5. Zou, H.: The adaptive lasso and its oracle properties. J. Am. Stat. Assoc. **101**(476), 1418–1429 (2006)
6. Zou, H., Hastie, T.: "Regularization and variable selection via the elastic net." J. R. Stat. Soc. Ser. B statistical Methodol, **67**(2), 301–320 (2005)
7. Hoeting, J.A., Madigan, D., Raftery, A.E., Volinsky, C.T.: Bayesian model averaging: a tutorial (with comments by M. Clyde, David Draper and EI George, and a rejoinder by the authors. Stat. Sci. **14**(4), 382–417 (1999)
8. Kapetanios, G., Papailias, F., et al.: Big data & macroeconomic nowcasting: methodological review. Econ. Stat. Cent. Excell. Natl. Inst. Econ. Soc. Res. (2018)
9. Do Van, T.: Dimensionality reduction performance of sparse PCA methods. In: Cong Vinh, P., Huu Nhan, N. (eds.) ICTCC 2021. LNICSSITE, vol. 408, pp. 138–148. Springer, Cham (2021). https://doi.org/10.1007/978-3-030-92942-8_12
10. Postma, E.: Dimensionality reduction : a comparative review dimensionality reduction : a comparative review. J. Mach. Learn. Res. 10, 1–35 (2007). October 2016
11. Zhong, X., Enke, D.: Forecasting daily stock market return using dimensionality reduction. Expert Syst. Appl. **67**, 126–139 (2017)

12. Shlens, J.: A tutorial on principal component analysis. *arXiv Prepr. arXiv1404.1100* (2014)
13. Schölkopf, B., Smola, A., Müller, K.-R.: Nonlinear component analysis as a kernel eigenvalue problem. Neural Comput. **10**(5), 1299–1319 (1998)
14. Schölkopf, B., Smola, A.J.: A short introduction to learning with kernels. In: Mendelson, S., Smola, A.J. (eds) Advanced Lectures on Machine Learning. Lecture Notes in Computer Science, vol. 2600, pp. 41–64. Springer, (2003). https://doi.org/10.1007/3-540-36434-X_2
15. Urasawa, S.: Real-time GDP forecasting for Japan: a dynamic factor model approach. J. Jpn. Int. Econ. **34**, 116–134 (2014)
16. Bok, B., Caratelli, D., Giannone, D., Sbordone, A.M., Tambalotti, A.: Macroeconomic nowcasting and forecasting with big data. Annu. Rev. Econom. **10**, 615–643 (2018)
17. Castle, J.L., Hendry, D.F., Kitov, O.I.: Forecasting and Nowcasting Macroeconomic Variables: A Methodological Overview (2013)
18. Bańbura, M., Rünstler, G.: A look into the factor model black box: publication lags and the role of hard and soft data in forecasting GDP. Int. J. Forecast. **27**(2), 333–346 (2011)
19. Foroni, C., Marcellino, M.: A comparison of mixed frequency approaches for nowcasting Euro area macroeconomic aggregates. Int. J. Forecast. **30**(3), 554–568 (2014)
20. Bai, J., Ghysels, E., Wright, J.H.: State space models and MIDAS regressions. Econom. Rev. **32**(7), 779–813 (2013)
21. Kim, H.H., Swanson, N.R.: Mining big data using parsimonious factor, machine learning, variable selection and shrinkage methods. Int. J. Forecast. **34**(2), 339–354 (2018)
22. Geweke, J.: The dynamic factor analysis of economic time series. Latent Var. socio-economic Model (1977)
23. Panagiotelis, A., Athanasopoulos, G., Hyndman, R.J., Jiang, B., Vahid, F.: Macroeconomic forecasting for Australia using a large number of predictors. Int. J. Forecast. **35**(2), 616–633 (2019)
24. Yu, Y., Samworth, R.J.: Discussion of Large Covariance Estimation by Thresholding Principal Orthogonal Complements by Fan, Liao and Mincheva (2013)
25. Stock, J.H., Watson, M.W.: Forecasting using principal components from a large number of predictors. J. Am. Stat. Assoc. **97**(460), 1167–1179 (2002)
26. Foroni, C., Marcellino, M.G.: A survey of econometric methods for mixed-frequency data (2013). SSRN 2268912
27. Ghysels, E., Kvedaras, V., Zemlys, V.: Mixed frequency data sampling regression models: the R package midasr. J. Stat. Softw. **72**(1), 1–35 (2016)
28. Zhang, Y., Li, S., Teng, Y.: Dynamic processes monitoring using recursive kernel principal component analysis. Chem. Eng. Sci. **72**, 78–86 (2012)
29. Kim, K.I., Franz, M.O., Scholkopf, B.: Iterative kernel principal component analysis for image modeling. IEEE Trans. Pattern Anal. Mach. Intell. **27**(9), 1351–1366 (2005)
30. Rathi, Y., Dambreville, S., Tannenbaum, A.: Statistical shape analysis using kernel PCA. In: Image Processing: Algorithms and Systems, Neural Networks, and Machine Learning, vol. 6064, p. 60641B (2006)
31. Erichson, N.B., Zheng, P., Manohar, K., Brunton, S.L., Kutz, J.N., Aravkin, A.Y.: Sparse principal component analysis via variable projection. SIAM J. Appl. Math. **80**(2), 977–1002 (2020)
32. Karatzoglou, A., Smola, A., Hornik, K., Zeileis, A.: kernlab-an S4 package for kernel methods in R. J. Stat. Softw. **11**(9), 1–20 (2004)
33. "UCI-Machine Learning Repository."
34. Wooldridge, J.M.: Introductory Econometrics: A Modern Approach. Nelson Education (2016)
35. Kedaras, V.K., Zemlys, V., Imports, M., NumDeriv, M.: Package midasr (2021)

Detecting Major Extrema in Streaming Time Series

Bui Cong Giao$^{(\boxtimes)}$ and Ho Van Cuu

Faculty of Electronics and Telecommunications, Saigon University,
Ho Chi Minh City, Vietnam
{bcgiao,cuuhovan}@sgu.edu.vn

Abstract. Time series are formed from data points collected over time. The prominent data points of time series are often minima or maxima; hence they have special values. Moreover, they are virtually turning points that change trend of time series. These prominent data points play an important role in determining the characteristics of time series so they are called important data points or major extrema. There are many methods to detect major extrema in time series in static context; however, in streaming context there have almost been no methods to carry out this task so far. In the paper, we propose a method for detecting major extrema in streaming time series. The method is of low computational time in identifying major extrema as soon as a newly in-coming data point of streaming time series is collected. The experimental results demonstrate that the proposed method exactly detects major extrema on the fly. Furthermore, the method could identify correlation of streaming time series thanks to their major extrema. An interesting application of the proposed method is to enable the task of online forecasting to predict future data points of streaming time series based on similarity search using major extrema.

Keywords: Major extrema · Streaming time series

1 Introduction

Problems of data mining on streaming time-series often appear in real-time processing applications which almost require fast and accurate response times. Solutions to these problems use frequently techniques to accelerate the computation of distances between time series [1,2], and appropriately segment streaming time series into subsequences [3] for further tasks of data mining on streaming time series. Therefore, the time-series segmentation is an important preprocessing step for such tasks, such as similarity search [4], anomaly detection [3], online forecasting [5], etc. The segmentation techniques employ frequently critical data points of time series, called major extrema, to improve the performance of these tasks.

supported by Saigon University.

Major extrema of time series are often prominent, distinct from data points of average amplitude. Moreover, they are often local important minimum or maximum data points. As for static setting, there are a lot of research studies on how to detect major extrema in time series [6,7]; however, there have virtually been not methods to perform the task in streaming time series up to now. Motivated by the above observation, in the paper we propose an efficient method to detect major extrema in streaming time series.

The main contributions of the paper are as follows:

i. A proposed method to identify major extrema in streaming time series on the fly. The method could detect major extrema quickly when there is a newly incoming data point of streaming time series.
ii. The application of major extrema to find out the correlation between two streaming time series, and to segment streaming time series into subsequences for online forecasting.

The paper is structured as follows. Section 2 reviews related works. Section 3 briefly describes some basic background. In Sect. 4 we present the proposed method. Section 5 reports the experimental evaluation. Finally, Sect. 6 gives conclusions and future work.

2   Related Works

There have been several typical research studies on major extrema and the application of major extrema for time-series data mining on both static and streaming background. These research studies would be reviewed in chronological order as below.

Fu et al. [6] claimed that data points with perceptually importance in the human visual identification process are more important than other data points in time series. The authors used perceptually important points (PIP) to build a framework representing financial time series. The framework helps to reduce the time-series dimension to different levels of detail based on PIP. PIPs of a time series are identified as follows. The first two PIPs are the starting point and the ending one of the time series. The successive PIP is the point with the greatest distance to the first two PIPs. The fourth PIP is the point with the greatest distance to its two adjacent PIPs. The process to find out remaining PIPs continues until all the points in the time series are visited or the required number of PIPs is reached. It is obvious that the method is solely suitable for static time series since in streaming scene, streaming time series are assumed that their data points come continuously and there is not the ending one.

Fink and Gandhi [7] presented the definitions of major extrema of time series and a one-pass algorithm to find major extrema. The algorithm is of low time complexity, $\mathcal{O}(n)$. Since the algorithm solely works on static background, it needs changing to identify major extrema of streaming time series.

Giao and Anh [5] proposed an online forecasting method in streaming time series based on similarity search [2]. The method takes every newly incoming time-series subsequence of a streaming time series, then finds k nearest neighbor subsequences. Future data points of the streaming time series are forecast based on the k best matches. Before the similarity search, these subsequences have been retrieved from the streaming time series by a segmentation technique using major extrema. Note that in the research study the authors have not yet presented the method of identifying major extrema in streaming time series.

Zhan et al. [4] introduced an online segmenting algorithm for streaming time series. The algorithm segments streaming time series by choosing the most important turning point, which enable to reflect the variation trend features of the streaming time series. The segmenting approach is an improvement of online Piecewise Linear Representation [8].

Thuy et al. [3] presented two methods, TopK-EP-ALeader and TopK-EP-ALeader-S, which combine segmentation and clustering for detecting top-k discords in static and streaming time series. The segmentation is based on the major extrema method of Fink and Gandhi [7]. However, like the article [5], the article [3] also do not present the technique of identifying major extrema in streaming time series.

3   Background

The section presents some definitions of streaming time series, major extrema, and online forecasting using major extrema to segment streaming time series into subsequences.

3.1   Streaming Time Series

Definition 1. *(Streaming time series)* A streaming time series X is a discrete, semi-infinite numerical sequence obtained from collecting or sampling a data stream at specific time ticks. Mathematically, X is represented by data points whose values are real numbers: $x_1, x_2, \ldots, x_n \ldots$, where x_n is the most recent data point, called the newly incoming one.

A subsequence C of X is a time series in X, i.e. $C = x_i, x_{i+1}, \ldots, x_j$ for $1 \leq i$ and $j \leq n$. For simplicity, let $(x_i : x_j)$ denote $\{x_i, x_{i+1}, \ldots, x_j\}$. It is noted that tasks of data mining on streaming time series often consider the newly incoming subsequence $(x_i : x_n)$.

3.2   Major Extrema

Extrema of a time series are data points of local minimum or maximum. According to Fink and Gandhi [7], *strict*, *left*, *right* and *flat* minima are defined as below.

Definition 2. *(Minima)* Given time series $X = (x_1 : x_n)$ and $1 < i < n$.

- x_i is strict minimum if $x_{i-1} > x_i < x_{i+1}$.

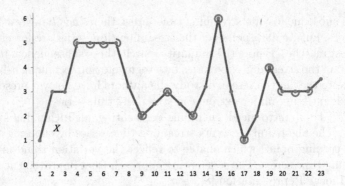

Fig. 1. An illustration of time series X and its extrema

- x_i is left minimum if $x_{i-1} > x_i$ and there is r, where $r > i$, such that $x_i = x_{i+1} = \cdots = x_r < x_{r+1}$.
- x_i is right minimum if $x_i < x_{i+1}$ and there is l, where $l < i$, such that $x_{l-1} > x_l = \cdots = x_{i-1} = x_i$.
- x_i is flat minimum if there are l and r, where $l < i < r$, such that $x_{l-1} > x_l = \cdots = x_{i-1} = x_i = x_{i+1} = \cdots = x_r < x_{r+1}$.

The definition of maxima is similar to that of minima. Figure 1 depicts time series X and its extrema as follows. Strict extrema are shown as circles, left and right as half-circles and flat extrema as downward half-circles.

A time series might have a lot of extrema; however, major extrema are often more interested. Fink and Gandhi [7] defined major extrema as below.

Definition 3. *(Important minima)* Given a distance function $d(a, b) = |a - b|$ and a positive value R, x_i is an important minimum if there are l and r, where $l < i < r$, such that x_i is a minimum among $x_l, \ldots, x_r$ and $d(x_i, x_l) \geq R$ and $d(x_i, x_r) \geq R$.

There are some important notes about Definition 3:

- The parameter R is a *compression rate* to determine important minima. The larger R is, the fewer the number of important minima is identified. To illustrate the compression rate, Fig. 2 depicts examples of the four types of important minima that are identified by R. Because major extrema are often prominent, different from data points of average amplitude, it is reasonable to set

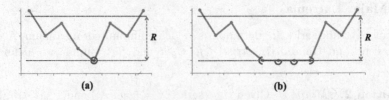

Fig. 2. (a) Strict important minimum (b) Left, flat, and right important minima [5]

$R = \beta \times \sigma$, where β is the *tuning* parameter and often larger than 1, and σ is the standard deviation of the time series. If a time series does not change much, β might be smaller than 1 to get more major extrema.

- Flat important minima can be derived from left important minima and right important minima in case they are consecutive as in Fig. 2 (b).
- The definition of important maxima can be inferred from Definition 3. Important minima and maxima are often called major extrema. Using major extrema of time series, we can segment time series sensibly and visually into subsequences

Given streaming time series X and a newly incoming data point x_n of X, the problem of our research study is how to fast detect major extrema right after the last major extremum x_k, where $k \leq n$.

The newly found major extrema often imply a certain special characteristic of X and they can be used to segment X for further data-mining tasks. The following online forecasting method [5] employs major extrema of X to segment a streaming time series into subsequences for the task of prediction.

3.3 Online Forecasting

Given streaming time series X and a newly incoming data point x_n of X, the aim of online forecasting is to predict x_{n+p} for $p \geq 1$.

The online forecasting method [5] has three main components: (i) k-NN or Simple Exponential Smoothing (SES), (ii) identifying major extrema, and (iii) similarity search under Dynamic Time Warping (DTW) [9].

To describe the method concisely, we need to review popular measures for evaluating accuracy of prediction, SES, and then introduce two definitions.

There are three common measures to evaluate accuracy of prediction: Mean Absolute Percentage Error (MAPE), Mean Absolute Deviation (MAD), and Mean Squared Error (MSE). For these measures, the smaller the value, the prediction method is more accurate. The meanings of the measures as follows. MAPE measures the accuracy of fitted time-series values. The accuracy is expressed as a percentage. MAD measures the accuracy of the prediction by averaging the alleged error. MSE measures the expected squared distance between the predicted value and the true one.

SES is a time-series forecasting method for univariate data without a trend or seasonality. The method is expressed by the following equation:

$$\hat{x}_{n+1} = \alpha x_n + (1 - \alpha)\hat{x}_n \tag{1}$$

where x_n is the most recent observation for time tick n, $\hat{x}_{n+1}$ is the smoothed value or the predicted value at time tick $n + 1$. α is a smoothing constant whose value domain is from 0 and 1.

From Eq. 1, the next equation is

$$\hat{x}_{n+1} = \alpha x_n + \alpha(1-\alpha)x_{n-1} + \alpha(1-\alpha)^2 x_{n-2} + \cdots + \alpha(1-\alpha)^{n-1}x_1 + (1-\alpha)^n x_0. \quad (2)$$

To use Eqs. 1 and 2, we need to determine α and x_0 beforehand. The minimum results of the triple (MAPE, MAD, MSE) can be used to determine α. For an initial estimate of x_0, let x_0 be x_1, or be an average of a few previous observations.

The following are three necessary definitions for the online forecasting.

Definition 4. *(Segment)* A *segment* of a time series is a subsequence determined by two successive important maxima or two successive important minima.

Definition 5. *(Target subsequence)* A *target* subsequence is a newly incoming subsequence whose left end is the latest segment.

Definition 6. *(Source subsequence)* Given a *target* subsequence C, a *source* subsequence S for C have to satisfy three conditions:

(i) The data points of S must be in a buffer containing collected data points of X,
(ii) The left end of S is a major extremum of the same type as the major extremum at the left end of C, and
(iii) The two subsequences are the same length.

The working setting of the online forecasting method [5] is illustrated in Fig. 3. In addition, the method consists of two phases:

- *Sampling Phase:* In the beginning, all available data points of X are loaded into the buffer. Subsequently, the standard deviation σ is computed from these data points. Given a specific tuning parameter β, the compression rate R is then calculated from σ and β. Next, major extrema and segments are determined from the available data points of X. Finally, the target subsequence and its source ones are determined and normalized using z-score.
- *Forecasting Phase:* There are two cases are
  i. The newly incoming data point x_n of X does not cause any new major extrema. In the case, the target subsequence and its source ones are extended one data point to the right. After that, these subsequences are incrementally normalized [2].
  ii. The arrival of the data point x_n incurs new major extrema. In the case, the target subsequence needs redefining using the latest segment of X combined with x_n. Next, the source subsequences for the new target subsequence are identified, and then all of them are normalized from the scratch.

Having the target subsequence and its source ones, the similarity search method SUCR-DTW [2] conducts k-NN search to find k nearest neighbor subsequences of the target subsequence from the set containing the source ones. Subsequently, x_{n+p} is computed from data points following these k subsequences as

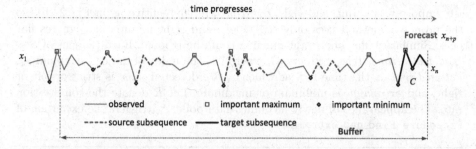

Fig. 3. The context for the operation of the online forecasting [5]

the following manner. Let S_i be one of the k nearest neighbor subsequences, and x_{si+p} be the data point following S_i by a distance of p time ticks. x_{si+p} is then normalized using the z-score coefficients of S_i. Let y_{si+p} be the normalized value of x_{si+p}. The normalized value y_{n+p} of x_{n+p} might be calculated in accordance with two ways:

The first way is average of the k normalized values.

$$y_{n+p} = \frac{1}{k} \sum_{i=1}^{k} y_{si+p}. \tag{3}$$

The second way is weighted average of the k normalized values.

$$y_{n+p} = \frac{2}{k \times (k+1)} \sum_{i=1}^{k} i \times y_{si+p}. \tag{4}$$

Having y_{n+p}, the data point x_{n+p} can be computed from the z-score coefficients of C. As for Eq. 4, it is worth noting that the closer to the target subsequence a resulting subsequence is, the greater the weight of the resulting subsequence is. Therefore, the online forecasting method has two variants, kNN-Av for Eq. 3 and kNN-WAv for Eq. 4. Furthermore, this method might hybridize with SES as follows.

$$y_{n+p}^{Hybrid} = \omega y_{n+p} + (1 - \omega) y_{n+p}^{SES} \tag{5}$$

where y_{n+p} is the normalized value by kNN-Av or kNN-WAv, y_{n+p}^{SES} is the normalized value by SES, and ω is a weighted parameter whose value is between 0 and 1.

The next section will reveal the proposed method to solve the problem of detecting major extrema in streaming time series on the fly.

4   Proposed Method

Let S be the ordered list of the major extrema of streaming time series X. The list follows an ascending index order of data points being major extrema. As mentioned earlier, flat important minima can be derived from the couples of left important minima and right one that are consecutive as in Fig. 2 (b), so the proposed method uses only strict, left, and right minima and ignores flat ones. Similarity, flat important maxima could be ignored. Each element of S is (i, *detected time, type, extremum*), where i is the index of major extremum x_i, *detected time* is the time tick at which x_i are detected, *type* is strict or left or right, and *extremum* is minimum or maximum. Let R denote the compression rate. The appearance of newly incoming data point x_n triggers the execution of Procedure Find_new_extrema.

Procedure Find_new_extrema

---

1. if $S = \varnothing$ then
2.   Find_first
3.   if $S \neq \varnothing$ then Find_minmax
4. else
5.   Find_minmax
6. end if

Procedure Find_first   // Find the first major extreme point

---

1. $lMin = rMin = lMax = rMax = i = 1$
2.   while $i < n$ and $d(x_{i+1}, x_{lMax}) < R$ and $d(x_{i+1}, x_{lMin}) < R$ do
3. i++
4.   if $x_{lMin} > x_i$ then $lMin \leftarrow i$
5.   if $x_{rMin} \geq x_i$ then $rMin \leftarrow i$
6.   if $x_{lMax} < x_i$ then $lMax \leftarrow i$
7.   if $x_{rMax} \leq x_i$ then $rMax \leftarrow i$
8.   end while
9. i++
10. if $i < n$ and $x_i > x_1$ then Output_ext($lMin, rMin$, minimum)
11. if $i < n$ and $x_i < x_1$ then Output_ext$lMax, rMax$, maximum)

Procedure Find_minmax   // Find the next major extreme point
                             // right after the newly found major one: x_k

---

```
1.  x_k ← the last item of S
2.  i ← k + 1
3.  if x_k is maximum then
4.     while i < n do
5.         i ← Find_min(i)
6.         if i < n then i ← Find_max(i)
7.     end while
8.  else
9.     while i < n do
10.        i ← Find_max(i)
11.        if i < n then i ← Find_min(i)
12.    end while
13. end if
```

Function Find_min(i)   // Find the next important minimum from
                              // x_i to x_{n-1}

```
1.  l = r = i
2.  while i < n and ( x_{i+1} < x_l or d(x_{i+1}, x_l) < R) do
3.     i++
4.     if x_l > x_i then l ← i
5.     if x_r ≥ x_i then r ← i
6.  end while
7.  if i < n then Output_ext(l, r, minimum)
8.  return i + 1
```

Function Find_max(i)   // Find the next important maximum from
                              // x_i to x_{n-1}

```
1.  l = r = i
2.  while i < n and ( x_{i+1} > x_l or d(x_{i+1}, x_l) < R) do
3.     i++
4.     if x_l < x_i then l ← i
5.     if x_r ≤ x_i then r ← i
```

```
6.   end while
7.   if i < n then Output_ext(l, r, maximum)
8.   return i + 1
```

```
Procedure Output_ext(l, r, extremum)        // Append the found major
                                            // extrema to S
```

```
1.   if l = r then
         // x_l is a major strict extremum
2.       Append (l, n, strict, extremum) to S
3.   else
         // x_l is a major left extremum
4.       Append (l, n, left, extremum) to S
         // x_r is a major right extremum
5.       Append (r, n, right, extremum) to S
6.   end if
```

Procedure Find_minmax shows that when a newly incoming x_n exists, the course of search for major extrema is conducted. Most frequently the search begins from x_{k+1}, where x_k is the newly found major extremum or the last item of S, to x_{n-1}. The time tick at which the major extrema are detected, that is n, is also recorded in Procedure Output_ext. The search is performed with the comparison operators (see lines 4 and 5 in Functions Find_min and Find_max) so the time complexity of Procedure Find_new_extrema is $\mathcal{O}(n - k) \approx \mathcal{O}(n)$. As for the memory used in the proposed method, it takes two buffers to contains data points. The first buffer stores data points of X. The buffer can be organized as a circular fashion and its size should be enough large to consists of data points which are still valuable. This means that the old data points of X that are not valuable would be deleted to make room for incoming data points. The second buffer is S consisting of major extrema. The buffer also works in a circular fashion as the first.

Note that the proposed method to identify major extrema in streaming time series can be used with the compression rate R as a constant or as a changeable value since some newly incoming data point. After a newly major extreme point x_i is found with a specific value of R, the successive major extreme point can be identified from the index $i + 1$ to the largest index n of X by another value of R. Besides, time-series data mining tasks using the proposed method need a sampling phase over the initial stage to emit data points of X so that σ can be computed on the corresponding initial subsequence of X. The size of the sampled subsequence is determined for each specific case study.

5   Experimental Evaluation

The section presents experiments on the proposed method with four streaming time series. These streaming time series are stimulated from static time series for working in streaming background. That is, there is a newly incoming data point collected from time series every time tick and the process of detecting new major extrema is performed immediately. Theses static time series may be downloaded from [10]. The experiments are divided into two kinds. The first illustrates results obtained from detecting major extrema in streaming time series of hydrology. The second shows an application of finding major extrema in streaming time series for prediction.

5.1   Detecting Major Extrema in Streaming Time Series of Hydrology

The two first experiments use time series of hydrology. They are *runoff_TriAn* and *runoff_PhuocHoa*. Theses time series are monthly runoffs from January 1978 to December 1993 collected by the two gauging-stations: Tri An and Phuoc Hoa located in the South of Vietnam. The data point 1 of *runoff_TriAn* is the runoff in January 1978 of Tri An. Likewise, the data point 2 of *runoff_TriAn* is the runoff in February 1978 of the gauging-station, etc. The time series thus has 192 data points. Similarity, *runoff_PhuocHoa* has 192 data points. The compression rate R is $\beta \times \sigma$, where σ is the standard deviation of time series, and β is the tuning parameter. In the two experiments, β is 1.1. Since the two time series are relatively short, we sampled entire data of them and got $\sigma = 236.684$ for *runoff_TriAn*, and $\sigma = 533.405$ for *runoff_PhuocHoa*.

Figure 4 shows the streaming time series presenting the monthly runoffs collected by Tri An and its major extrema. The important minima often happen in

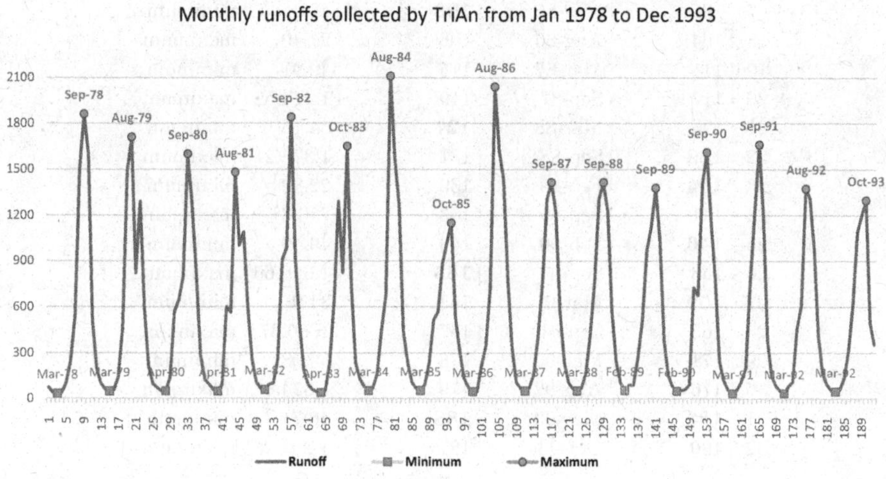

Fig. 4. Visualization of streaming time series *runoff_TriAn* and its major extrema

March and the important maxima often occur in August or September. Tri An records one minimal runoff and one maximal one for each year. Tri An gauges the highest runoff in August 1984.

Table 1 shows statistical results of the proposed method in streaming time series *runoff_TriAn*. The table identifies that the streaming time series has 16 important minima and 16 important maxima. Column Data point presents the index of the data points that are major extrema. Column Month-Year indicates the months corresponding to the data points being major extrema. Column Time tick of Detection depicts the time ticks at which the major extrema are discovered. For instance, the data point 3 corresponding to Mar-78 is an important

Table 1. Statistics of detecting major extrema in streaming time series *runoff_TriAn*.

No	Data point	Month-Year	Time tick of Detection	Runoff	Extremum
1	3	Mar-78	10	32	minimum
2	9	Sep-78	11	1,860	maximum
3	**15**	Mar-79	19	47.6	minimum
4	20	Aug-79	21	1,710	maximum
5	28	Apr-80	**31**	48.9	minimum
6	33	Sep-80	35	1,600	maximum
7	40	Apr-81	**44**	46.7	minimum
8	44	Aug-81	**47**	1480	maximum
9	51	Mar-82	55	58.6	minimum
10	57	Sep-82	58	1,840	maximum
11	64	Apr-83	**68**	38.5	minimum
12	70	Oct-83	**71**	1,650	maximum
13	75	Mar-84	**79**	50.7	minimum
14	80	Aug-84	**82**	2,110	maximum
15	87	Mar-85	92	52.1	minimum
16	94	Oct-85	**95**	1,150	maximum
17	**99**	Mar-86	**103**	44.4	minimum
18	104	Aug-86	106	2,040	maximum
19	111	Mar-87	115	49.91	minimum
20	117	Sep-87	119	1,414.59	maximum
21	123	Mar-88	**127**	54.16	minimum
22	**129**	Sep-88	131	1,378.21	maximum
23	**134**	Feb-89	139	22.82	minimum
24	141	Sep-89	143	710.37	maximum
25	**146**	Feb-90	150	49.49	minimum
26	153	Sep-90	**155**	1,610.66	maximum
27	**159**	Mar-91	163	34.9	minimum
28	165	Sep-91	167	1660.37	maximum
29	171	Mar-92	176	33.98	minimum
30	176	Aug-92	179	1,374.48	maximum
31	**183**	Mar-93	**188**	46.71	minimum
32	190	Oct-93	191	1,298.28	maximum

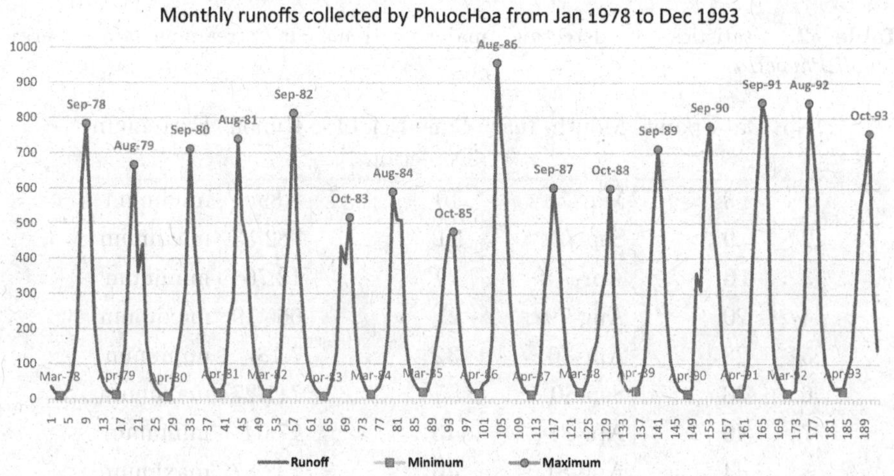

Fig. 5. Visualization of streaming time series *runoff_PhuocHoa* and its major extrema

minimum. The major extremum is detected at time tick 10. Column Runoff shows the values of major extrema.

Figure 5 represents the streaming time series indicating the monthly runoffs collected by Phuoc Hoa and its major extrema. The important minima often take place in March or April, and the important maxima appear frequently from August to October. Like Tri An, each year Phuoc Hoa has one important minima and one important maximal. Phuoc Hoa gauges the highest runoff in August 1986.

Table 2 illustrates statistical results of the proposed method in streaming time series *runoff_PhuocHoa*. The table also identifies that the streaming time series has 16 important minima and 16 important maxima. Note that the time ticks that appear major extrema of the two streaming time series are nearly the same. There are solely 8 times in which the major extrema of the two streaming time series take place in different months; however, the differences are negligible. For example, the 3rd major extremum of *runoff_TriAn* occurs in March 1979, whereas the 3rd major extremum of *runoff_PhuocHoa* takes place in April 1979. In addition, the time ticks at which the proposed method detects major extrema of the two streaming time series are nearly the same. There are only 12 out of 32 cases in which this method detects major extrema of the two streaming time series are different. For instance, the 5th major extremum of *runoff_TriAn* are identified at time tick 31 whereas the 5th major extremum of *runoff_PhuocHoa* are identified at time tick 32. It is obvious that the difference of the two detection time ticks is small. These differences are emphasized by the bold fonts in the two tables.

Table 2. Statistics of detecting major extrema in streaming time series *runoff_PhuocHoa*.

No	Data point	Month-Year	Time tick of Detection	Runoff	Extremum
1	3	Mar-78	10	8.89	minimum
2	9	Sep-78	11	782.33	maximum
3	16	Apr-79	19	12.76	minimum
4	20	Aug-79	21	666.19	maximum
5	28	Apr-80	32	7.18	minimum
6	33	Sep-80	35	711.27	maximum
7	40	Apr-81	43	17.04	minimum
8	44	Aug-81	46	738.87	maximum
9	51	Mar-82	55	15.24	minimum
10	57	Sep-82	58	811.87	maximum
11	64	Apr-83	68	8.01	minimum
12	70	Oct-83	72	516.66	maximum
13	75	Mar-84	80	13.58	minimum
14	80	Aug-84	83	588.94	maximum
15	87	Mar-85	92	20.15	minimum
16	94	Oct-85	96	475.84	maximum
17	100	Apr-86	104	16.8	minimum
18	104	Aug-86	106	955.9	maximum
19	112	Apr-87	115	12.03	minimum
20	117	Sep-87	119	600.63	maximum
21	123	Mar-88	128	20.05	minimum
22	130	Oct-88	131	598.06	maximum
23	136	Apr-89	139	22.82	minimum
24	141	Sep-89	143	710.37	maximum
25	148	Apr-90	150	13.94	minimum
26	153	Sep-90	154	775.27	maximum
27	160	Apr-91	163	16.82	minimum
28	165	Sep-91	167	843	maximum
29	171	Mar-92	176	16.45	minimum
30	176	Aug-92	179	841.68	maximum
31	184	Apr-93	187	22.02	minimum
32	190	Oct-93	191	754.77	maximum

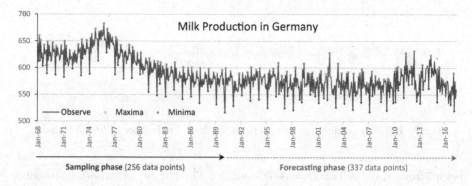

Fig. 6. Streaming time series *Milk Production in the Germany* and its major extrema

The appearance periods of the major extrema of the two streaming time series demonstrate that they have nearly the same trend. For this reason, these streaming time series have a strong correlation.

5.2 Online Forecasting in Streaming Time Series Using Major Extrema

The following are two experiments of the online forecasting method [5] to demonstrate an application of major extrema, which are detected on the fly, in segmenting streaming time series into subsequences. Note that only *single-step-ahead* prediction is considered in the experimental evaluation, that mean the online forecasting method tries to predict x_{n+1} where x_n is a newly incoming data point of streaming time series X.

Milk Production in the Germany. The dataset from the web page [11] is a time series of raw cows' milk productions in the Germany from January 1968 to May 2017. The time series thus has 593 data points. In the experiment, the size of the buffer is 256 and the tuning parameter β is 1.3. The standard deviation σ computed in the sampling phase is 29.733 so the compression rate R is 39.654. Figure 6 shows the monthly observations of the time series, the number of data points of the two phases, and the two working phases. The forecasting phase

Table 3. The best test cases of each method

Method	MAPE	MAD	MSE
kNN-Av with $k = 4$	2.183	12.455	286.928
kNN-WAv with $k = 5$	2.135	12.162	274.506
SES with $\alpha = 0.1$	2.667	15.154	383.638
Hybrid with $\omega = 0.9$	**2.130**	**12.138**	**268.198**

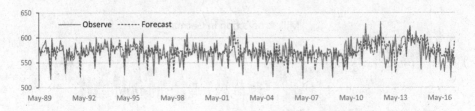

Fig. 7. The observations and predictions for *Milk Production in the Germany*

begins from May 1989 and spans 337 months. The number of important minima and maxima are 72, and 71, respectively.

It can be seen from Table 3, the hybrid method with $\omega = 0.9$ is the best test case. Notice that the hybrid method combines kNN-WAv with $k = 5$ and SES with $\alpha = 0.1$. The predictions obtained in the best test case of the hybrid method are illustrated in Fig. 7. The figure shows that the prediction time series and the observation time series have nearly the same fluctuation; however, their major extrema seldom coincide.

Temperatures at Savannah International Airport. The dataset from the web page [12] is a time series of monthly temperatures from January 1874 to May 2011. Therefore, the time series has 1,649 data points. In the experiment, the size of the buffer is 1,024, β is 1.3 and σ computed in the sampling phase is 6.327. Hence R is 8.225. Figure 8 shows the monthly observations of the time series and the number of data points of the two phases. The figure also shows the major extrema in the time series. The number of important minima and maxima are 138, and 144, respectively. The forecasts have been carried out since May 1959.

Table 4 shows the best prediction quality for each method. Note that although the hybrid method combines kNN-WAv with $k = 5$ and SES with $\alpha = 0.5$, the hybrid method with $\omega = 0.9$ does not give better results. kNN-WAv with $k = 5$ gives the best results. The predictions obtained in the best test case of kNN-WAv with $k = 5$ are illustrated in Fig. 9. The figure shows that the predictions are

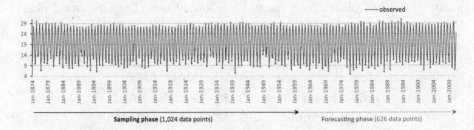

Fig. 8. Streaming time series *Temperatures at Savannah International Airport* and its major extrema

Table 4. The best test cases of each method

Method	MAPE	MAD	MSE
kNN-Av with $k = 4$	11.116	1.167	4.728
kNN-WAv with $k = 5$	**10.898**	**1.609**	**4.402**
SES with $\alpha = 0.5$	32.557	5	32.233
Hybrid with $\omega = 0.9$	10.982	1.837	5.799

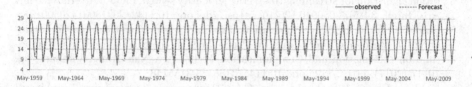

Fig. 9. The observations and predictions for *Temperatures at Savannah International Airport*

nearly the same observations although there are also many significant differences between the observation and the prediction at some important maxima.

6   Conclusions

The paper has introduced a new method to identify major extrema in streaming time series. The proposed method is a modification of the major extrema method [7], which works solely with static time series, to enable the task of finding major extrema in streaming time series. The proposed method is of low time complexity so it could detect major extrema quickly when a newly incoming data point of streaming time series has been just collected. Finding major extrema on the fly enables subsequent tasks of data mining on streaming time series to be performed efficiently and effectively such as determining correlation between streaming time series, segmenting streaming time series into subsequences more conveniently and sensibly for online forecasting, etc.

As for future work, we plan to use the proposed method to segment streaming time series for the task of subsequence join in streaming context.

Acknowledgement. This research is funded by Saigon University (SGU) under grant number CSA2022-06.

References

1. Rakthanmanon, T., et al.: Searching and mining trillions of time series subsequences under dynamic time warping. In: Proceedings of the 18th ACM SIGKDD Conference on Knowledge Discovery and Data Mining (KDD 2012), Beijing, China, pp. 262–270 (2012). https://doi.org/10.1145/2339530.2339576

2. Giao, B.C., Anh, D.T.: Similarity search for numerous patterns over multiple time series streams under dynamic time warping which supports data normalization. Vietnam J. Comput. Sci. **3**(3), 181–196 (2016). https://doi.org/10.1007/s40595-016-0062-4

3. Thuy, H.T.T., Anh, D.T., Chau, V.T.N.: Segmentation-based methods for top-k discords detection in static and streaming time series under euclidean distance. In: Cong Vinh, P., Rakib, A. (eds.) ICCASA 2021. LNICST, vol. 409, pp. 147–163. Springer, Cham (2021). https://doi.org/10.1007/978-3-030-93179-7_12

4. Zhan, P., Sun, C., Hu, Y., Luo, W., Zheng, J., Li, X.: Feature-based online representation algorithm for streaming time series similarity search. Int. J. Pattern Recognit Artif Intell. **34**(5), 2050010 (2020). https://doi.org/10.1142/S021800142050010X

5. Giao, B.C., Anh, D.T.: An application of similarity search in streaming time series under DTW: online forecasting. In: Proceedings of the 8th International Symposium on Information and Communication Technology. Nha Trang, Vietnam, pp. 10–17 (2017). https://doi.org/10.1145/3155133.3155148

6. Fu, T.C., Chung, F.L., Luk, R., Ng, C.M.: Representing financial time series based on data point importance. Eng. Appl. Artif. Intell. **21**(2), 277–300 (2008). https://doi.org/10.1016/j.engappai.2007.04.009

7. Fink, E., Gandhi, H.S.: Compression of time series by extracting major extrema. J. Exp. Theor. Artif. Intell. **23**(2), 255–270 (2011). https://doi.org/10.1080/0952813X.2010.505800

8. Keogh, E., Smyth, P.: A probabilistic approach to fast pattern matching in time. In: Proceedings of 3rd International Conference Knowledge Discovery and Data Mining, California, USA, vol. 1997, pp. 24–30

9. Berndt, D., Clifford, J.: Using dynamic time warping to find patterns in time series. In: Proceedings of AAAI Workshop on Knowledge Discovery in Databases, Seattle, Washington, USA, pp. 359–370 (1994)

10. Giao, B.C: Time-series datasets. https://www.researchgate.net/publication/361923578_Time-series_datasets. Accessed 01 Jun 2022

11. Eurostat. Cows' milk collection and products obtained - monthly data. http://appsso.eurostat.ec.europa.eu/nui/show.do?dataset=apro_mk_colm. Accessed 31 Jul 2017

12. Hyndman, R.: Time series data library. https://datamarket.com/data. Accessed 01 Aug 2017

Use of Raman Spectroscopy to Diagnose Diabetes with SVM

Le Anh Duc and Nguyen Thanh Tung[(✉)]

International School, Vietnam National University, Ha Noi, Vietnam
me@anhducle.com, tungnt@isvnu.vn

Abstract. In this work, investigations were made for exploring the potential of machine learning in predicting Type 2 Diabetes Mellitus patients. In overall, 20 patients were assessed. The Raman spectrum was observed in four anatomical locations of the body: ear lobe, inner arm, thumb nail and cubital vein. The measurements were taken to examine the difference between Control and DM2 (9 well-controlled patients and 11 diabetic patients). To create effective diagnostic algorithms for categorization among these categories, multivariate approaches such as principal component analysis (PCA) paired with support vector machine (SVM) were applied. Based on the implemented classification systems, diabetic patients are classified using PCA-SVM shows the best potential of 80% in accuracy. Therefore, the taken approach successfully creates a classification and evaluation system. Overall, our findings show that the combination of Raman spectroscopy, PCA-SVM has several advantages in terms of preciseness and is suggested as a viable non-invasive diagnostic technique for diabetes.

Keywords: Diabetes · Raman spectroscopy · Machine learning · SVM · Diagnose

1 Introduction

Diabetes is a dangerous, chronic disease that arises when the pancreas fails to generate enough insulin (a hormone that regulates blood sugar, or glucose) or when the body fails to utilise the insulin that is produced adequately. Diabetes is a major public health issue, and it is one of four priority noncommunicable diseases (NCDs) that world leaders have identified for action. Diabetes has been progressively increasing in both the number of cases and the prevalence during the last few decades [1].

In Vietnam, diabetes cases have more than doubled in the previous ten years, with nearly twice as many patients diagnosed. According to the International Diabetes Federation, diabetes-related treatment expenditures in Vietnam averaged US$ 162.7 per patient per year [2], while average income was averaged at US$ 182.7 per month in 2020 [3]. Furthermore, the number of individuals with pre-diabetes is three times that of those with diabetes [4].

Early detection for diabetes can be achieved with relatively inexpensive blood sugar monitoring. Nowadays, invasive blood glucose detection technology is now commonplace, convenient, and practical in both hospitals and home by glucometers that employ the procedure of blood sample first and then analyzing it in vitro for blood glucose measurement. Traditional glucose monitoring devices employ the electrochemical approach [5], which needs a certain amount of blood to be extracted out of the body through finger pricking or a thin lancelet placed subcutaneously. Unfortunately, most diabetics find it unpleasant to check their blood glucose levels on a regular basis since blood extraction is required many times each day for monitoring purposes.

2   Related Work

Recent studies show that blood glucose monitoring can be accomplished using non-invasive methods [6]. With the rise of worldwide diabetes in recent years, an increasing number of people have experienced discomfort and infections as a result of the intrusive nature of popular commercial glucose meters. Non-invasive blood glucose monitoring technology has become a global research focus as well as a novel way that might help a large number of patients. Based on the detection principle, researchers have been working on major problems of non-invasive blood glucose detection technology. Medical, materials, optics, electromagnetic waves, chemistry, biology, computational science, and other sectors are covered by this new method. The advantages and limitations of non-invasive and invasive technologies, as well as electrochemistry and optics in non-invasives were discussed in [7]. Therefore, non-invasive blood glucose monitoring will become more efficient, inexpensive, robust, and competitive on the market as wearable technology and transdermal biosensors advance.

In the last 20 years, a lot of researches has been conducted in non-invasive blood glucose testing. For non-invasive measurements, the researchers discovered a variety of optical techniques such as near-infrared (NIR) [8], photoacoustic spectroscopy, Raman spectroscopy [9], polarization techniques, and light scattering techniques [10]. A transilluminated laser beam is used to monitor glucose levels.

Non-invasive glucose monitoring is obviously the most attractive approach for diabetic patients, allowing for more frequent, if not continuous, assessments without discomfort or sensation. Until now, various approaches for non-invasive blood glucose testing have been proposed. However, the key challenge with non-invasive procedures is ensuring high accuracy of test result.

3   Machine Learning

There is no use in offering a definition for Machine Learning (ML) without first addressing the larger context in which it exists: the domain of Artificial Intelligence.

Artificial Intelligence (AI) is a notion that refers to any approach that allows computers to mimic human behavior in order to address and solve problems. Machine Learning, which uses statistical approaches to enable machines to recognize certain patterns by learning and improving through experience on a set of provided data, became more widespread in the 1980s.

In the decades afterwards, AI has been praised as the key to our civilization's brightest future, and derided as a harebrained idea of over-reaching propellerheads. Until 2012, there was a little bit of both. AI has surged in the last several years, particularly after 2015 [11]. Much of this is due to the widespread availability of GPUs, which makes parallel computing quicker, cheaper, and more powerful. It also has to do with the simultaneous one-two punch of almost endless storage and a deluge of data of all kinds (the whole Big Data movement)—photos, text, digital signal, transactions, mapping data, etc. (Fig. 1).

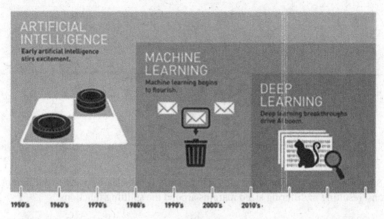

Fig. 1. Relationship between Artificial Intelligence, Machine Learning and Deep Learning

Machine Learning is a subset of AI. As defined by Wikipedia, Machine learning is the subfield of computer science that "gives computers the ability to learn without being explicitly programmed" [12]. Simply put, Machine Learning is a subfield of Computer Science that has the ability to learn on its own based on input without having to be specifically programmed.

Machine Learning has gone a long way and is a new subject in recent years, as computing power has been boosted to a new level and massive amounts of data have been collected by large technological businesses, Deep Learning (DL) was born. Deep Learning has enabled computers to perform tasks that were previously impossible: classifying hundreds of distinct objects in photographs, creating captions for images, imitating human voices and handwriting, communicating with humans, and even composing literature or music [13, 14].

4 Support Vector Machine

Support Vector Machine (SVM) is a linear model for classification and regression issues. It can handle linear and non-linear problems and is useful for a wide range of practical applications. The SVM concept is straightforward: The method draws a line or a hyperplane that divides the data into classes. The fundamental method to data classification begins with attempting to develop a function that divides the data points into the relevant labels with (a) the fewest possible mistakes or (b) the greatest feasible margin. This is because larger vacant spaces around the splitting function result in less error since the labels are easier to differentiate from one another.

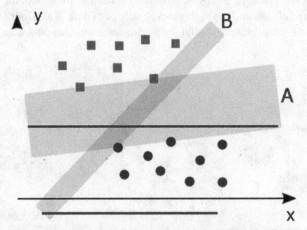

Fig. 2. Support Vector Machine separating a data set into two classes using two different linear separations, resulting in differing sized margins around the splitting functions.

Figure 2 shows that a data set may be separated by numerous functions with no errors. As a result, the margin surrounding a separating function is utilized as an extra parameter to assess separation quality. In this situation, separation A is preferable since it differentiates the two classes more precisely.

The objective of this algorithm is to achieve a hyperplane in an n-dimensional space that connects the data points to their possible classes. The hyperplane should be positioned as close to the data points as possible. The data points having the shortest distance to the hyperplane are referred to as Support Vectors [15]. Because of their near proximity, their effect on the exact position of the hyperplane is greater than that of other data points. The Support Vectors are the three points (2 blue, 1 green) laying on the lines in Fig. 3.

Any hyperplane can be written as the set of points x' satisfying

$$\mathbf{w}^T \mathbf{X} - b = 0$$

where $\mathbf{w}$ is the (not necessarily normalized) normal vector to the hyperplane. The input space consists of $\mathbf{x}$ and $\mathbf{x}'$. Therefore, $\Phi(\mathbf{x_i})$ represents the kernel function that turns the input space into a higher-dimensional space, so that not every data point is explicitly mapped. The kernel function can also be written as: $k(\mathbf{x}, \mathbf{x}')$.

5 Experimental Setup and Design

At the University of Guanajuato in Mexico, 11 patients with type 2 diabetes (DM2, 7 females, Age: 49.5 ± 6.7 years) and 9 healthy volunteers (Ctrl, 7 females, Age: 33.2

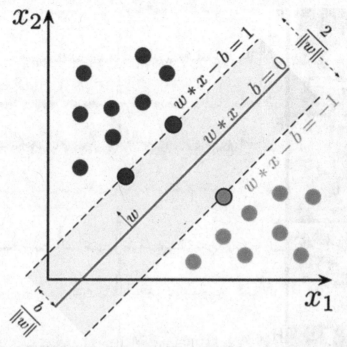

Fig. 3. Maximum-margin hyperplane and margins for an SVM trained on two classes of data. The support vectors are samples on the margin [15].

± 4.9 years) were investigated [16]. Before individuals were enrolled, the Institutional Review Board authorized the study and all subjects supplied informed consent. All DM2 patients in this research were previously diagnosed by their doctors using normal procedures such as a fasting plasma glucose test. Since the traditional method of monitoring HbA1C in human blood sample is regarded as the gold standard for long-term glycemic management in diabetic patients [17]. To evaluate HbA1C levels, a sample volume of 5 µl of blood was taken from each patient and analyzed using boronic acid affinity chromatography (LabonaCheck MH-200, Ceragem Medisys Inc.) (Fig. 4).

6 Implementation for PCA-SVM

Given 1000 dimension for each observation, it is hard to fit into an estimator with large number of features. The main idea of principal component analysis (PCA) is to reduce the dimensionality of a data set consisting of many variables correlated with each other, either heavily or lightly, while retaining the variation present in the dataset, up to the maximum extent. The same is done by transforming the variables to a new set of variables, which are known as the principal components (PCs) and are orthogonal, ordered such that the retention of variation present in the original variables decreases as we move down in the order. So, in this way, the 1st principal component retains maximum variation that was present in the original components. The principal components are the eigenvectors of a covariance matrix, and hence they are orthogonal.

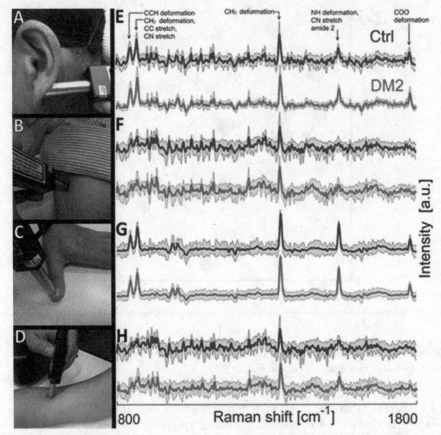

Fig. 4. Skin site images for in vivo Acquisition of Raman spectra: (A) ear lobe, (B) inner arm, (C) thumb nail, and (D) median cubital vein. The equivalent Raman observations (mean standard deviation) collected at an excitation wavelength of 785 nm (E-H) are also presented on the right side, with control spectra displayed in blue and DM2 spectra displayed in red [16].

As described previously, a PCA step is necessary to solve problems with high dimension data. Figure 5 shows an example of data acquired after being processed with Sci-kit Learn library in Python:

As can be seen in Fig. 6, particularly in ear lobe dataset, the initial number of components is chosen to match 99% explained variance ratio so that PCA compresses the main information in original dataset to produce new data that has 17 dimension. The explained variance ratio is the percentage of variation assigned to each of the chosen components. To minimize overfitting, the number of components should be selected to include in the ML model by adding the explained variance ratio of each component until it reaches a total of roughly 99%. After this processing step, the data is ready to be fed into a SVM model (Table 1).

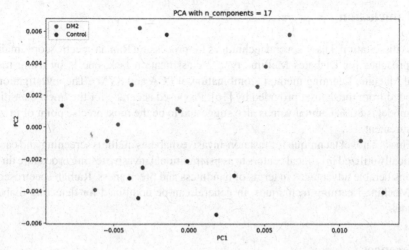

Fig. 5. Visualization of 2 first PCs obtained with total of 17 components in ear lobe dataset.

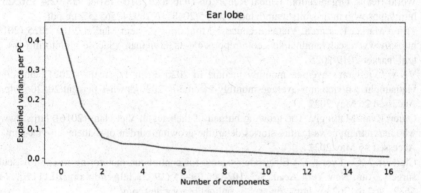

Fig. 6. Explained variance ratio for each PC.

Table 1. Experimental result of PCA-SVM.

| | Mean accuracy (%) | |
	5-fold mean accuracy	10-fold mean accuracy
Ear lobe	65	60
Inner arm	65	65
Thumb nail	70	70
Cubital vein	80	75

7 Conclusion

In this dissertation, I have several techniques for processing Raman spectroscopy, mainly 2 approaches for Diabetes Mellitus type 2 classification task, one is by using traditional Machine Learning method (combination of PCA and SVM). The investigation is extended from the dataset provided by [16]. Proposed accuracy for the finest classification model is 80%. Cubital vein is also suggested to be the most precise point of in vivo measurement.

This is a novel technique for fast non-invasive diabetes mellitus screening and can be practically utilized in clinical centers to assist traditional invasive testing procedure due to its considerable advantages in terms of handiness and preciseness. Raman spectroscopy and Machine Learning techniques, in general can be combined for detecting diabetic patients.

References

1. World Health Organization. Global Report on Diabetes (2016). ISBN 978 92 4 156525 7. http://apps.who.int/iris/bitstream/handle/10665/204871/9789241565257eng.pdf
2. Triton Market Research. Vietnam Glucose Monitoring System Market 2019–2025 (2019). https://www.researchandmarkets.com/reports/4803838/vietnam-glucose-monitoring-system-market-2019-2025
3. VNA. "Vietnam's average monthly income in 2020 down 1 percent" (2021). https://en.vietnamplus.vn/vietnams-average-monthly-income-in-2020-down-1-percent/204206.vnp. Accessed 25 May 2022
4. Quinn Ryan Mattingly. The growing burden of diabetes in Viet Nam (2016). https://www.who.int/vietnam/news/feature-stories/detail/the-growing-burden-of-diabetes-in-viet-nam. Accessed 25 May 2022
5. Clark Jr, L.C., Lyons, C.: Electrode systems for continuous monitoring in cardiovascular surgery. Ann. New York Acad. Sci. **102** (1), 29–45 (1962). https://doi.org/10.1111/j.1749-6632.1962.tb13623.x, https://nyaspubs.onlinelibrary.wiley.com/
6. Caduff, A., Etienne Hirt, Y., Feldman, Z.A., Heinemann, L.: First human experiments with a novel non-invasive, non-optical continuous glucose monitoring system. Biosens. Bioelectron. **19**(3), 209–217 (2003)
7. Tang, L., Chang, S.J., Chen, C.J., Liu, J.T.: Non-invasive blood glucose monitoring technology: a review. Sensors, **20**(23), 6925 (2020). ISSN 1424–8220. https://www.mdpi.com/1424-8220/20/23/6925
8. Menon, K.U., Hemachandran, D., Abhishek, T.K.: A survey on non-invasive blood glucose monitoring using NIR (2013). https://doi.org/10.1109/iccsp.2013.6577220
9. Abdallah, O., Bolz, A., Hansmann, J., Walles, H., Hirth, T.: Design of a compact multi-sensor system for non-invasive glucose monitoring using optical spectroscopy (2012)
10. Anas, M.N., Nurun, N.K., Norali, A.N., Normahira, M.: Non-invasive blood glucose measurement. In: 2012 IEEE-EMBS Conference on Biomedical Engineering and Sciences, pp. 503–507 (2012)
11. Machine learning in healthcare – a brief introduction (2021). https://genomed4all.eu/2021/06/08/machine-learning-in-healthcare-a-brief-introduction/
12. Machine learning (2022). https://en.wikipedia.org/wiki/Machine_learning
13. LeCun, Y., Bengio, Y., Hinton, G.: Deep learning. Nature **521**(7553), 436–444 (2015)

14. Brownlee, J.: Inspirational applications of deep learning (2019). https://machinelearningmas tery.com/inspirational-applications-deep-learning/
15. Support-vector machine (2022). https://en.wikipedia.org/wiki/Support_vector_machine
16. Guevara, E., Torres-Galván, J.C., Ramírez-Elías, M.G., Luevano-Contreras, C., González, F.J.: Use of Raman spectroscopy to screen diabetes mellitus with machine learning tools. Biomed. Opt. Express 9(10), 4998–5010 (2018)
17. Jeppsson, J.O., et al.: Approved IFCC reference method for the measurement of hba1c in human blood (2002)

A New Approach for Visual Analytics Applying to Multivariate Data of Student Intakes in the University

Dang Van Pham[1,2,3]($\boxtimes$) ![ORCID], Vinh Cong Phan[1] ![ORCID], and Nam Hoang Do[1] ![ORCID]

[1] Faculty of Information Technology, Nguyen Tat Thanh University, Ho Chi Minh City, Vietnam
pvdang.tps@gmail.com, {pvdang,pcvinh,namdh}@ntt.edu.vn
[2] Graduate University of Science and Technology, Vietnam Academy of Science and Technology, Hanoi, Vietnam
[3] Institute of Applied Mechanics and Informatics, Ho Chi Minh City, Vietnam

Abstract. Human always has the ability to view things and phenomena, but to understand about it that depends on the ability to perceive as well as combine with existing experiences and knowledge which is available in every human to understand it. This research studies the human vision organs, infographics capture characteristics of the human eye, human vision awareness progress, and human visual viewing - thinking mechanisms to design visual analytics system of multivariate data (mdVAS), model of viewing - thinking visually analyzing, and visual graphs for discovering knowledge from multivariate data (mD). This mdVAS will support to upgrade human vision awareness progress that includes stages such as viewing - perceiving - cognizing - analyzing - understanding - remembering (vpcaurH$_S$). This progress, especially the analysis stage plays a key that opens the door for human to understand the profound significance of things. Humans who want to understand the profound insights of things must bring out questions, at that time the mdVAS will enhance knowledge for humans to answer questions that humans themselves brought out. This approach will help humans, especially leaders, who have a profound insight into mD. This research illustrates experiments on educational data to manage the student intakes to help leadership on policy and decision making.

Keywords: Human vision awareness progress · Visual analytics system of multivariate data · mdVAS · Model of viewing - Thinking visually analyzing · Visual graph · Educational data

1 Introduction

Due to human demand wanting to discover the profound insights hidden within mD, human has used many methods in combination with different tools to collect data from various data sources in the real-world. Therefore, human is facing enormous challenges in extracting information and discovering knowledge from within these data sources. The

C. V. Phan and T. D. Nguyen (Eds.): ICTCC 2022, LNICST 473, pp. 88–120, 2023.
https://doi.org/10.1007/978-3-031-28790-9_7

data is analyzed and converted into many different formats to display on a 2D computer screen, but it depends on discovering purposes of every human. At that time, human will represent it in whatever forms to suit their purpose, such as visual graphs, images, symbols, etc. to help human perceive more and more significance as deep inside data as possible. This is the basis for answering the question, why do humans understand so quickly some forms of data representation and others don't? This question is extremely important for data scientists who are pursuing the design of mdVAS that exploits mD.

For having the formats as above, there are two approaches to transform data into information and knowledge in mdVAS that are approach according to the mathematics and visualization methods [1–3]. With the mathematics method, system discovered knowledge from data by providing algorithms to answer analytical questions but without the participation of users. With the visualization method, human is reputed the most important component in mdVAS to answer analytical questions through experiences and knowledge available in every human to perceive visually. Human looks at visual graphs representing data to perceive the deepest significance about data from which to support of policy making and makes decision.

Human always has the ability to view, deduce, remember based on deductive mechanisms, remind memory and with the great operation of the human vision organs (hVO_s) that the Creator bestows on human, it is also a means for human to think, create, accumulate knowledge and is able to contemplate the colorful beauty of nature. This research studies the hVO_s, human vision awareness progress ($hVAP_s$), infographics capture characteristics of the human eye ($hIGCE_s$) and human visual viewing - thinking mechanisms ($hVTM_s$) to design mdVAS that services users for extracting information and discovering knowledge from mD. Vision is the most important sensory organ, the channel that receives the most data. On those bases, this research proposes to make mdVAS that human is able to use and connect components as model of viewing - thinking visually analyzing (visVTM), computer science methodologies to support visual viewing – thinking, questions and answers, how to fit the visual graphs that support to human adapt to the $hVAP_s$ that includes stages such as $vpcaurH_s$ to extract information and discover knowledge from mD.

The remainder of this paper is organized as follows. Section 2 focuses on the discovery the hVO_s for the direction of the visual analysis of student intakes in the university in progresses by $hVAP_s$. Section 3 provides an overview of the research related to discover knowledge from mD and focuses on presenting concepts related to visual analysis of mD including visual analytics approach and question types applied on a mdVAS. Section 4 proposes to build a mdVAS, human observation abilities, visVTM, and visual analysis of the university data. Section 5 focuses on visual analysis of student intakes by using the types of questions that visually analyze mD. Section 6 presents the conclusions and development direction in the future.

2 Human Vision Organs

2.1 The Amazing Possibilities of Human Vision

2.1.1 The Main Components of the Human Eye

Look at the main components of the human eye (hE_s) in Fig. 1, we have a clear picture of the major components of the hE_s that the Creator bestows on humans and through a lot of time analyzed by scientists including components such as focusing optics and objects. With a focusing optic consisting of layers like layers of transparent lens, transparent corneas, iris, and pupil. The transparent lenses are able to pick up the light rays from the object to the convergent point focusing on the retina. With a focusing object having a retina layer which is behind focusing optic of the vision organs. In other words, light rays coming from objects through the cornea are focused on the retinal layer to create a visual image of the object. Thus, we see that each component of the hEs has distinct functions and tasks. To concretize the analysis of the main components of the hEs and the hVOs, we look at Fig. 1 and specifically in Fig. 2 to understand how the sublime functioning of the hVOs.

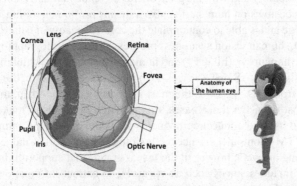

Fig. 1. Topology relational diagram of nine - time units

2.1.2 Human Vision Organs

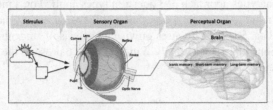

Fig. 2. The human visual perception organs [4, 5]

Look at the Fig. 2, we perform a survey of a light ray from a point on a certain object to the hEs that light ray may be emitted by itself or reflected into that object from another light source. According to electromagnetic wave, light rays are electromagnetic waves that carry data of object points. In theory, electromagnetic waves are called modulated data, while light rays are called carrier wares. When reaching the hE_s, light rays converge on the fovea layer in the retina layer to be demodulated by rod-shaped photoreceptors and cone-shaped photoreceptors to separate data from the carrier ware. One of both two types of photoreceptors has its own demodulation function. Rod-shaped cells are very sensitive to light, allowing them to see things in low light conditions and to help them see further. Cone-shaped cells need more light, but they tell us very small details of things when we look at them. The data is driven to the iconic memory (IM) of brain by optic nerve. At IM, the data is perceived to quickly select which data should be transferred to short-term memory (STM). Processing data of IM is understood as categorizing which data is of interest and which is not. Data of interest is transferred to STM. At STM, the data is identified cognition about object. This cognized data is exchanged with information and knowledge available in long-term memory (LTM), collated, filtered carefully and combined with the data stored in LTM to synthesize meaning, thus, the profound understanding of human data is enhanced by the combination of new data and previously available data stored in LTM. At this point, human has awaked to the profound significance hidden within the data, meaning awareness of things. After that, the data is uploaded to LTM in order to update awareness and long-term storage for later reuse or also known as the reminiscent of memories. This is a $hVAP_s$, also known as the progress of transferring data from objects to the human brain, which the hVO_s were progressed naturally by themselves.

2.1.3 Discovering the Efficiency of the hEs

With the ability to perceive the very rich light of the hE_s, the hE_s can distinguish light having different intensities from light to dark. If the light has too high intensity, the iris layer will adjust automatically the size of the pupil layer so that there is enough light reaching the retina. If the convergent point of light rays emitted by objects through the transparent cornea is not on the retina layer, at that time, the eye muscles will automatically adjust the lens that is attached behind the cornea to change the curvature and thickness of the cornea, and cause the convergent point to be shifted back into position on the retinal layer during the progress of receiving objects from the outside into the hVO_s [4–6]. Scientists still do not understand a lot of the mystery of human vision. One of the mysteries is the small number and size of PN_s, so how PN_s of the retina can be able to perform above magical and extremely complex abilities efficiently, accurately and quickly even before these signals are move to the central brain to form vision and control the organs of the hE_s or other parts of the human body. How the hE_s can adapt itself to the intensity and color of the ambient light in many different situations to always accurately and faithfully record the nature of the captured image is a mystery and are major challenges for scientists.

The hE_s can perceive images in a very detailed way thanks to the huge number of photoreceptor neurons (PN_s) that surround the fovea layer. The hE_s can also distinguish very precisely the depth, width and height of a scene thanks to the depth of the fovea layer on the retina. In order to analyze the received signals, each PN of the hE_s acts as a separate element, it performs an accurate sense of size, shape, position, depth, width, height, amplification and color of the landscape outside the real-world and many other complex mysteries that scientists have not yet discovered. The PN_s network system of the hE_s works so sophisticated and complicated in the progress of image perception that scientists still don't understand its details today.

2.2 Human Vision Awareness Evolution

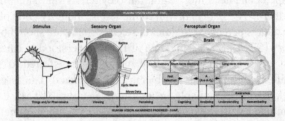

Fig. 3. Integrating human vision awareness progress in the hVO_s

Human perceives things with the five senses. Each sense is compared to a data acquisition system that supports very powerful and very sophisticated for human brain to perceive the real-world. Each sense has different amazing abilities. *Hearing* perceives sound in the real-world with ears. *Touch* perceives objects that exist in the real-world with touching the skin. *Smell* perceives objects and phenomena in the real-world with nose. *Taste* perceives the sweet and sour taste of dishes with tongue. *Vision* perceives things in the real-world with eyes. Among these senses, vision is considered to be the most important one and is carefully analyzed and studied in the section on the great abilities of human vision. Since then, we have found that in this hVOs having hidden superpowers such as the $hVAP_s$, the $hVTM_s$, and the $hIGCE_s$ to awake to things in the real-world, this progress includes stages as $vpcaurH_s$ (Fig. 3).

The analytical stage of the $hVAP_s$ is a core stage for upgrading human understanding, this stage is called the stage of data VA (A-a-A-Q_s) (Fig. 3). At this stage, we perform the combination and integration into the mdVAS with four components such as the component of questions and answers bank system, $hVTM_s$, and the component of $hIGCE_s$ in order to support human extracts information and discovers knowledge from data. With the component of question bank system is embedded in the mdVAS, it will help human answer the questions how to understand things in the real-world? To answer this question, humans must either bring out questions themselves or use the exist questions in system to understand things in the real-world that if you want to understand, you have to ask. With the component of answer system is embedded in the mdVAS, it will help human clearly understand about things in the progress of data VA based on visual graphs.

2.3 Human Visual Viewing-Thinking Mechanisms

To transform objects in the real-world into forms of information and knowledge representation that conform to the $hVTM_s$ as well as their goals are major challenges for scientists. Humans have used many methods, specifically mathematical modeling method and data visualization method [1–3]. Through these methods, people choose the mode of representation and its presentation tools in accordance with the $hVTM_s$. With the existing system of great senses, people can sometimes use their five senses simultaneously to perceive things in the real-world. To aspect of viewing-thinking, vision is seen as the channel receiving the most information and knowledge compared with the rest of the human senses and previous studies have also shown that formats such as images, graphs, diagrams will be the easily forms conveying and representing the most information and knowledge [7]. Therefore, we choose the format graphs to represent data in this study in order to help human perceive the most information and knowledge from mD.

Through analysis of the hVO_s and the $hVAP_s$ that we performed above, hE_s perceives objects with the rays emitted by the object that reach the eyes, this light is led to the brain by the nervous system to processed into information and knowledge. Based on studies, we found that the brain analyzes information that leads to the eyes at two general and detailed levels. With the level of general, by parallel method the brain quickly analyzes the outstanding characteristics of objects. With the level of detail, the brain analyzes by serial method to detect specific details of an object [4, 8, 9]. The $hVTM_s$ of objects of the hE_s are carried out automatically. We discovered that the hE_s has a mechanism for seeing the whole and the mechanism for seeing the details of objects. With respect to the whole overall mechanism, the hE_s perceives the whole object, that is, it receives light rays coming from the object to provide the brain with processing, the brain draws information at the most general level as the main components of the object present on the representational forms. With respect to the detailed vision mechanism, the hE_s perceives details from the whole perception, the brain analyzes and processes it in more detail in the overall perception, based on the serial method, the hE_s identifies variables, characteristics of variables and detailed components on the representational forms. Through the overall perception and the detailed perception of representation forms of the objects, by viewing-thinking, each person, depending on their knowledge and experience, will perceive the relationship between the variables, between the components of the physical representation forms at different angles of vision with the expectation of discovering new relationships and knowledge available on the representational forms.

Visual analytics system discovers data applying methods of data analysis [2, 3, 10, 11] to render forms of data visual representation from that human can apply viewing - thinking mechanisms, in which contains a lot of information and knowledge. With ability of overall viewing-thinking as soon as detailed viewing-thinking, people will apply the ability to perceive the whole, perceive details and perceive the relationships among the available components on data representations to discover information and the knowledge hidden within it.

2.4   The Infographics Capture Characteristics of the hEs

The hE_s is a vision organs like an optical machine [5, 12, 13], having a very complex structure, having a task for capturing visual information of an object and then converting it to the brain, the brain is in charge of perceiving, cognizing, analyzing, understanding, remembering and synthesizes images acquired and stored in LTM sent from millions of photoreceptors located on the retina to create a profound visual perception of object images. Environmental factors in which the presence of objects will greatly determine humans' cognitive abilities. Therefore, the selection of data representation formats to suit the human visual perception ability and the $hIGCE_s$ of the hE_s plays an extremely important role in extracting information and discovering knowledge from data. Through the aforementioned analysis and the $hIGCE_s$ of the hE_s are clearly shown through the following five characteristics [4, 6, 12].

- **The hE_s is sensitive to light.** The hE_s having automatic sensitivity to light is sophisticated and impeccable which is shown through aspects of capturing images and image quality are lifelike and almost instantaneous.
- **The hE_s automatically adjusts light.** The hE_s is able to automatically adjust the light of an object from light to dark and vice versa when this light enters the eye because the iris layer automatically performs enlargement or contraction.
- **The hE_s automatically focuses the image.** The hE_s is capable of autofocusing the image of an object very flexibly using a light-sensitive retina surface. The lens layer combines with the muscles in orbit to constantly change the shape of the lens layer to create flexibility in focusing images of objects.
- **The hE_s automatically balances the colors.** The hE_s from the moment it receives light, it automatically balances the colors according to the context in which the light enters the eye. The hE_s always creates harmony and combination closely with the brain to create visual images that help the brain maximize the perception of object images.
- **The hE_s automatically adjusts the focus of the image.** The hE_s automatically adjusts the focal of object images by bending the light through the lens so that it enters focus on the retina, and then received by the vision nerve system and transferred to the brain to analyze and process cognition of object images.

With the $hIGCE_s$ that we analyzed above, the hE_s is really regarded as a powerful and very sophisticated vision organs. Thus, the acquisition of image information of the object is almost perfect, so that this approach is complete and more perfect. Our mission is to make human view-to-think the image of the object on the representations in a more meaningful and profound way, based on the philosophy of Albert von Szent-Gyorgyi points out that "Discovery consists of seeing what everybody has seen and thinking what nobody has thought." [14] is very essential and highly practical science in the field of data visual analytics. To do this, we focus on building a visual analytics system that explores mD by combining and integrating into this system with five components such as the component of banking question system, answer system, the $hVTM_s$, the $hIGCE_s$, and visVTM to assist human in extracting information and discovering knowledge from data. Especially, today when human is more inclined to wake up the mind of each person, extremely important to support the leaders in policy and timely decision making.

3 Related Words

3.1 Discovering Knowledge from Multivariate Data

Extracting information and discovering knowledge from mD is a major challenge in analyzing data visual for researchers on data science and is a problem which is concerned now. In respects of data, data always exists in many different forms as writing, image, sound, light, etc. that its usefulness lies implicit within it which is endless. It challenges people to explore it that means information and knowledge hidden in the data is endless, it challenges people to explore it. According to Andrienko [15], the data represents the results of observations or measurements of phenomena. By means of data analysis, people can study these phenomena. Data analysis is to find answers to various questions related to things and phenomena. For data mining methods, from the past to the present, there are many methods of mining information and knowledge from the data, in there includes algorithmic methods, modeling methods, visual presentation method, visualization method, visual analysis method [1–3, 10]. Each method has different special abilities and will be presented in the next paragraphs and then we will propose to choose one of these methods as the basis for the research on the subject about extracting information and discovering knowledge from data.

Algorithm is a method that can extract information and discover knowledge from data by algorithms. To develop the algorithms, we must rely on the knowledge and experience of computer science specialists to understand and develop it. However, when the data arises quickly, specially, the data is in many different forms and accompanied by the generation of complex data at different times, leading to the method of algorithm development not in time and not timely analysis to respond the need to explore knowledge from data. On the other hand, algorithmic methods cannot mobilize the intelligence of all experts in many areas, also known as interdisciplinary as enrollment, epidemiology, weather, climate change, etc. to analyze and develop algorithms. Modeling is a method that can extract information and discover knowledge from data by modeling. Modeling one or more real-world contexts into a model is a huge challenge for researchers. In there, a data model is a model that provides forms of symbols to describe datasets and sets of behaviors on these datasets. The data model summarizes the data from outside reality and provides an overview of the data to represent a specific range and a limited range of real-world [16]. From the modeling method, researchers have come up with a variety of data models to extract information and discover knowledge from data, such as TLODs model [17], expanded CityGML model [18], ELUDM model for 2.5-3D objects [19], a new LoD and multi-representational concept for the CityGML model [20], etc.

Based on the philosophy of von Szent-Gyorgyi [14], from this philosophy, it paved the way for data visual representation, visualization and visual analytics method born. The visual representation method is data representation in a display form [21, 22], which allows users to view data visually, but limiting is the users haven't understood a lot of the datasets represented here. Data visual analytics and visualization method makes it possible for people to see what everyone saw and understands what people understand. The special point of data visual analytics and visualization method is thanks to the knowledge and experience of analysts in many areas, also known as interdisciplinary (enrollment, epidemiology, weather, etc.). Data visual analytics is analytical theoretical science major supported by interactive visual interface [22]. There are now more specific definitions of data visual analytics [10] as follows data visual analytics is a combination of automated analytical techniques with visual interaction images to help people understand and reason more easily and make more effective decisions about large and complex datasets. The goal of visual analytics (VA) is to create tools and computer techniques that allows people to synthesize information and have wide and deep insight from large datasets, datasets that change over time, unclear dataset, and conflict datasets, detect what is already there hidden in the data and discover unexpected things from the datasets and provides timely and easy-to-understand assessments from datasets, effectively communicates the evaluation of human activities.

According to the team of Sun.G.D and his colleagues express that VA is the use of visual image of interaction to integrate human's knowledge and reasoning into analytical processes data. This is a dynamic and innovative field of research that is currently applied in a different variety of areas and has many applications in the area, such as security, finance, business, etc. [23]. According to the team of G.Andrienko, VA is aimed at combining human strong points and processing electronic data [24]. Visualization is a method for people and computers to be able to collaborate with each other through a computer graphic interface or being called a means whereby this collaboration can be achieved require. Researchers should find approached methods to solve the complexity of current data and find ways to create data visual analysis tools that are accessible and usable for the potential user community and contribute to resolve some of the big problems.

In today's applications, data volume is created at an unprecedented speed [1]. The ability to collect and store data in applications is increasing rapidly, while the ability of human analyzing this large amount of data to discover knowledge increases at a much lower level. This gap leads to enormous challenges for data scientists, data analysis experts, policy and decision making or in-depth research teams in data analysis that face the process of data analysis, extract information and discover the knowledge hidden in data. Today, with the emergence of a area of VA focused on data processing at different levels such as huge data volumes, heterogeneous data volumes and especially these data volumes change continuously over time. With the advantage of that area of VA is to have the integration of human judgment, existing knowledge as well as human experience from which humans apply data visual representation methods, visual interaction techniques for data visual analysis process is an innovative and scientific approach. The VA area is a combination of many other related research areas including visualization, information analysis, scientific analysis, knowledge discovery, visual interaction, knowledge representation, data management, cognitive and perceived sciences, spatial analysis and statistical analysis [1] that can upgrade VA into a area of full prospecting research and trends in the future.

3.2   Taxonomy of the Models Discovering Knowledge from Multivariate Data

Human's daily activities always take place in many different contexts, this is the basis for human to receive information and knowledge from many different data sources, leading to decision-making on problems that are great challenges for human. Therefore, the study of methodologies, data visual analytics system, data analysis processes, data analysis models, or information extraction and knowledge discovery tools from data are promising and challenging works for data scientists. Especially today, humans are increasingly aiming to awaken each person's mind to make decisions about financial policies and improve the quality of training based on useful information and discovered knowledge that can be strategic for their units. This research systematizes study works related to areas such as data visualization, analysis of exploratory data, knowledge discovery in the database, and data mining.

Information extraction and knowledge discovery from mD by visual methods and VA of data have been proposed by many groups of authors [2, 3, 13, 25–27], these two areas are currently having a very strong development trend. Humans take advantage of data visualization and their own pre-existing knowledge to be able to perform information extraction and knowledge discovery from data based on visual graphs representing mD. Visual graphs should be designed to best visualize the range of mD visual representations, without omitting any useful information and knowledge, and without misunderstanding non-existent meanings in the data, whereby helping the analyst to observe and empathize the visual graphs using the visual viewing - thinking method to extract information and discover knowledge. During the length of the development history of the areas of data analysis, many groups of authors have researched and proposed models and processes of data analysis by visualization and VA. VA of data is based on the existing knowledge base of each person combined with computer science methods in the data discovery process. With visualization, this approach allows the creation of visual images and graphs that represent information and illustrate data in a way that is easy to understand and must reflect the truthfulness of the datasets to the user. Data visualization uses tools that support data processing and analytics to answer, clarify defined goals, and show current potential through the easiest acquired presentation most absorbed by the model of viewing – thinking and the vision method. Hereafter, we conduct a survey of some of the researches related to discover knowledge from data with the presence of human in the data analysis process.

Discovering knowledge from data is a challenging task for data analysts. Analysts must devise strategies for discovering knowledge from data, where data is transformed into information and knowledge by mathematical model, visualization and VA. With the mathematical model approach to help the analyst discover information and knowledge using mathematical model, this further confirms that the information and knowledge discovered have great useful value related to the support and improvement the quality of education in order to attract a steady and increasing annual student intake entering, and as a basis for maintaining the confidence of students studying at faculties in the university to aim at limiting the remaining student intakes occur. With the visualization approach, this approach applies the available knowledge and experience of humans and cooperates with computers in the process of discovering knowledge from data by vision methods. More specifically, in this research, we will combine mathematical model, visualization, and VA in extracting useful information and discovering knowledge from mD of the student intake types entering the university will give analysts the most insights into what they discover. In the context of increasingly focusing on influencing the minds of each human to help them in decision making, development strategies and other policies in the unit. Therefore, data analysis systems require the presence of humans to cooperate with computers in the process of discovering knowledge from data, this approach not only brings new prospects, but also presents huge challenges for data analysts who aspire to design and build data analysis systems that focus on taking human as the core of the system. In the following, we analyze a number of studies related to data analysis that have been proposed by many groups of authors and make some comments as a premise for new proposals.

Approaching to extract information and discover knowledge from data by models and processes, the visual method and mathematical model are the most suitable choice and considered the key to success in the knowledge discovery process from data. This approach is the basis for the authors to propose the roles of humans and computers to cooperate with each other in data analysis models and processes including the reference visualization model proposed by Stuart Card et al. [28] to perform from the data transformation stage to the interactive visual form stage by means of visual mappings controlled by humans; The visual analysis process proposed by Keim et al. [10] was built from the visualization model proposed by Wijk [29], this process represents stage one of receiving data sources, stage two applies visualization to transform data into interactive visualization, stage three helps the analyst to apply the viewing - thinking method to perceive the deepest meaning of newly discovered knowledge, and the analyst can rely on the newly discovered knowledge and existing assumptions to continue the analysis further with the technical characteristics applied to the visualization of stage two; The VA process proposed by Keim et al. [30] helps human combine modeling and visualization methods to discover knowledge from data where modeling methods are carried out automatically data analysis while the visualization methods are conducted visual data exploration by human vision; Quality-metrics-driven automation pipeline is extended from the reference visualization model with a quality-metrics-driven automation proposed by Bertini et al. [31] helps the analyst to interact and control the entire process, and finally the analyst obtains the results which are visual structures that are displayed in different ways; The model of arising knowledge in the field of VA proposed by Sacha et al. [32] proposes the role of human involved in the implementation of the mining process, the testing process, the process of arising knowledge and the rest is a visual analysis system automatically performed by a computer; The data analysis system proposed by ThiNguyen et al. [2] has the ability to convert data into information and knowledge by modeling method to build mathematical models combined with visualization that help humans and computers work together with the available knowledge and experience of each human involved in discovery knowledge from data; The visual analytics system that mines mD based on visual graphs proposed by VanPham et al. [3] has two main layers, layer one combines mathematical model and visualization method to render visual graphs, layer two helps the analysts to interact on the visual graphs by asking questions and self-answering with a step-by-step visual viewing - thinking process, step one with the appearance of analysts and visual graphs, step two analysts view the visual graphs, step three analysts understand visual graphs to crystallize information and knowledge, step four analysts again interact with the visual graphs by asking and answering data analysis questions while observing the visual graphs, and the process continues to repeat step one if the human wants to do it for the next times.

Through the systematization and analysis of the above research works helped us get an overview of the area of data analysis by taking models and processes as the focus of the process of extracting information and discovering knowledge from data. In the research works that we have analyzed above, there is a research work by ThiNguyen [2] and VanPham [3] that mentions the types of elementary questions, variation questions, and relation questions used for visual analysis of data based on visual graphs. However, the data analysis system by ThiNguyen's group [2] mentions the types of elementary, variation, and relation questions but does not specify where to use it on the data analysis system, while the research work of VanPham's group [3] uses type of elementary, variation and relation questions to coordinate with criteria in visual analysis discovering knowledge from mD. Based on the survey results of the above research works, we propose a mdVAS applied on the mD of student intakes in the university. To build a mdVAS, we study the hVO_s, $hVAP_s$, $hVTM_s$, $hIGCE_s$ of the hE_s, and build visVTM to integrate into the mdVAS to help the analyst to $vpcaurH_s$. The mdVAS is an approach that thanks to the analyst's available experience and knowledge is used to contribute to the process of uncovering the deep meanings hidden in the data and allows analysts to easily understand data visual forms by using their memory, thinking and imagination ability.

3.3 Related Concepts

3.3.1 Data Analysis

Analyzing data for the purpose of extracting information, exploring knowledge and finding new laws from diverse data sources is an extremely difficult and challenging job for data analysts. The analysis of data is carried out by analysts in a multi-step process [3, 15], each step demonstrates the efficiency and flexibility in data visual analysis. Flexible and effective data analysis not only helps strategy analysts and strategy administrators achieve their desired goals, but also demonstrates the reliability and accuracy of information extraction, explore knowledge, and discover new rules from multivariate datasets for policy making and decision making. Each of these real-world objects has a certain use meaning, it is used for different purposes that people want to explore it. The analyst perceives it through the vision organs, visual information-gathering properties of the eye, visual viewing - thinking mechanisms, and vision awareness progress to view and think visually the existing image of objects in the real-world. From there, analysts will ask visual analysis questions of mD based on the objects that they see because of the need to discover objects and find out new rules of objects.

In visual analytics, we find that visual analysis questions of mD are the only clue, and also the most practical scientific approach to visual analysis of mD. In which, the characteristics of the visual analysis questions of mD include two main parts, that is the assumption and the conclusion [3]. In data visual analysis, question building is the first step and basis for the data visual analysis process to proceed. It can be said that it is impossible to perform data analysis if no questions are asked. Based on the relevance of the question to the data variables, the values of the data variables, and especially the related variables. Therefore, analysts play a central role in the process of visualizing data discovering knowledge and exploiting new rules from mD by applying a data visual analysis process that includes the following steps [3, 15].

- **Step 1:** Analyst proceeds to collect data through a number of specific legitimate sources. After the data has been collected, the analyst performs the removal of the unrelated types of data that are necessary for research purposes, and retain only those types of data for analysis by their purpose.
- **Step 2:** Analyst must focus on building questionnaires and then proceed to use these questionnaires to analyze data to explore knowledge and find new rules hidden within mD in step 1.
- **Step 3:** Analysts have to select reasonable methods they can choose mathematical modeling methods to extract information and explore knowledge from data. The analysts can choose the visual analysis method, especially this method of which is the coordination between computers and humans, apply human knowledge and experience to extract information, discover knowledge, find new rules hidden within mD.
- **Step 4:** Analysts apply the method they have chosen to apply it to the datasets collected in step 1 into the data analysis process.
- **Step 5:** Analysts look at visual graphs to extract information, discover knowledge, find out new laws and then conduct an evaluation of the results achieved to make specific decisions and employment policy for its unit.

3.3.2 Data Visual Analytics

VA is considered as a science of analytical theory, proven by scientists as one of the scientific methods of analyzing data visual analysis. This method uses an intuitive interface to assist the analyst in interacting with the intuitive interface in representing information and knowledge from variable datasets [22]. Therefore, we believe that the tools support efficiently in analyzing visual data are interactive visual interfaces. Interactive visual interfaces are means to represent visual objects that are surveyed, analyzed, designed, evaluated, and implemented by scientists in visual analysis systems that help analysts in extracting information, exploring knowledge, and finding out new rules hidden in multivariate datasets [2, 3]. Today, visual analysis is viewed by data scientists as a promising, prospecting, and challenging field in the future, concretely for strategic analysts, senior leaders of corporations, companies, and universities have to face and use it in data visual analysis [1, 10, 17, 22, 33].

3.3.3 The Types of Analysis Questions of Multivariate Data

To build types of analysis questions of data for mdVAS, we systematize some types of analysis questions suggested by many groups of authors for the category destination extracting information, discovering knowledge, and uncovering new laws from data. This is also the basis for us to propose more general types of analysis questions and are widely applied in the mdVAS of a university that we propose at the next sections of this research. In 2006, Andrienko author and colleagues [15] carried out dividing the questions of data analysis into two levels, level 1 is an elementary level question which is a question related to value of a certain variable, level 2 is a synoptic level question which is a type of question related to a group of values of a certain variable or a question type related to all values of a certain variable. In 2011, Bertin author [8] carried out dividing the questions of data analysis into levels. With level 1 is an elementary level question which is a question related to value of a certain variable, with level 2 is a synoptic level question of Andrienko author [15]. After that, Bertin divided the synoptic level question of Andrienko into two levels. With level 1 is an intermediate level question which is a question related to value of a certain variable. With level 2 is a global level question which is a question type related to all values of a certain variable. In 2019, ThiNguyen [2] and VanPham [3] author groups also proposed types of analysis questions divided into three levels. With level 1 is an elementary question which is a type of question related to value of a certain variable. With level 2 is a global question which is a type of question related to a group of values of a certain variable or a question type related to all values of a certain variable to understand the characteristics of variables or to understand the law of variation. With level 3 is a relation question which is a type of question related to multiple data variables, used to find correlations between variables to help us discover new relational rules among variables as well as between datasets of related variables.

4 Visual Analytics System

4.1 Visual Analytics System of Multivariate Data

Humans (analysts, data scientists, or senior leaders) inherently have his/her own wonderful abilities that the Creator has bestowed upon their including his/her vision organs, $hIGCE_s$ of their eyes, $hVAP_s$, $hVTM_s$, and their existing experiences and knowledge. Based on these excellent capabilities, the analyst can apply it for both ask and answer his/her own questions while also having good support of the questionnaire and answer set components. These two components have been integrated in the mdVAS (see Fig. 4) in the knowledge discovery progress and draw new rules from the mD represented on the visual graphs. Through the studies above, we discovered that the philosophy of Szent-Gyorgyi [14] the more clarifying the profound meaning of seeing, everyone has the ability to seeing, but thinking the real-world objects they are seeing is a big challenge for the data analysts explore knowledge and find new relationships and rules hidden within objects. Based on this philosophy, we propose building a mdVAS that extracts information, discovers knowledge and draws new rules from mD as an urgent research direction and high practical scientific.

Looking at mdVAS we see that, at the computer layer, there is an external environment that includes many important data sources that need to be collected for the purpose of extracting information and discovering knowledge of data analysts. The visualization method in coordination with mathematical model method [1–3, 10, 13, 23, 25–27, 34] to render the mD into visual graphs to suit the possibility human visual perception. In the VA layer, the analyst plays a central role in the data VA process. In this process includes components such as the visual graph component, the data analyst component by the viewing - thinking method, the component of the analyst who observes the visual graphs by three seeing (see Fig. 5) such as whole seeing, partial seeing and partial detailed seeing, the $hVAP_s$ component, the questions component, and the answers component that the analyst can be used for knowledge discovery purposes and find new rules from visual graphs. At this layer of VA of mdVAS, the $hVAP_s$ component is shown through an automatic progress consisting of the following stages as $vpcaurH_s$. In this evolution, especially the analyzing phase is very important and a big challenge for analysts, in data

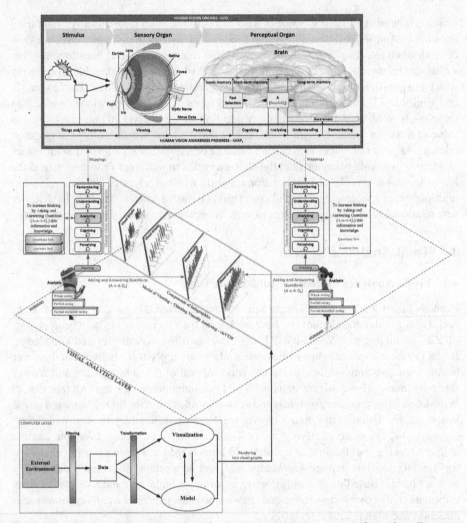

Fig. 4. The visual analytics system of multivariate data (mdVAS) extracts information, discovers knowledge and finds new rules from mD based on visual graphs, where the mdVAS indicates computer layer and VA layer (humans, visual graphs, detailed questionnaire component and the corresponding answers component, visVTM, and $hVAP_s$).

analysis consists of two important aspects, which are question and answer, if we want to understand, we must ask and answer ourselves. To solve this phase of analyzing, we integrated into the mdVAS as a detailed questionnaire component and the answers set correspondingly. Data analysts will use these two components to discover knowledge themselves and find new rules according to their wishes.

From mdVAS, we see that the biggest challenge in a mdVAS is the VA layer, especially the trend to solve the noticeable current problem is according to the approach that awakens the human mind in making decisions to satisfy a certain purpose. Therefore,

VA is understood as the dialogue between the analyst and the data visual representations that the data depends on the applications and according to the performer that the analyst must interpret and must be adapted to those data visual representations. In VA, analysts have a need to observe data visual representations, from which they think and interpret if they want to understand the profound meaning of what they see and next they will think about the next questions to ask. At this point, the types of analysis questions will arise in many different respects for the analyst, and new elements in the data visual representations will have to be considered further. The representations in this dialogue are visual interactions between the analyst and with the data visual representations, in particular, a visual graph representing mD.

To better understand the mdVAS clearly, especially in the VA layer, the types of analysis questions are conducted through many stages, each stage relies on the form of visual representation to questions, the viewing stage of analysts is to ask and answer questions themselves. The data analysis strategy using the VA method is by using the analyst as a key component of the mdVAS that searches for information, discovers knowledge, and discovers generate new rules from mD (Fig. 4). In the computer layer, the computer supports the analyst by displaying mD as visual graphs, the analyst views at the visual graph with his/her knowledge and experience and coordinate with the questions component and different information to think and understand the content hidden within the datasets by visual graphs. This combination is the questionnaire and corresponding answer set for that questionnaire, which means that the analyst understands the deep meaning hidden in the related datasets by a visual graph that the mdVAS provided, which is the questions and the answers component. The scientific and creative nature of this mdVAS is to take advantage of the hVO_s to analyze data visually, these advantages are expressed through the components such as the components of $hIGCE_s$, $hVAP_s$, and $hVTM_s$.

4.2 Human Observation Abilities

Following this, we propose a classification approach for seeing and types of analysis questions. With the above mdVAS, the analyst often performs the progress of observing the visual graph in the following ways as whole seeing (WS_q), partial seeing (PS_q), and partial detailed seeing (PDS_q) (see Fig. 5). The analyst can use the analytical questions available in the mdVAS to analyze the data, subsequent analysis questions will be generated by themselves during the analysis of the data, and the data analysis questions are classified into the following types of questions as elementary questions, variable questions, relationship questions, hierarchical questions, visually thinking questions, overall questions between variables and between datasets of one variable. We have the following conventions, human collectively known as the analyst will have ability whole seeing with forms $WS_q | q = 1, 2, 3, \ldots, n$; partial seeing with forms $PS_q | q = 1, 2, 3, \ldots, n$; partial detailed seeing with forms $PDS_q | q = 1, 2, 3, \ldots, n$; in which $\{q_1, q_2, q_3, \ldots, q_n\}$ are visual analysis questions of mD. Thus, humans can see real-world objects with $S = \{WS_q, PS_q, PDS_q\}$ in process of data visual analysis.

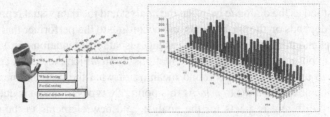

Fig. 5. Humans have the ability to see whole, partial, and partial detailed of real-world objects in progress of analyzing visually multivariate data.

4.3 Visual Analytics of a University Data

Einstein's theory of relativity says that time is relative and indefinite. The elapsed time depends on your frame of reference [35]. In managing any job, time management can be seen as a challenging job. Because the time it takes to complete something is an indefinite time. In structured datasets, time structure has semantics related to time distribution such as discrete time, continuous time, and absolute time [36]. On the time axis, discrete time means that there is a definite number of points between any two points on that axis; while continuous time means that between any two points on the time axis there is an indefinite number of points and it is suitable for representing constantly changing objects such as change of courses in a university; absolute time means to show a perfectly definite object as majors or faculties in a university. Time data types include time point, time segment, and time period. Time point means describing a point on the time axis, giving an example of a meeting that took place at 14:00 on January 12, 21 at the office of faculty of information technology (FIT), Nguyen Tat Thanh University (NTTU). Time segment means describing a time segment on the time axis and is limited by two points of time, for an example of a course year starting from 2020 ending until 2024; for example, the time for submitting online homework of students is from January 9, 21 to January 20, 21. Thus, the data of courses belongs to time segment is represented in the following formats: the discrete time format is 14, 15, 16, etc.; the absolute time format is 14–18, 15–19, 16–20, etc.; 14–15, 15–16, 16–17, etc. A period of time to describe an indeterminate segment of time, giving the example of a student who has been in college for 5 years and has not graduated from university.

Data of a university belongs to many different fields, including the part of data on the intake of students entering and leaving at a university according to each academic year which occurs regularly and continuously, a piece of data of particular interest to school leaders. In this research, which focuses on analyzing this data piece and student intakes are represented by the form of ratio data. The main purpose is to help school leaders know the student intakes by each course that the faculties are managing so that they have a basis to compare and make improvement decisions to improve the quality of training to meet all labor resource needs of society. Student intake entering means that every year after graduating from high school, students will perform a special task in their future that is to apply for admission into universities by many different university admission methods. The intake of students making reservation means that in the learning process, for some reason, students cannot continue to study anymore, at that time, students can make a record to reserve their academic results. In the future, when possible, students can use this reservation to ask the school to go back to school. The intake of graduated students means students who have received a university diploma. The intake of current students means students who are studying a particular major in a department of a university. The intake of suspended students means students who are in violation of school rules and regulations. The intake of students withdrawing fees means students may encounter some personal problems, they cannot continue to study, according to the school's rules and regulations, at that time, students may be entitled to withdraw tuition. The intake of students dropping out means students making an announcement to the university that the student has stopped studying. This is voluntary of students and students can carry out the prescribed formalities of giving up university. The intake of students studying in excess of training time means that each student has a prescribed study period, which is a general regulation of the ministry of education and training. If during a period of study that a student has not completed the prescribed university program that student is called a student exceeding the training period. The intake of students transferring majors means students apply to transfer to another major. The school allows students to have one time transfer but can only transfer major within the internal university.

In this research, the data source is explored from the training management system (TMS) of NTTU, Hochiminh City, Vietnam where we are working. To secure this data source we have encrypted it. The research focuses on exploring the data sources of 6 majors including Information Technology (IT), Software Engineering (SE), English Language (ES), Business Administration (BA), Logistics and Supply Chain Management (LSCM), Finance and Accounting (FB), in which each major has opened 7 training courses including 14, 15, 16, 17, 18, 19 and 20. The above six majors are managed by 4 respective faculties after the FIT, the Faculty of Foreign Languages (FFL), the Faculty of Business Administration (FBA), the Faculty of Finance and Accounting (FFA). In the 7 courses of each major, there are 9 student intakes, including student intake in admission, student intake with retention of academic results, student intake of graduates, student intake studying, student intake of suspended, student intake of withdrawals, student intake dropping out, student intake studying beyond the prescribed training time, and student intake changing majors. Through exploiting this educational data sources (EDS), we have discovered that this data source needs to be divided into 9 types of student intakes for 7 courses, 6 majors and 4 faculties. From that, we calculate 7 courses × 6 majors = 42 data tuples and also from here we calculate 7 courses × 6 majors × 19 data domain variables = 798 data cells in the EDS.

4.4 Structured Hierarchical Tree by Multivariate Groups

Based on the above data structures, we have discovered 19 important data variables used to represent the student intakes participating in the university courses from here creating relations. The relations between the variables make a hierarchical tree (hTree) by multivariate groups (MG_s) (Fig. 6). The relations between variables on a hTree by MG_s are structured into a visVTM of mD, the correlation between variables on this model helps to upgrade the $hVAP_s$ of the analyst includes stages such as $vpcaurH_s$ in extracting information and discovering new knowledge from mD.

The hTree by MG_s helps the analyst to understand the degree of association between the new knowledge latent variables and especially where the correlation between variables of different student intake is hidden for which the analyst wants to discover knowledge. The faculty variable containing the dataset of faculties in the university, is called vF_s. There are two relational variables linked together by faculties, called vF_p and vF_c. The course variable contains the dataset of courses of each faculty in the university and is collectively referred to by the research as the temporal variable (vT_s). The major variable (vD_s) contains the data domain that is the majors in the university. The student intake variable (vI_s) contains a set of nine sub variables containing the data domains, these sub variables are variables that directly affect the student intakes participating in the majors and courses that help the analyst cover and enhance visual analysis of data. The data subdomain variables include vE_s which is the domain variable containing the dataset of enrolled students, vZ_s is the domain variable containing the dataset about students with retention of academic results, vP_s is the domain variable containing the dataset about students who have received diplomas, vS_s is the domain variable containing the dataset of students studying, vU_s is the domain variable containing the dataset of suspended students, vW_s is the domain variable containing the dataset about students applying for tuition withdrawal, vA_s is the domain variable containing the dataset of students withdrawing from school, vK_s is the domain variable containing the dataset of students studying beyond the training period, and vM_s is domain variable containing the dataset of students applying to change majors. All subdomain variables of this data correspond to each number of students enrolled in the university described by the variable vI_{Num}. The following are specific descriptions and classifications of data domain variables, data tuple variables, data relational variables, and relations related.

vF_s is a data domain variable belonging to the relation vF, but in the relation vD it is named vF_{ds} used to describe university faculties. At this point, vF_{ds} becomes the relational domain variable of data between the two relations vF and vD. In which, vF_s and vF_{ds} contain the datasets {'FIT', 'FBA', 'FFA', 'FFL', etc.} but may not be equal in number of corresponding relations in the two relations vF and vD. vF_p is a data domain variable belonging to the relation vF_{pc}, also this variable in the relation vF_{pc} we duplicate it into a data relation domain variable named vF_c, these two variables work together to create a hierarchical grouping relationship of faculties in the university. vT_s is a data domain variable belonging to the relation vT, but in the relation vI it is named vT_{is} used to describe university courses. At this point, vT_{is} becomes the data relation domain variable between the two relations vT and vI. In which, vT_s and vT_{is} contains the same datasets {14, 15, 16, 17, 18, 19, 20, etc.} but may not be equal in the number of corresponding relations in the two relations vT and vI. vD_s is a data domain variable belonging to the relation vD, but in the vI relation it is named vD_{is} used to describe the fields of study in the university. At this point, vD_{is} becomes the data relation domain variable between the two relations vD and vI. In which, vD_s and vD_{is} contains the same datasets {'IT', 'SE', 'BA', 'ES', 'FB', 'LSCM', etc.} but may not be equal in the number of corresponding relations in the two relations vD and vI. vI_s is a data domain variable belonging to the relation vI, this variable has data subdomain variables vE_s, vZ_s, vP_s, vS_s, vU_s, vW_s, vA_s, vK_s, and vM_s used to describe the student intakes of courses and majors in the university. vE_s, vZ_s, vP_s, vS_s, vU_s, vW_s, vA_s, vK_s, vM_s are data domain variables belonging to the relation vI used to describe the student intakes corresponding to each number of students described by the vI_{Num} variable of majors according to university courses. In which, the corresponding student intakes variables have tasks such as containing the dataset of enrolled students (vE_s), containing the dataset about students with retention of academic results (vZ_s), containing the dataset about students who have received diplomas (vP_s), containing the dataset of students studying (vS_s), containing the dataset of suspended students (vU_s) containing the set data about students applying for tuition withdrawal (vW_s), containing the dataset of students withdrawing from school (vA_s), containing the dataset of students studying beyond the training period (vK_s), and containing the dataset of students applying to change majors (vM_s). With t, p, q, b, c are the contextual variables of the data visual analysis that these variables take a role as free variables or bound variables used in data tuples and domains relational calculus expressions.

The hTree by MG_s (Fig. 6) is structured according to the characteristics of hierarchical groups of multivariate. We conduct visual analysis of MG_s on the hTree, the MG_s on the left side of the hTree include variables vF_p, vF_c, vF_s, vFd_s, vD_s representing the roles of related faculties and majors associated with the respective faculties. The MG_s on the right side of the hTree include variables vM_s, vK_s, vA_s, vW_s, vU_s, vZ_s, vP_s, vS_s, vE_s, vI_{Num}, and vI_s representing the correlation with each other to compare the student intakes participating in the courses of each major and representing the dependent constraint between the student intakes studying and the student intakes enrolled by using the quartet variables vE_s, vS_s, vI_{Num}, and vI_s. This MG_s on the right side have features such as the higher the enrollment of students, the higher the characteristics of students studying. The MG_s in the middle of the hTree of variables vD_s, vD_{is}, vT_{is}, vT_s, and vI_s representing a major association will correspond to multiple courses represented by the student intakes participating in the university. From here, this study integrates the three MG_s on the left side, MG_s on the right side and MG_s in the middle of the hTree to create a visVTM of mD (Fig. 7), this approach is the scientific basis for improving cognitive progresses for analysts. The visVTM exploring information and knowledge from EDS is proposed, based on this model and depending on the nature of the MG_s, we perform the structure to visual graph (Fig. 8) in information extraction and knowledge discovery from EDS of the TMS of NTTU. The relationships between MG_s, the hierarchies of MG_s, the in-out of data sources, and the correlations between MG_s are generated on the hTree is the basis for structuring into a visVTM that will help analysts know many ways to approach information extraction and discover hidden knowledge on this model.

After analyzing the MG_s on the hTree, naming the variables and briefly describing the capabilities of the MG_s, we found that the variables vF_s, vF_p, vT_s, vD_s, vI_s, vI_{Num}, vF_{ds}, vF_c, vD_{is}, vT_{is}, vE_s, vZ_s, vP_s, vS_s, vU_s, vW_s, vA_s, vK_s, vM_s are called data domain variables. We choose a new approach by using the hierarchical group method of the above variables to create a hTree for managing of student intakes of the university. The hTree clearly shows the grouping of variables to display data domains to create related data domains. With data domain variables, we have the following variables vF_s, vF_p, vT_s, vD_s, vI_s, vI_{Num}, vF_{ds}, vF_c, vD_{is}, vT_{is}, vE_s, vZ_s, vP_s, vS_s, vU_s, vW_s, vA_s, vK_s, vM_s. With data tuple variables, we have the following variables t, p, q, b, and c. These variables have two types, which are free and bound variables depending on the form of visual analysis of mD, sometimes it is a free variable and sometimes it is a bound variable.

The variables vF_p, vF_c, vF_{ds}, vT_{is}, vD_{is} make up the correlation relations between the relations corresponding following vF_{pc}, vD, vI, and vT. From here, analysts can visually analyze multivariate data based on relational calculus expressions on the data tuples and domains. Each group of multivariate put together has the ability to visually represent multivariate datasets, closely related MG_s, and the combination of variables helps the analyst to answering his/her own questions of mD.

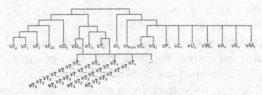

Fig. 6. Hierarchical tree (hTree) by multivariate groups in VA of mD of student intakes participating in each course in the major of each faculty in the university.

4.5   Viewing – Thinking Model Visually Analyzing Multivariate Data

From mdVAS (Fig. 4), data analysts can conduct knowledge discovery according to data tuples and domains relational calculus [37]. To visually analyze mD in extract information and discover new knowledge in the form of tuples, the analyst uses a data tuple relational calculus expression with form $\{t_1.A_i, t_2.A_j, ..., t_n.A_k | P(t_1, t_2, t_3, ..., t_n)\}$, in which $\{t_1, t_2, t_3, ..., t_n\}$ are tuple variables, $\{A_i, A_j, ..., A_k\}$ are the attributes in the t tuple variables correspondingly, and P is the formula formed from the prime formulas. To visually analyze mD in information extraction and discovery of new knowledge in the form of data domains, the analyst uses a relational calculation expression on data domains of the form $\{x_1, x_2, x_3, ..., x_n | P(x_1, x_2, x_3, ..., x_n)\}$, in which $\{x_1, x_2, x_3, ..., x_n\}$ are domain variables that receive a value as a domain of attribute values, P is a formula formed from prime formulas, finally the return result set of values $\{x_1, x_2, x_3, ..., x_n\}$ such that when the values are substituted for $\{x_i\}$ then P is true. The approach to using relational calculus expressions on the data tuples and domains in the data visual analytics of various student intakes of a university is the scientific basis in the VA of mD to help school leaders in implementing financial policies and making timely decisions.

This visVTM of mD of the university was integrated by us into the mdVAS (Fig. 4). With its strengths, in the analysis progress, the analyst applies available knowledge, the hVO_s, the $hIGCE_s$, the $hVAP_s$, and $hVTM_s$ for extracting information and discovering knowledge from mD. The visual analysis questions of mD will be formed based on the visVTM multivariate data presented in two aspects, the first aspect is the visual analysis questions of mD built on this system, the second aspect is the visual analysis questions of mD that will be generated in the progress of vision awareness of the analyst, depending on the topic of data they are analyzing, this progress will upgrade the analyst's knowledge and automatically generate questions and answers corresponding to the data topic they are discovering.

The visVTM multivariate data about student intakes of courses in each faculty of a university used to represent information extraction and knowledge discovery through formal queries of relational calculus expressed on data tuples and domains. These formal queries representation helps the analyst to extract information and discover new knowledge. Through this visual analysis, leaders see useful and unhelpful pieces of information and knowledge to make the right decisions for each faculty in the university about managing student intakes in different courses. From that, faculties have taken measures to upgrade their approaches to student data management. The visual analysis of data by relational calculus expressions on data tuples and domains is shown in the next sections.

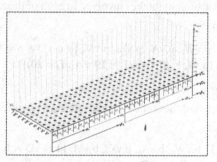

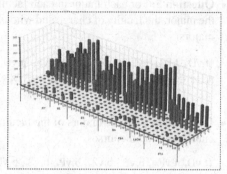

Fig. 7. Model of viewing - thinking visually analyzing (visVTM) multivariate data integrated by MG_s of hierarchical tree by MG_s related to student intake types of courses and majors.

Fig. 8. A visual graphical representation of multivariate data of different the student intakes participating in the university by a viewing-thinking model analyzing in mdVAS.

4.6 Questions with Relational Calculus Expressions on Tuples and Domains

- **Question 1:** Indicate the faculties having majors and the student intakes opened for training in courses 18, 19 and 20. This question is conducted visual analysis including the following parts.

$\{t.vD_s, b.vE_s, b.vZ_s, b.vP_s, b.vS_s, b.U_s, b.W_s, b.vA_s, b.vK_s, b.vM_s \mid t \in vD \wedge b \in vI \ (b.vD_{is} = t.vD_s) \wedge (\exists p \in vI \ (t.vD_s = p.vD_{is} \wedge p.vT_{is} = 18) \vee \exists q \in vI \ (t.vD_s = q.vD_{is} \wedge q.vT_{is} = 19) \vee \exists c \in vI \ (t.vD_s = c.vD_{is} \wedge c.vT_{is} = 20))\}$

$$(1)$$

- **Question 2:** Indicate the majors of the faculties with the student intakes entering or the student intakes changing majors. This question is analyzed visually through the following sections.

$\{t.vF_s, b.vD_s, c.vE_s, c.vM_s \mid t \in vF \wedge b \in vD \wedge c \in vI \ (t.vF_s = b.vF_{ds} \wedge b.vD_s = c.vD_{is}) \wedge (\exists p \in vI \ (b.vD_s = p.vD_{is} \wedge p.vE_s > 0) \vee \exists q \in vI \ (b.vD_s = q.vD_{is} \wedge q.vM_s > 0))\}$

$$(2)$$

- **Question 3:** Indicate the faculties and majors that have both the student intakes suspended and the student intakes exceeding the training period.

$\{t.vF_s, b.vD_s \mid t \in vF \wedge b \in vD \ (t.vF_s = b.vF_{ds}) \wedge (\exists p \in vI \ (b.vD_s = p.vD_{is} \wedge p.vU_s > 0) \wedge \exists q \in vI \ (b.vD_s = q.vD_{is} \wedge q.vK_s > 0))\}$

$$(3)$$

- **Question 4:** For course 20, please indicate the majors that have the student intakes studying (vS_s) and the student intakes exceed the training time but do not have the student intakes suspended.

$$\{t.vD_s, p.vS_s, p.vK_s, q.vU_s \mid t \in vD \wedge (\exists p \in vI \ (t.vD_s = p.vD_{is} \wedge p.vS_s > 0) \wedge \neg \exists q \in vI$$
$$(t.vD_s = q.vD_{is} \wedge q.vU_s \leq 0) \wedge p.vI_{is} = 20)\}$$

$$(4)$$

- **Question 5:** For each major in each faculty of courses 17, 19 and 20, please indicate the major, the faculty of charge and whole of student intakes involved in each of those majors.

$$\{t.vD_s, t.F_{ds}, p.vE_s, p.vZ_s, p.vP_s, p.vS_s, p.vU_s, p.vW_s, p.vA_s, p.vK_s, p.vM_s \mid t \in vD \wedge p \in vI$$
$$\wedge \exists q \in vT \ (q.vT_s = p.vT_{is} \wedge p.vD_{is} = t.vD_s \wedge (q.vT_s = 17 \vee q.vT_s = 19 \vee q.vT_s = 20))\}$$

$$(5)$$

- **Question 6:** Find the majors of the faculties and the student intakes that are open for enrollment in all courses.

$$\{t.vD_s, t.vF_{ds}, b.vE_s, b.vZ_s, b.vP_s, b.vS_s, b.vU_s, b.vW_s, b.vA_s, b.vK_s, b.vM_s \mid t \in vD \wedge b \in$$
$$vI \ (b.vD_s = b.vD_{is}) \wedge \forall p \ vT \ (\exists q \in vI \ (q.vT_{is} = p.vT_s \wedge q.vD_{is} = t.vD_s))\}$$

$$(6)$$

- **Question 7:** Indicate the majors of the faculties and the student intakes that are open for enrollment in all courses offered by the FIT, by the FFL, or by the FFA management.

$$\{t.vD_s, t.vF_{ds}, b.vE_s, b.vZ_s, b.vP_s, b.vS_s, b.vU_s, b.vW_s, b.vA_s, b.vK_s, b.vM_s \mid t \in vD \wedge b \in$$
$$vI \ (b.vD_s = b.vD_{is}) \wedge \forall p \ vT(t.vF_{ds} = \text{'FIT'} \vee t.vF_{ds} = \text{'FFL'} \vee t.vF_{ds} = \text{'FFA'} \Rightarrow (\exists q \in vI$$
$$(q.vT_{is} = p.vT_s \wedge q.vD_{is} = t.vD_s)))\}$$

$$(7)$$

- **Question 8:** Indicate faculties, majors and student intakes in which have the student intakes entering greater than 200 students participating in the university.

$$\{vF_{ds}, vD_s, vE_s, vZ_s, vP_s, vS_s, vU_s, vW_s, vA_s, vK_s, vM_s \mid \exists vD_s \ (<vF_{ds}, vD_s> \in vD \wedge \exists vD_{is},$$
$$vE_s \ (<vD_{is}, vE_s, vZ_s, vP_s, vS_s, vU_s, vW_s, vA_s, vK_s> \in vI \wedge vE_s > 200 \wedge vD_s = vD_{is}))\}$$

$$(8)$$

- **Question 9:** Indicate the majors of the faculties having the student intake studying, the student intake being suspended, the student intake applying for tuition withdrawal, the student intakes withdrawing from school, and the student intakes changing majors all of these types of intakes are greater than or equal to 1 participating in the majors of the courses 15, 16, 17, 18, 19, or 20.

$$\{vF_{ds}, vD_s, vS_s, vU_s, vW_s, vA_s, vM_s \mid \exists vD_s \ (<vF_{ds}, vD_s, vS_s, vU_s, vW_s, vA_s, vM_s> \in vD \wedge$$
$$\in vI \wedge vD_s = vD_{is} \wedge \exists vS_s, vU_s, vW_s, vA_s, vM_s, vD_{is}, vT_{is} \ (<vE_s, vZ_s, vP_s, vS_s, vU_s, vW_s,$$
$$vA_s, vK_s, vM_s, vD_{is}, vT_{is}> \in vI \wedge vD_s = vD_{is} \wedge vS_s > 0 \wedge vU_s > 0 \wedge vW_s > 0 \wedge vA_s > 0 \wedge$$
$$vM_s > 0 \wedge (vT_{is} = 15 \vee vT_{is} = 16 \vee vT_{is} = 17 \vee vT_{is} = 18 \vee vT_{is} = 19 \vee vT_{is} = 20))\}$$

$$(9)$$

- **Question 10:** Indicate the faculties, the majors and the courses having the student intake changing majors, the student intake withdrawing from school, the student intake being suspended, and the student intake reserving academic results.

$\{vF_{ds}, vD_s, vT_{is}, vM_s \mid \exists vF_{ds}, vD_s\ (<vD_s, vF_{ds}> \in vD \wedge \exists vD_{is}, vM_s\ vA_s, vU_s, vZ_s\ (<vE_s, vZ_s, vP_s, vS_s, vU_s, vW_s, vA_s, vK_s, vM_s, vT_{is}, vD_{is} > \in vI \wedge vD_s = vD_{is} \wedge vM_s > 0 \vee (vA_s > 0 \vee vU_s > 0 \vee vZ_s > 0))\}$

$$(10)$$

- **Question 11:** Please indicate the majors of each faculty not having the student intake exceeds the training time and indicate extra the student intake entering, the student intake studying, the student intake applying for tuition withdrawal and the student intake changing majors in courses belonging to faculties in the university.

$\{vD_s, vF_{ds}, vK_s \mid \exists vD_s, vF_{ds}\ (<D_s, vF_{ds}> \in vD \wedge \neg\exists vD_{is}, vK_{is}\ (<vE_s, vZ_s, vP_s, vS_s, vA_s, vK_s, vM_s, vD_{is}> \in vI \wedge vD_s = vD_{is} \wedge vK_s > 0))\}$

$$(11)$$

- **Question 12:** For each major that is open for training according to each course having the student intake more than 180 students, please indicate the majors, courses, the student intake studying and the student intake entering and indicate extra the types of student intakes remaining belonging to faculties in the university.

$\{vD_{is}, vT_{is}, vS_s, vE_s, vF_{ds}, vZ_s, vP_s, vU_s, vW_s, vA_s, vK_s, vM_s \mid \exists vS_s\ (<vD_{is}, vE_s, vZ_s, vP_s, vS_s, vU_s, vW_s, vA_s, vK_s, vM_s, vT_{is}> \in vI \wedge \exists vD_s, vF_{ds}\ (<D_s, vF_{ds}> \in vD \wedge vD_s = vD_{is} \wedge vS_s > 180))\}$

$$(12)$$

- **Question 13:** Indicate the faculties which has the majors having the student intake entering between 1 and 300 students and having the student intake graduated between 1 and 200 students.

$\{vF_{ds}, vD_s, vE_s, vP_s \mid \exists vD_s\ (<vD_s, vF_{ds}> \in vD \wedge \exists vD_{is}, vE_s\ (<vD_{is}, vE_s, vZ_s, vP_s, vS_s, vU_s, vW_s, vA_s, vK_s, vM_s, vT_{is}> \in vI \wedge vD_s = vD_{is} \wedge vE_s \geq 1 \wedge vE_s \leq 300) \wedge \exists vD_{is}, vP_s\ (<vD_{is}, vE_s, vZ_s, vP_s, vS_s, vU_s, vW_s, vA_s, vK_s, vM_s, vT_{is}> \in vI \wedge vD_s = vD_{is} \wedge vP_s \geq 1 \wedge vP_s \leq 200))\}$

$$(13)$$

- **Question 14:** With each major belonging to FIT and FBA faculties managing, please indicate the student intake entering, the student intake receiving diplomas, the courses and enclosed the majors.

$\{vE_s, vP_s, vT_{is}, vD_{is}, vF_{ds} \mid \exists vD_{is}, vT_{is}\ (<vD_{is}, vE_s, vZ_s, vP_s, vS_s, vW_s, vA_s, vT_{is}> \in vI \wedge \exists vD_s, vF_{ds}\ (<vD_s, vF_{ds}> \in vD \wedge vD_{is} = vD_s \wedge (vF_{ds}=\text{'FIT'} \vee vF_{ds}=\text{'FBA'})))\}$

$$(14)$$

- **Question 15:** For each course 14, 16, 18 and 20 having the student intake studying greater than or equal to 100 students of each faculty, please indicate the faculties, the majors, the student intake entering and the student intake studying in the majors of faculties belonging to each course.

$\{vF_{ds}, vD_s, vT_{is}, vE_s, vS_s \mid \exists vD_s, vF_{ds}, vE_s\ (<vF_{ds}, vD_s, vS_s, vE_s> \in vD \wedge vI \wedge vD_s = vD_{is} \wedge \exists vS_s, vD_{is}, vT_{is}\ (<vD_{is}, vE_s, vZ_s, vP_s, vS_s, vU_s, vW_s, vA_s, vK_s, vM_s, vT_{is}> \in vI \wedge vD_s = vD_{is} \wedge vS_s > 100 \wedge vT_{is} = 14 \vee vT_{is} = 16 \vee vT_{is} = 18 \vee vT_{is} = 20))\}$

$$(15)$$

5 Visually Analyzing of University Multivariate Data

5.1 Visually Analyzing Multivariate Data with Questions and Answers

The $hVAP_s$ has many different stages in which the analysis stage is one of the most important stages of the progress of perceiving objects that exist in the real-world of humans. Humans perceive the real-world objects with the vision organs with the desire to discover the objects, but also to understand the objects, humans have to analyze it. Therefore, the analytical stage is the stage in which humans ask and answer questions themselves in the process of discovering new knowledge, the philosophy of Szent-Gyorgyi [14] pointed out that humans want to understand objects, they must ask questions, because questions are the first step and the basis for motivating humans to carry out the process of analyzing and discovering objects.

In the analytical stage of the humans' visual perception progress, if humans want to understand objects, they must ask and answer questions to extract information and discover new knowledge. Therefore, developing a questionnaire is an important initial step and is the basis for accelerating the data analysis process to be conducted. Research shows that data scientists cannot perform data analysis without questions which were asked with the desire to discover objects. Types of analysis questions have been proposed by many authors in the past to discover knowledge from data based on the relationships between variables and the values of data variables. From here, we propose to create a visVTM as a foundation for integrating visual graphs representing mD. The group of authors Andrienko has divided the data analysis questions into two groups as one is elementary questions and the other is synoptic questions [15]. The author Bertin has divided data analysis questions into three levels as elementary level, intermediate level, and overall level [8]. The group of authors ThiNguyen has divided the questions into 3 levels, level 1 is elementary questions, level 2 is variation questions, and level 3 is relationship questions [2].

Through surveying related research works, we draw the most important point in data analysis that if humans want to extract information and discover knowledge from data, they must perform data visual analysis by using question types and accompanying answers. We survey the data variables to create a hTree by MG_s from which to combine the variables and the data of these variables to answer questions for the purpose of extracting information and discovering new knowledge from data. Based on the types of questions proposed by the group of authors above, we find the elementary questions, the variable questions, and the relational questions are suitable for this study, so we choose these three types of questions to apply to the mdVAS. In addition, we propose the types of elementary questions (Q_{es}), variation questions (Q_{vs}), relationship questions (Q_{rs}), hierarchical questions (Q_{hs}), visual thinking questions (Q_{vts}), and overall questions (Q_{os}) to applying for mdVAS. To become a component capable of classifying standard visual analysis questions of mD, we provide specific definitions of question types used in mdVAS (Fig. 4) as follows.

- **Definition 1:** Q_{es} include questions regarding a value of a variable or regarding a value of many variables combined together to help the analyst understand the value of a variable or mD.

- **Definition 2:** Q_{vs} include questions regarding a value group of a variable or variables that combine together to help the analyst understand the variational rules of variables.
- **Definition 3:** Q_{rs} include questions regarding many data variables that help the analyst find correlations and relationships between variables to discover correlation and new relational rules between data variables.
- **Definition 4:** Q_{hs} include questions regarding many data variables that help the analyst find hierarchies between variables.
- **Definition 5:** Q_{vts} include questions regarding abstraction between data variables that help the analyst visualize new knowledge in data abstraction.
- **Definition 6:** Q_{os} include questions regarding overall datasets of relational variables that help the analyst see the overall work of an object in the work process.

5.2   Visually Analyzing Multivariate Data of the Student Intakes

For visually analyzing of mD of student intakes in a university, we have conducted research to make a visVTM to integrate into the mdVAS. From visVTM, we apply relationship expressions on the data tuples and domains to help the analyst extract information and explore new knowledge. The visual graphs visually representing mD in Fig. 8 about student intakes participating in the university is rendered from visVTM in mdVAS to help the analyst easily explore new knowledge. Based on this basis, we have applied relational calculation expressions on the data domains and tuples to assist the analyst in extracting information and discovering knowledge about student intakes participating in the university shown in visually analyzing data.

For mdVAS, humans play the most important role in the process of analyzing extracting information and discovering knowledge from data. To evaluate the student intakes participating in the university to find out which types of intakes directly affect the financial policy and making decision of school leaders, we survey data variables, subgroup hierarchy by MG_s to create hTree to make visVTM, from that visually representing the student intakes on the visual graphs, through which we pose some analytical questions to verify the effectiveness of the visual graphs representing mD. The analyst looks at visual graphs and with the powerful support of components in mdVAS can ask questions themselves and also can answer these questions themselves when interacting with visual graphs to extract information and discover new knowledge. Let's observe together to investigate the visual graphs that visually represent the student intakes of a university in Fig. 8 above it which is the result rendering from visVTM in the mdVAS.

For visual analysis questions of mD are questions asked by the analysts with the desire to extract information and discover new knowledge while observing visual graphs. Depending on the data characteristics the analysts can ask appropriate analytical questions when observing the visual graphs. The visual analysis questions of mD are divided into six categories of questions that we have defined standard above, and for each visual analysis question of mD including an assumptive and conclusive part. The assumptive part is the data that the analyst will have to provide when the question begins to be asked, the conclusive part is the results obtained after the question is analyzed visually. In the following, we focus on visual analysis of different student intakes by coordinating with all components on the mdVAS (see Fig. 4) to extract information and discover new knowledge.

5.3 Strategy for Answering Visual Analysis Questions

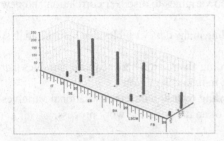

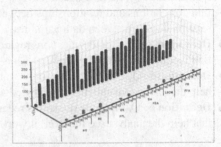

Fig. 9. Visual representation of the student intakes studying, the student intakes suspended, and the student intakes exceed the training time in course 20 of majors in the university by visual graph representing of mD.

Fig. 10. Visual representation of the student intakes entering and student intakes changing majors of courses belonging to the majors of faculties in the university by visual graph representing of mD.

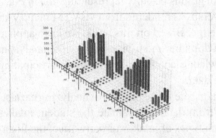

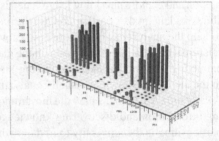

Fig. 11. Visual representation of the student intakes in courses 18, 19 and 20 of IT, SE, ES, BA, LSCM and FB majors belonging to FIT, FFL, FBA and FFA faculties respectively managed by visual graph representing of mD.

Fig. 12. Visual representation of each major is open to training belonging to each course having the student intake studying more than 180 students and the student intake entering enclosed the student intakes remaining in courses of majors of faculties in the university.

5.3.1 Elementary Questions

Approaching to extract information and discover knowledge from mD of student intakes using strategy of combining Q_{es} with relational calculus expressions on data tuples on the visual analytics system to apply for question $4^{(4)}$ having given assumption is course 20, the student intakes studying, the student intakes exceed the training time and the student intakes suspended. The conclusion of the analysis process is the majors, the student intakes studying, the student intakes exceed the training time and the student intakes suspended. The analyst views and thinks the visual graph in Fig. 8 and then conducts visual analysis of mD on this visual graph. The results of visual analysis of mD in Fig. 9 help the analyst to answer this question, they discover that course 20 has the student intakes studying and the student intakes exceed the training time, but there are no the student intakes suspended. Course 20 of any majors also has the student intakes

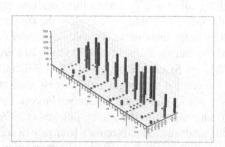

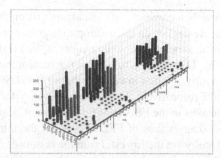

Fig. 13. Visual representation whole of the student intakes in course 17, 19 and 20 of majors belonging to the faculties in the university by visual graph representing of mD.

Fig. 14. Visual representation of the majors that are open for enrollment in all courses offered by the managed by the FIT, FFL and FFA faculties enclosed with all student intakes in the university.

exceed the training time, except for the course 20 of ES major, which there is no the student intakes exceed the training time. The analyst can easily see that the student intake exceeding the training time is much lower than the student intake studying in course 20 of majors.

5.3.2 Variable Questions

Using relational calculus expressions on data tuples combine with Q_{vs} to extract information and discover knowledge from mD of student intakes on the visual analysis system applying for question $2^{(2)}$ having given assumption is the student intakes entering and the student intakes changing majors. The conclusion of the analysis process is faculties, majors, the student intakes entering and the student intakes changing majors. The analyst views and thinks the visual graph in Fig. 8 and then conducts visual analysis of mD on this visual graph. To answer this question, they rely on the assumptions given to explore the student intakes entering and the student intakes changing majors in the university. The results of visual analysis of mD in Fig. 10 help the analyst to see the variation of the increasing the student intakes entering for each course 14, 15, 16, 17, 18, 19 and 20 in contrast to the student intakes changing majors, there is no variation by course and shows that the student intakes changing majors is not significant. From the results of this analysis, the university's leaders understand the period variation of the student intakes in courses which are most important to promptly invest in developing all resources for the units directly under the university.

5.3.3 Relationship Questions

To extract information and discover knowledge from mD of student intakes, this research combines Q_{rs} with relational calculus expressions on tuples of data on the visual analysis system to apply for question $1^{(1)}$ having given assumption is the courses 18, 19 and 20. The conclusion of the analysis process is faculties, majors and student intakes for each of 18, 19 and 20 courses respectively. The analyst views and thinks the visual graph in Fig. 8

and then conducts mD visual analysis on this visual graph. To answer this question, the analyst relies on the assumptions given for courses 18, 19 and 20 to explore the student intakes belonging to the majors of the faculties in the university. The analysis results in Fig. 11 help them to see that the student intakes entering and studying FB major of FFA faculty is much lower than that of BA, LSCM, ES, SE and IT majors of FBA, FFL and FIT respectively. In addition, it is easy for the analyst to recognize the largest student intakes in the FBA faculty, the student intakes of FIT faculty are the second largest, the student intakes of FFL faculty are the third largest, while the student intakes of FFA faculty are the lowest. From the results of this analysis, the university's leaders will see the correlation between the student intakes at the faculties to help them make appropriate financial investments policing for each faculty in the university.

5.3.4 Hierarchical Questions

Strategies for visual analysis of mD of student intakes using Q_{hs} combine with relational calculus expressions on domains of data on the visual analysis system to apply for question 12[12] having given assumption is the student intake studying more than 180 students. The conclusion of the analysis process is the majors, courses, the student intake studying, the student intake entering and the student intakes remaining belonging to faculties. From Fig. 8 and the assumptions that this question has allowed the analyst to discover the student intake studying, the student intake entering and the student intakes participating visually performed in course 20 of IT major, in courses from 17 to 20 of SE major, in courses 18 and 20 of ES major, in courses 17, 19, 20 of BA major, and in courses from 18 to 20 of LSCM major (see result in Fig. 12). In addition to these two student intakes studying and entering, the student intake showed insignificant student intake remaining in courses of majors belonging to faculties in the university.

5.3.5 Visually Thinking Questions

Approaching to combine Q_{vts} with relational calculus expressions on tuples of data on the visual analysis system to apply for question 5[5] having given assumption is the courses 17, 19 and 20. The conclusion of the analysis process is the majors, the faculty of charge, whole of student intakes involved in each of the majors. The analyst views and thinks the visual graph in Fig. 8 and then conducts visual analysis of mD on this visual graph. To answer this question, the analysts based on given assumptions help them easily to discover some important information such as no the student intakes graduated in courses 17, 19 and 20 also in these courses showing them that there are equal correlations the student intakes studying compared to the student intakes entering, see result in Fig. 13. Especially, the student intakes changing majors of IT, SE, BA and FB majors in course 20 did not occur, which proves that these majors are showing a very high resource demand of the labor market and a trend strong development direction in the future, on the contrary, these majors have the student intakes exceed the training time, which proves that these majors are very difficult to study, requiring students to have a high sense of self-study and to spend more time studying. In addition, the student intakes in the remaining courses 17, 19 and 20 occurred but has negligible intake.

5.3.6 Overall Questions

From on the visual analysis system combining Q_{os} with relational calculus expressions on data tuples to extract information and discover knowledge from mD of student intakes applying for question $7^{(7)}$ having given assumption is the FIT, FFL, FFA, and courses. The conclusion of the analysis process is the majors are open for training in all courses offered by the FIT, FFL, and/or FFA. The analyst views and thinks the visual graph in Fig. 8 combining with all components in the mdVAS, then they conduct VA of mD on this visual graph. From the assumptions that this question has allowed the analyst to discover all three faculties of FIT, FFL, or/and FFA having in turn IT, ES and FB majors are all open for training in all courses 14, 15, 16, 17, 18, 19 and 20. By observing the results of extracting and exploring IT, ES and FB majors, we see that the student intakes including vE_s, vP_s and vS_s of two majors IT and ES are much larger than those of the FB major, the remaining the student intakes including vK_s and vM_s of these three majors are quite similar. The student intakes vZ_s, vU_s, vW_s and vA_s remaining of the IT, ES and FB faculties all have intakes happening but are insignificant, so they do not affect the development of faculties and university, see result in Fig. 14.

6 Conclusions

This paper has systematized research works related to data mining, data visualization, data analysis processes, and visual analysis from different data sources. This research conducts analysis of educational data on student intakes, hierarchizes multivariate groups to create a hierarchical tree (hTree), and conducts restructuring the hierarchical tree to build a viewing - thinking model analyzing visually of mD of student intakes. Since then, this paper has focused on exploring vision organs, infographics capture characteristics, vision awareness progress, and visual viewing-thinking mechanisms of human to create a visual analytics system of multivariate data (mdVAS) of student intakes to help upgrade the human visual perception progress such as $vpcaurH_s$ in information and knowledge discovery, and find out new rules.

Visual graphs represent student intakes where there is a lot of latent information, containing a lot of new knowledge and rules that humans wish to discover. The analyst has the ability to observe visual graphs and then conducts data visual analysis by asking and answering corresponding questions based on relational calculations on tuples and domains of data, at the same time, flexible support of all components on a mdVAS, thereby not only helping analysts visually analyze data and compare the correlation between data variables to discover new patterns in student intakes according to courses of majors of faculties in the university so that there are solutions to promote the strengths as a premise to overcome the outstanding points in the university, but also especially support the leaders in the university to better understand the discovered information and knowledge to make financial policies and make timely decisions for each unit in the school. In addition, the mdVAS can be developed and extended to always adapt to multidimensional datasets, multiple data sources, and especially in exploiting data sources on school finances and comparing the learning outcomes of many students in the same subject, class, or the same course to help schools and parents have orientations to develop knowledge chains as well as career orientations for students in the future.

References

1. Keim, D.A., Mansmann, F., Schneidewind, J., Thomas, J., Ziegler, H.: Visual analytics: scope and challenges. In: Simoff, S.J., Böhlen, M.H., Mazeika, A. (eds.) Visual Data Mining. LNCS, vol. 4404, pp. 76–90. Springer, Heidelberg (2008). https://doi.org/10.1007/978-3-540-710 80-6_6
2. Thi Nguyen, H., Thi Pham, T.M., Thi Nguyen, T.A., Thi Tran, A.V., Vinh Tran, P., Van Pham, D.: Two-stage approach to classifying multidimensional cubes for visualization of multivariate data. In: Cong Vinh, P., Alagar, V. (eds.) ICCASA/ICTCC 2018. LNICSSITE, vol. 266, pp. 70–80. Springer, Cham (2019). https://doi.org/10.1007/978-3-030-06152-4_7
3. Van Pham, D., Vinh Tran, P.: A system and model of visual data analytics related to junior high school students. In: Vinh, P.C., Rakib, A. (eds.) ICCASA/ICTCC 2019. LNICSSITE, vol. 298, pp. 105–126. Springer, Cham (2019). https://doi.org/10.1007/978-3-030-34365-1_9
4. Fairchild, M.D.: Color Appearance Models, 2nd edn. Association with the Society for Imaging Science and Technology (USA Wiley–IS&T Series in Imaging Science and Technology) (2005)
5. Few, S.: Tapping the Power of Visual Perception. Perceptual Edge, pp. 1–8 (2004)
6. Kuehni, R.G.: Color An Introduction to Practice and Principles, 3rd edn. Wiley, Hoboken (2013)
7. Few, S.: Data visualization for human perception. In: Soegaard, M., Dam, R.F. (eds.) The Encyclopedia of Human-Computer Interaction, Aarhus, Denmark, 2nd edn. (2014)
8. Bertin, J.: General theory, from semiology of graphics. In: Perkins, M.D.R.K.C. (ed.) The Map Reader: Theories of Mapping Practice and Cartographic Representation, pp. 8–16. Wiley (2011)
9. Green, M.: Toward a perceptual science of multidimensional data visualization: bertin and beyond. In: ERGO/GERO Human Factors Science. Citeseer (1998)
10. Keim, D., Andrienko, G., Fekete, J.-D., Görg, C., Kohlhammer, J., Melançon, G.: Visual analytics: definition, process, and challenges. In: Kerren, A., Stasko, J.T., Fekete, J.-D., North, C. (eds.) Information Visualization. LNCS, vol. 4950, pp. 154–175. Springer, Heidelberg (2008). https://doi.org/10.1007/978-3-540-70956-5_7
11. Feldkamp, N., Bergmann, S., Strassburger, S.: Visual analytics of manufacturing simulation data. In: The 2015 Winter Simulation Conference (WSC), Huntington Beach, CA, USA, 6–9 December 2015, pp. 779–790. IEEE (2015). https://doi.org/10.1109/WSC.2015.7408215
12. Francois, G., Gautron, P., Breton, G., Bouatouch, K.: Image-based modeling of the human eye. IEEE Trans. Visual. Comput. Graph. 15(5), 815–827 (2009). https://doi.org/10.1109/TVCG.2009.24
13. Thi Nguyen, H., et al.: Integrating retinal variables into graph visualizing multivariate data to increase visual features. In: Vinh, P.C., Rakib, A. (eds.) ICCASA/ICTCC 2019. LNICSSITE, vol. 298, pp. 74–89. Springer, Cham (2019). https://doi.org/10.1007/978-3-030-34365-1_7
14. von Szent-Gyorgyi, A.: American (Hungarian-born) Biochemist (Nobel Laureate 1937), "who said: Discovery consists of seeing what everybody has seen and thinking what nobody has thought," Edited by Irving Good. The Scientist Speculates (1962)
15. Andrienko, N., Andrienko, G.: Exploratory Analysis of Spatial and Temporal Data - A Systematic Approach. Springer, Heidelberg (2006)
16. Schneider, M.: Spatial and Spatio-Temporal Data Models and Languages. In: Liu, L., Özsu, M.T. (eds.) Encyclopedia of Database Systems, pp. 2681–2685. Springer, Boston (2009). https://doi.org/10.1007/978-0-387-39940-9_360
17. Van Pham, D., Vinh Tran, P.: Visually analyzing evolution of geographic objects at different levels of details over time. In: Cong Vinh, P., Alagar, V. (eds.) ICCASA/ICTCC 2018. LNIC-SSITE, vol. 266, pp. 98–115. Springer, Cham (2019). https://doi.org/10.1007/978-3-030-061 52-4_9

18. Kolbe, T.H.: Representing and exchanging 3D city models with CityGML. In: Lee, J., Zlatanova, S. (eds.) 3D Geo-Information Sciences. LNGC, pp. 15–31. Springer, Heidelberg (2009). https://doi.org/10.1007/978-3-540-87395-2_2

19. Tuan Anh, N.G., Tran Vinh, P., Vu, T.P., Van Pham, D., Sy, A.T.: Representing multiple levels for objects in three-dimensional GIS model. Presented at the the 13thInternational Conference on Information Integration and Web-based Applications & Service (iiWAS2011) (2011)

20. Löwner, M.O., Gröger, G., Benner, J., Biljecki, F., Nagel, C.: Proposal for a new LOD and multi-representation concept for CITYGML. ISPRS Ann. Photogrammetry Remote Sens. Spat. Inf. Sci. **IV-2/W1**, 3–12 (2016). https://doi.org/10.5194/isprs-annals-IV-2-W1-3-2016

21. Dang, P.V., Phuoc, T.V., Phuoc Tuyen, H.N.: Visual representation of geographic objects in 3D space at levels of different details. Presented at the FAIR - Fundamental and Applied Information Technology (2017)

22. Thomas, J.J., Cook, K.A.: Illuminating the Path the Research and Development Agenda for Visual Analytics. IEEE Computer Society Press, Los Alamitos (2005)

23. Sun, G.-D., Wu, Y.-C., Liang, R.-H., Liu, S.-X.: A survey of visual analytics techniques and applications: state-of-the-art research and future challenges. J. Comput. Sci. Technol. **28**(5), 852–867 (2013). https://doi.org/10.1007/s11390-013-1383-8

24. Andrienko, G., et al.: Space, time and visual analytics. Int. J. Geograph. Inf. Sci. **24**(10), 1577–1600 (2010). https://doi.org/10.1080/13658816.2010.508043

25. Vinh Tran, P., Xuan Le, T.: Approaching human vision perception to designing visual graph in data visualization. Concurr. Comput. Pract. Experience, no. Special Issue Paper (2020). https://doi.org/10.1002/cpe.5722

26. Thi Nguyen, H., Xuan Le, T., Vinh Tran, P., Van Pham, D.: An approach of taxonomy of multidimensional cubes representing visually multivariable data. In: Vinh, P.C., Rakib, A. (eds.) ICCASA 2019, pp. 90–104. Springer, Cham (2019). https://doi.org/10.1007/978-3-030-34365-1_8

27. Nguyen, H.T., Tran, A.V.T., Nguyen, T.A.T., Vo, L.T., Tran, P.V.: Multivariate cube integrated retinal variable to visually represent multivariable data. EAI Endorsed Trans. Context-Aware Syst. Appl. **4**(12) (2017). https://doi.org/10.4108/eai.6-7-2017.152757

28. Card, S.T., Mackinlay, J.D., Scheiderman, B.: Readings in Information Visualization: Using Vision to Think. Academic Press (1999)

29. van Wijk, J.J.: The value of visualization. In: IEEE Visualization, VIS 2005, 23–28 October 2005, pp. 79–86 (2005). https://doi.org/10.1109/VISUAL.2005.1532781

30. Keim, D., Kohlhammer, J., Ellis, G., Mansmann, F.: Mastering the Information Age: Solving Problems with Visual Analytics. Eurographics Association, Goslar (2010). https://diglib.eg.org/handle/10.2312/14803. ISBN 978-3-905673-77-7

31. Bertini, E., Tatu, A., Keim, D.: Quality metrics in high-dimensional data visualization: an overview and systematization. IEEE Trans. Vis. Comput. Graph. **17**(12), 2203–2212 (2011). https://doi.org/10.1109/TVCG.2011.229

32. Sacha, D., Stoffel, A., Stoffel, F., Kwon, B.C., Ellis, G., Keim, D.A.: Knowledge generation model for visual analytics. IEEE Trans. Vis. Comput. Graph. **20**(12), 1604–1613 (2014). https://doi.org/10.1109/TVCG.2014.2346481

33. Andrienko, G., Andrienko, N., Burch, M., Weiskopf, D.: Visual analytics methodology for eye movement studies. IEEE Trans. Vis. Comput. Graph. **18**(12), 2889–2898 (2012). https://doi.org/10.1109/TVCG.2012.276

34. Von Landesberger, T., et al.: Visual Analysis of large graphs: state-of-the-art and future research challenges. Comput. Graph. Forum **30**(6), 1719–1749 (2011)

35. Part of the Einstein exhibition. "A Matter of Time." The Museum. https://www.amnh.org/exhibitions/einstein/time/a-matter-of-time#:~:text=In%20the%20Special%20Theory%20of,on%20your%20frame%20of%20reference.&text=The%20faster%20a%20clock%20moves,a%20different%20frame%20of%20reference

36. Ning, Z.: Spatio-temporal cadastral data model: geo-Information management perspective in China. Master thesis, International Institute for Geo-Information Science and Earth Observation, Enschede, The Netherlands (2006)
37. Codd, E.F.: Relational compleness of database sublanguages. In: Rustin, R. (ed.) Database Systems, pp. 65–98. Prentice Hall and IBM Research Report RJ 987, San Jose, California (1972)

Machine Learning, Deep Learning

Predicting Academic Performance of High School Students

Nguyen Dinh-Thanh[1] and Pham Thi-Ngoc-Diem[2(✉)]

[1] Song Doc High School, Ca Mau, Ca Mau Province, Vietnam
ndthanh@camau.edu.vn
[2] College of Information and Communication Technology,
Can Tho University, Can Tho, Vietnam
ptndiem@ctu.edu.vn

Abstract. Students' weak learning ability is a problem that occurs in most countries around the worldwide and leads to many bad effects on students such as boredom leading to dropout, guilt with friends and with many other students. Students' poor academic results will greatly affect the teaching effectiveness and the reputation of the school. Therefore, predicting the student learning outcomes in high school can help educators to find innovative and effective solutions to support teachers, students in improving the learning and teaching quality in high schools. In this work, machine learning models were used to predict academic performance of high school students. These models were built from a dataset of 21,222 student records with 2,545 (11.99%) very good students, 7,859 (37.03%) good students, 8,099 (38.16%) average students, 2,531 (11.93%) poor students and 188 (0.89%) very poor students in high schools in Ca Mau province, Vietnam. With the use of the Synthetic Minority Over-sampling TEchnique algorithm to balance the dataset before putting it into the machine learning models, the results have shown that the Random Forest, XGBoost, Light GBM models give the best results with the Accuracy of 81.69%, 80.86% and 80.82%. In addition, important features that contribute decisively in predicting academic performance were also extracted, including Grade Point Average (GPA) of semester 1 and 2, Age, Class, Academic Performance of semester 1 and 2, Father's occupation, Mother's occupation and Learning online.

Keywords: Academic performance prediction · Students' academic performance · Features extraction · Machine learning models

1 Introduction

Martinez considers academic performance is "the product given by the students and it is usually expressed through school grades" [11]. In this way, in Vietnam, academic performance of high school students is measured mainly by GPA and is divided into 5 levels of Very good, Good, Average, Poor, Very Poor, described in Table 1.

© ICST Institute for Computer Sciences, Social Informatics and Telecommunications Engineering 2023
Published by Springer Nature Switzerland AG 2023. All Rights Reserved
C. V. Phan and T. D. Nguyen (Eds.): ICTCC 2022, LNICST 473, pp. 123–135, 2023.
https://doi.org/10.1007/978-3-031-28790-9_8

Table 1. Academic levels and conditions

Academic performance	Condition
Very Good	The GPA of all subjects is from 8.0, in which score of each subject is from 6.5, the score of one of the three subjects of Literature, Mathematics, and Foreign Language is at least 8.0 and Physical Education is rated as Passed
Good	The GPA of all subjects is from 6.5, in which score of each subject is from 5.0, the score of one of the three subjects of Literature, Mathematics, and Foreign Language is at least 6.5 and Physical Education is rated as Passed
Average	The GPA of all subjects is from 5.0, in which the score of each subject is from 3.5, the score of one of the three subjects of Literature, Mathematics, and Foreign Language is at least 5.0 and Physical Education is rated as Passed
Poor	Students meet one of the following conditions: – The GPA of all subjects is not enough 5.0 – The score of one of three subjects Literature, Mathematics, and Foreign Language is less than 5.0 – At least one subject has a score of 2.0 to less than 3.5 – Physical Education is not passed
Very Poor	All remaining cases

In addition, there are some cases that are temporarily called downgrade in academic performance levels:

✓ Students are graded as Very Good, but due to a certain subject is graded as Average, so their academic performance is adjusted as Good.
✓ Students are graded as Very Good, but due to a certain subject is graded as Poor, so their academic performance is adjusted as Average.
✓ Students are graded as Good, but due to a certain subject is graded as Poor, so their academic performance is adjusted as Average.

Academic performance plays an important role in a student's subsequent decisions like continuing to go to school or leaving school. In Vietnam's Ca Mau province, high school dropout rate was 5.61% in 2019–2020 school year [9]. This rate is relatively high. Among the factors affecting students' dropping out of school, poor academic performance is the most important factor [2,11]. Moreover, [7,12,14,18] have determined that students' academic performance dramatically influences dropping out of school. The problem of low academic performance can cause negative effects on the family, the school and society such as the emergence of cases of violence, imbalance and in harmonic among the community members, the emergence of social classes, ... [2]. Therefore, early predicting the risk of poor academic performance in high school can help learners to improve their learning and educators to have interventions and efficient solutions in reducing the highs school dropout rate. This is the main goal of this study.

Nowadays, machine learning has many applications in education such as enrollment management [1], enrollment prediction [13], predicting dropout [4], predicting learning outcomes [10,15], ... In this paper, machine learning algorithms have been applied to build models for predicting student academic performance in high school. They are Decision Tree (DT), Random Forest (RF), XGBoost (XGB), Light GBM (LGBM), Artificial Neuron Network (ANN) and Multilayer Perceptron (MLP). This is a multi-label classification problem where students are classified by the levels of Very Good, Good, Average, Poor, Very Poor.

Single machine learning models as well as machine learning models combined with Bagging were used in this study. The dataset to train and test the models was collected from 12 high schools in Ca Mau province [4]. The data collected include the student's personal information and their academic performance in the two semesters adjacent (called GPA 1 and 2, academic performance 1 and 2) to the semester in which the student academic performance is predicted. This dataset contains 21,222 students, in which the number of Very Good, Good, Average, Poor and Very Poor students are 2,545, 7,859, 8,099, 2,531 and 188 respectively. The experiment results have shown that the RF model is best with 81.69% in Accuracy, 81.47% in Precision, 81.62% in Recall and 81.53% in F1-Score.

This paper is organized as follows. Literature review is presented at Sect. 2, our method is described in Sect. 3. Our experimental results are demonstrated in Sect. 4 and finally, the conclusion and future works are drawn in Sect. 5.

2   Related Work

There are a variety of researches for student academic performance prediction by using machine learning in the recent years. [16] focused on discussing the important attributes used in predicting students' performance and prediction methods used for students' performance. In the secondary education, [19] used decision tree, random forest, and naive Bayes to predict the five-level final grade of students based on their historical data. The experiment results showed the effectiveness of machine learning techniques when predicting the performances of students on two educational datasets related to mathematics lesson and Portuguese language lesson with 33 attributes each. [17] applied three single classifiers including a MLP, J48, and PART, three ensemble algorithms encompassing Bagging, MultiBoost and Voting and nine models developed by the fusion of single and ensemble-based classifiers to predict student performance. The experiment results on 1227 records and 16 attributes showed that MultiBoost with MLP achieved 98.7% Accuracy, 98.6% Precision, Recall, and F1-Score. In high school, [12] presented a use of machine learning for the student performance prediction in technical high school using tree-based methods and obtained prediction results over 89% Accuracy, etc.

Most of the researches focused on predicting student performance in higher education [3,8]. Only some works related to high school [2,12] and secondary school [17,19] students. These studies have used machine learning algorithms as well as deep learning to build student performance prediction models. The GPA, gender, age, income, nationality, marital status, employment status, attendance are attributes used in predicting student academic performance [3]. In addition, academic performance prediction can be conducted with only one subject or based on many subjects. The prediction results depend on many different factors such as the size of the dataset, the student's features, the machine learning techniques, data processing methods, etc. Furthermore, the machine learning techniques can be used individually or in combination with others. This paper presents a comparative analysis of six machine learning algorithms for early detection at the risk of low academic performance of high school students in the next semester using a dataset collected in the two previous semesters and student features related to academic performance, personal information, and family and high schools, etc.

3   Proposed Method

The main flow of the student academic performance prediction system is shown in Fig. 1. The gathered data were divided into two datasets, one for training, and the other for testing with machine learning algorithms such as DT, RF, XGB, LGBM, ANN and MLP.

The raw data is collected from a variety of high schools in Ca Mau. Each data item in this raw dataset contains many attributes of a student including the academic performance attribute. An attribute can take a numeric, string, or character value. Then, this raw dataset cannot be used to build machine learning models. The pre-processing of this dataset is necessary. The dataset obtained after pre-processing is separated into two datasets, called the D_train and D_test. During the training phase, the D_train is used to train and build the models. In the testing phase, the trained models are tested with all data point in the D_test. Every model produces a predictive value called P_predict indicating student's academic performance.

In this research, metrics of Accuracy, Precision, Recall, F1-Score are used to evaluate models while the selection of an appropriate model for predicting student academic performance in high school in Ca Mau province is based on D_test dataset and P_predict. The following sections presents the methods implemented in detail.

3.1   Data Collection

The dataset to train and test the models was collected from 12 high schools in Ca Mau province in the 2019–2020 school year [4]. This dataset is supplemented with student records in 2020–2021 school year and with many attributes. These data were processed and converted to .xlsx format. This .xlsx file called raw dataset. The details of attributes in the raw dataset are described in Table 2.

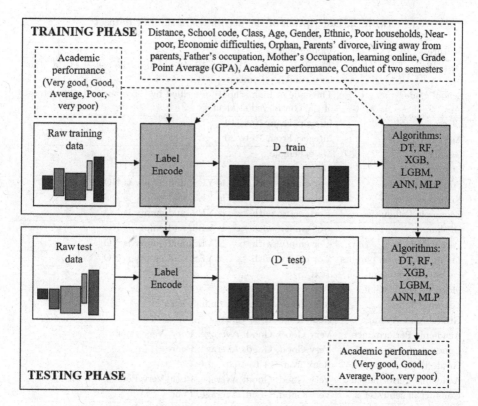

Fig. 1. Framework for student academic performance prediction

3.2   Data Pre-processing

The label encoding (LabelEncode) [5] method is applied on raw dataset before it is used to build machine learning models. An attribute in the raw dataset may have a defined set of available values. Each of these values will be encoded with a number. The resulting dataset is called the label-encoded dataset. For example, an academic performance attribute may be limited to the values Very Good, Good, Average, Poor and Very Poor in the raw dataset, then it will take one of the corresponding values of 4, 3, 2, 1 and 0 in the label-encoded dataset. The latter one includes feature vectors, each of which has the form (Distance, School Code, Class, Age, Gender, Ethnic, Poor households, Near-poor, Economic Difficulties, Orphan, Parents' divorce, Live away from parents, Father's occupation, Mother's occupation, learning online, GPA 1, Academic Performance 1, Conduct of semester 1, GPA 2, Academic Performance 2, Conduct of semester 2, and Academic Performance). More specifically, a data item in the label-encoded dataset looks like (24, 006, 10, 16, 0, 1, 0, 0, 0, 0, 1, 1, 0, 1, 0.5, 6.5, 2, 3, 7.5, 3, 3).

Table 2. Description of the attributes in the raw dataset

Feature	Value range
Distance	The distance from the student's school to the center of Ca Mau City (unit is kilometers).
School Code	The code of high school (described by three numeric characters) of the considered student
Class	Integer: From 10 to 12
Age	Integer: From 16 to 20
Gender	Male/Female
Ethnic	Text
Poor households	x or empty, with "x", is YES, and empty is NO
Near poor	x or empty, with "x", is YES, and empty is NO
Economic Difficulties	x or empty, with "x", is YES, and empty is NO
Orphan	x or empty, with "x", is YES, and empty is NO
Parents' divorce	x or empty, with "x", is YES, and empty is NO
Living away from parents	x or empty, with "x", is YES, and empty is NO
Father's occupation	Text
Mother's occupation	Text
Learning online	Real: Rate of learning online time
Grade Point Average 1	Real: from 0.1 to 10.0
Academic Performance 1	Very Good, Good, Average, Poor, Very Poor
Conduct of semester 1	Very Good, Good, Average, Poor
Grade Point Average 2	Real: from 0.1 to 10.0
Academic Performance 2	Very Good, Good, Average, Poor, Very Poor
Conduct of semester 2	Very Good, Good, Average, Poor
Academic Performance	Very Good, Good, Average, Poor, Very Poor

3.3   Using Machine Learning Models

In this work, machine learning algorithms used for predicting academic performance are DT, RF, XGB, LGBM, ANN and MLP. The Grid-search model hyper-parameter optimization technique was chosen to find the best set of hyper-parameters for each model. The latter one with different parameters was also executed. After testing, the values of parameters are adjusted according to Table 3. With ANN, the network was chosen with 4 layers: the input layer, two hidden layers with 64 neurons each and the output layer with 5 neurons for 5 labels (Very good, Good, Average, Poor, Very Poor) to predict. With MLP, default values are used.

3.4   Processing Imbalance Dataset

The data used in this study includes 21,222 students. Figure 2 shows the number of students in each academic level. It can be concluded that the majority of students are in the Average and Good grades.

As illustrated in Fig. 2, the dataset is imbalanced between the output classes for prediction. Then, the method of balancing the dataset with SMOTE [6]

Table 3. Parameters of the models

Model	Parameters
Decision Tree	max_depth = 21
Random Forest	n_estimators=2000
XGBoost	default
Light GBM	default
Artificial Neural Network	model = tf.keras.models.Sequential() model.add(tf.keras.layers.Dense(64, activation='relu')) model.add(tf.keras.layers.Dense(64, activation='relu')) model.add(tf.keras.layers.Dense(5, activation='sigmoid')) model.compile(optimizer='adam', loss='categorical_crossentropy', metrics=['accuracy'])
Multilayer Perceptron	hidden_layer_sizes=(100, 100, 100), max_iter=500, alpha=0.0001, solver='adam', verbose=10, random_state=21, tol=0.000000001

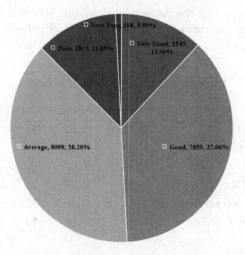

Fig. 2. The graph of the number and percentage of students at different academic levels

is used before putting this dataset into machine learning algorithms to build models. There are many methods of balancing the dataset [6], SMOTE is used because it does not change the original dataset. Moreover, the dataset is small, if Under sampling method is applied, there is not enough data to train the model. After balancing, the size of the dataset is 40,495 (8,099*5=40,495) for 5 labels.

4   Experimental Result

4.1   Machine Learning Model Evaluation

In this study, the dataset is divided into two parts, training and testing at the rate of 30% used as a test set. Several metrics are used to compare and evaluate the performance of the machine learning algorithms. The dataset for the experiment is imbalanced and processed into a balanced dataset. So, the evaluation measures such as Accuracy, Precision, Recall and F1-Score [5] are applied. Besides, important features are also extracted using the Gini index.

4.2 Experimental Result

The experiment was done in Python programming language (version 3.10) and the scikit-learning library [5] (version 1.0.2). This experiment uses the dataset presented in Sect. 3.1 and machine learning algorithms including DT, RF, XGB, LGBM, ANN and MLP for building models to predict student academic performance levels. Each student record consists of 21 features presented in Sect. 3.1. The experiment is run on a personal laptop configured with Chipset Intel i7 10750H 6-cores 2.6 GHz, 24 GB of memory, and a Windows 10 Home Single operating system.

The method of dividing the dataset by Hold-out [5] is used to split the dataset into a training set at the rate of 70% and testing set. Predictive results are shown in Table 4.

Table 4. Predictive results of all models

Model	Accuracy	Precision	Recall	F1-score
Decision Tree	73.65	73.49	73.58	73.52
Random Forest	81.69	81.47	81.62	81.53
XGBoost	80.86	80.81	80.81	80.78
Light GBM	80.82	80.62	80.76	80.66
Artificial Neural Network	73.04	72.89	72.96	72.86
Multilayer Perceptron	74.32	74.16	74.27	73.92

The Accuracy measure of all models is the best (more than 73%), followed by recall, precision and F1-score measure (more than 72%). The lowest value of recall measure is 72.96% for the ANN model. The high Accuracy measure indicates that the Accuracy of predicting student academic performance is high. Some models have F1-score value that is higher 80% as RF, XGB, LGBM. This result is suitable to evaluate the models as good. A high recall value of these models also shows that the wrong predictive rate is low.

A comparison of Accuracy of all models was illustrated in Fig. 3. Each model has a column representing Accuracy as a percentage (%). Only the Accuracy measures are shown in Fig. 3 because the dataset used in the models has been balanced using SMOTE. So, the values of the Accuracy, Precision, Recall measures or F1-Score are almost the same. Three models with over 80% Accuracy are RF, XGB and LGBM, in which the RF model obtained the highest value (81.69%), while the ANN model obtained the lowest value (73.04%). If the 80%

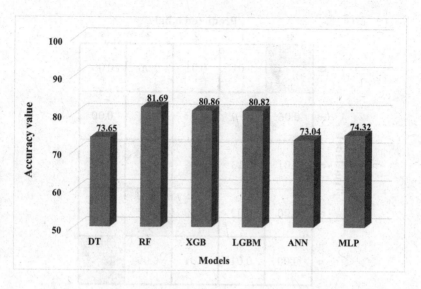

Fig. 3. Comparison of Accuracy of all models

standard is taken at the measures to select the model, the Fig. 3 shows that RF, XGB and LGBM models are qualified. The normalized confusion matrix results of three models are presented in Fig. 4, Fig. 5 and Fig. 6.

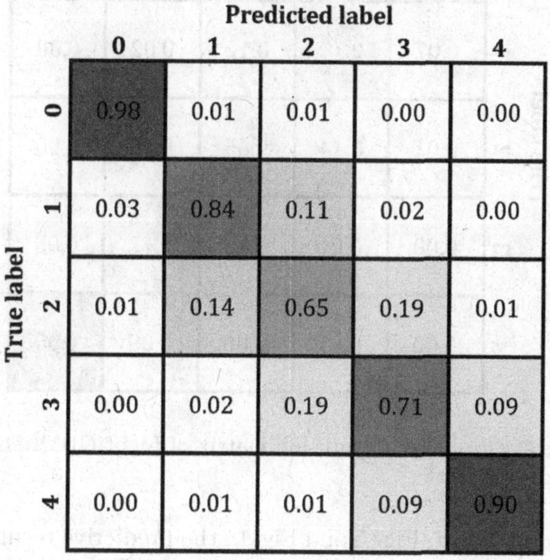

	Predicted label				
	0	**1**	**2**	**3**	**4**
0	0.98	0.01	0.01	0.00	0.00
1	0.03	0.84	0.11	0.02	0.00
2	0.01	0.14	0.65	0.19	0.01
3	0.00	0.02	0.19	0.71	0.09
4	0.00	0.01	0.01	0.09	0.90

Fig. 4. Normalized confusion matrix of Random Forest model

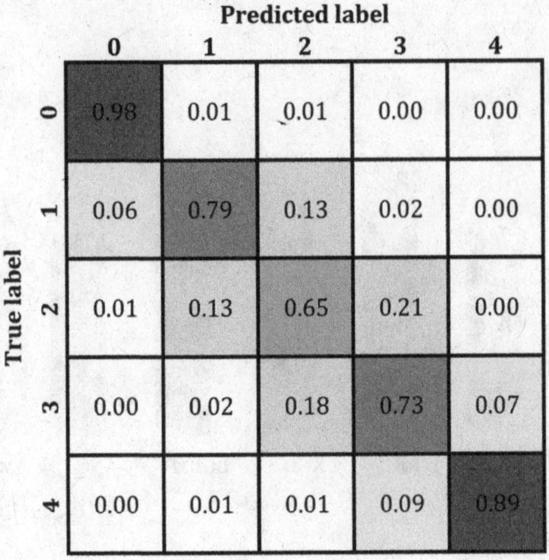

Predicted label

	0	1	2	3	4
0	0.98	0.01	0.01	0.00	0.00
1	0.06	0.79	0.13	0.02	0.00
2	0.01	0.13	0.65	0.21	0.00
3	0.00	0.02	0.18	0.73	0.07
4	0.00	0.01	0.01	0.09	0.89

True label

Fig. 5. Normalized confusion matrix of XGBoost model

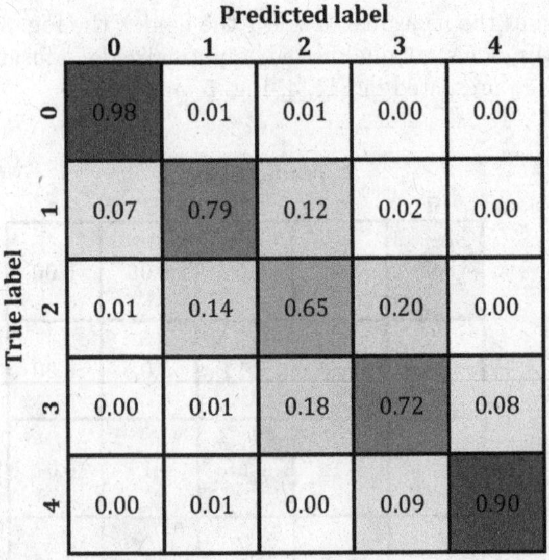

Predicted label

	0	1	2	3	4
0	0.98	0.01	0.01	0.00	0.00
1	0.07	0.79	0.12	0.02	0.00
2	0.01	0.14	0.65	0.20	0.00
3	0.00	0.01	0.18	0.72	0.08
4	0.00	0.01	0.00	0.09	0.90

True label

Fig. 6. Normalized confusion matrix of Light GBM model

As illustrated in Fig. 4, Fig. 5 and Fig. 6, the predictive results of Very Good (4) and Very Poor (0) levels are very high (over 90% except for the XGBoost model). The Average level is the lowest (only 65%). The objective of this study is to predict students with low academic performance (Poor and Very Poor levels) so that teachers and educators take appropriate measures to improve students learning outcomes. The prediction Accuracy at these two levels is high (over 79% for Poor level and 98% for Very Poor level). The prediction error through the Average and Good levels is small (from 0.14% to 0.16%). That means with this prediction result, teachers can focus more on most students at risk of low academy performance to help learners to improve their learning. So, for this study, RF, XGB and LGBM models are selected in predicting student academic performance in high school.

Furthermore, the Accuracy measure in Average level is not good (65%). This can be explained as follows. The score range between Average and Good levels as well as between Average and Poor levels is quite unclear. Because students can be downgraded from Good level to Average level, so the error of predicting a student from Average to Good level is still high (approximately 0.21% in XGBoost model).

4.3 Important Features

The technique of extracting the features aims to find important features and to reduce the number of features in a dataset. During the experimental process, the features extraction was also performed. The RF model was chosen to extract essential features because this model is the best among three models RF, XGB and LGBM. The weight by Gini index operator is applied to calculate the weights of attributes used to build the RF model.

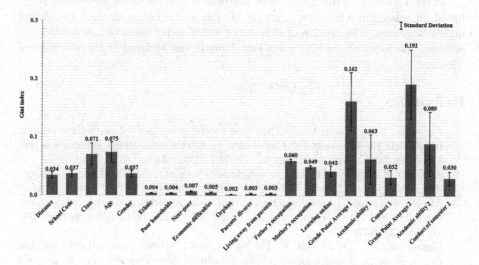

Fig. 7. The result of features extraction in model Random Forest

Figure 7 has illustrated the weights of features in the dataset. The GPA 1 and GPA 2 features are the most important with a Gini coefficient of 0.162 and 0.192, while the Orphan feature is the least important because Gini score is the smallest (0.002). As shown in Fig. 7, GPA (GPA1 and GPA 2), Age, Class, Academic performance (1 and 2), father's occupation and mother's occupation, learning online are decisive features that play a significant role in determining student academic performance from the dataset.

5   Conclusion and Future Work

In this research, an experiment was done with six machine learning models to predict student academic performance. As a result, three models RF, XGB and LGBM have been chosen. These models obtained performance measures over 80%. More specifically, the RF model is the best among the three models. This model achieved Accuracy, Precision, Recall, F1-Score more than 81% and a higher Accuracy than the two XGB and LGBM models. Moreover, the essential features that significantly influence student academic performance have been also extracted. They are GPA (1 and 2), Age, Class, Academic Ability (1 and 2), father's occupation, mother's occupation and learning online. These futures play an important role in teachers' decision making as well as considering factors affecting student learning.

Predicting student learning results as soon as possible is useful for school administrators as well as educational managers and teachers. Using predicted results, they can recommend remedial strategies and suitable solutions to improve the quality of learning and teaching in their high schools.

In the future, a learning outcomes prediction in each subject will be studied based on using more machine learning models and a bigger dataset to achieve higher measures. The results of this study can also be improved to predict the academic performance of high school students in the Mekong Delta provinces of Vietnam.

References

1. Aksenova, S.S., Zhang, D., Lu, M.: Enrollment prediction through data mining. In: 2006 IEEE International Conference on Information Reuse Integration, pp. 510–515 (2006). https://doi.org/10.1109/IRI.2006.252466
2. Al Zoubi, S., Younes, M.: Low academic achievement: causes and results. Theory Pract. Lang. Stud. **5**, 2262–2268 (2015). https://doi.org/10.17507/tpls.0511.09
3. Alturki, S., Hulpus, I., Stuckenschmidt, H.: Predicting academic outcomes: a survey from 2007 till 2018. Technol. Knowl. Learn. **27** (2022). https://doi.org/10.1007/s10758-020-09476-0
4. Dinh-Thanh, N., Thanh-Hai, N., Thi-Ngoc-Diem, P.: Forecasting and analyzing the risk of dropping out of high school students in Ca Mau Province. In: Dang, T.K., Küng, J., Chung, T.M., Takizawa, M. (eds.) FDSE 2021. CCIS, vol. 1500, pp. 224–237. Springer, Singapore (2021). https://doi.org/10.1007/978-981-16-8062-5_15
5. Fabian, P., et al.: Scikit-learn: machine learning in Python. J. Mach. Learn. Res. **12**(85), 2825–2830 (2011). http://jmlr.org/papers/v12/pedregosa11a.html
6. Fernández, A., García, S., Galar, M., Prati, R.C., Krawczyk, B., Herrera, F.: Learning from Imbalanced Data Sets. Springer, Cham (2018). https://doi.org/10.1007/978-3-319-98074-4

7. Goulet, M., Clément, M.-E., Helie, S., Villatte, A.: Longitudinal association between risk profiles, school dropout risk, and substance abuse in adolescence. Child Youth Care Forum **49**(5), 687–706 (2020). https://doi.org/10.1007/s10566-020-09550-9

8. Hellas, A., et al.: Predicting academic performance: a systematic literature review. In: Proceedings Companion of the 23rd Annual ACM Conference on Innovation and Technology in Computer Science Education, pp. 175–199 (2018). https://doi.org/10.1145/3293881.3295783

9. Hoang Du, L.: Report No. 1495/BC-SGDDT dated July 28, 2020, on assessing the performance of tasks for the 2019–2020 school year (2020)

10. Huynh-Ly, T.N., Thai-Nghe, N.: A system for predicting student's course result using a free recommender system library - MyMediaLite. In: Information Technology Conference (2013)

11. Lamas, H.: School performance. Propóitos y Representaciones **3**, 351–386 (2015). https://doi.org/10.20511/pyr2015.v3n1.74

12. de Melo Junior, G., Oliveira, S., Ferreira, C., Filho, E., Calixto, W., Furriel, G.: Evaluation techniques of machine learning in task of reprovation prediction of technical high school students. In: 2017 CHILEAN Conference on Electrical, Electronics Engineering, Information and Communication Technologies (CHILECON), pp. 1–7 (2017). https://doi.org/10.1109/CHILECON.2017.8229739

13. Nandeshwar, A., Chaudhari, S.: Enrollment prediction models using data mining. In: 2006 IEEE International Conference on Information Reuse and Integration (2009)

14. Ogresta, J., Rezo, I., Kožljan, P., Pare, M.H., Ajduković, M.: Why do we drop out? Typology of dropping out of high school. Youth Soc. **53**, 934–954 (2020). https://doi.org/10.1177/0044118X20918435

15. Phuoc Hai, N., Tian-Wei, S.: Predicting the student learning outcomes based on the combination of Taylor approximation method and grey models. VNU J. Sci. Educ. Res. **31**, 70–83 (2015)

16. Shahiri, A., Husain, W., Abdul Rashid, N.: A review on predicting student's performance using data mining techniques. Procedia Comput. Sci. **72**, 414–422 (2015). https://doi.org/10.1016/j.procs.2015.12.157

17. Siddique, A., Jan, A., Majeed, F., Qahmash, A., Quadri, N.N., Wahab, M.: Predicting academic performance using an efficient model based on fusion of classifiers. Appl. Sci. **11**, 11845 (2021). https://doi.org/10.3390/app112411845

18. Stevenson, N., Swain-Bradway, J., LeBeau, B.: Examining high school student engagement and critical factors in dropout prevention. Assess. Effective Interv. **46**(2), 155–164 (2021). https://doi.org/10.1177/1534508419859655

19. Ünal, F.: Data mining for student performance prediction in education. Data Mining - Methods, Applications and Systems, pp. 1–9 (2020). https://doi.org/10.5772/intechopen.91449

Gross Domestic Product Prediction in Various Countries with Classic Machine Learning Techniques

Chi Le Hoang Tran[1], Trang Huyen Phan[1], Pham Thi-Ngoc-Diem[2],
and Hai Thanh Nguyen[2(✉)]

[1] FPT Polytechnic, Can Tho, Vietnam
[2] Can Tho University, Can Tho, Vietnam
{ptndiem,nthai.cit}@ctu.edu.vn

Abstract. Gross Domestic Product (GDP) is an indicator used to measure the total market value of all final goods and services produced within a national territory during a given period. This is an essential indicator for formulating macroeconomic policies. This study presents a classical machine learning algorithm to forecast GDP in countries from 2013 to 2018 (with Economic Freedom Index's Predicting GPD dataset). We use the Feature importance technique and incorporate other methods such as PCA and KBest; simultaneously, we tune the hyperparameters for the model to have more optimal results. We compare the predictive accuracy of Random Forest (RF) with other classical models such as Support Vector Machines (SVM). We find that RF KBest outperforms RF and SVM. The forecast accuracy is measured by R^2 has reached 0.904 in predicting GDP in 186 countries. This study encourages increasing the use of machine learning models in macroeconomic forecasting. Besides, we present GDP growth rates (as a percentage) by region. We also analyze and find some critical factors that can significantly affect GDP, such as Freedom from Corruption, Property rights, and the unemployment rate.

Keywords: GDP Prediction · Economic · Classical Machine Learning

1 Introduction

Gross Domestic Product (GDP) is an indicator used to measure the total market value of all final goods and services produced within a national territory during a given period. Therefore, GDP is an economic indicator of the most interest. This index is given to assess the overall growth rate of the economy and the level of development of a region or a country. For economic development, GDP is a critical macroeconomic indicator that reflects the size and potential of the economy and serves as the basis for calculating many socio-economic indicators. GDP is influenced by many different factors within the territory of that country. However, three factors affect the GDP index: population, Foreign Direct

© ICST Institute for Computer Sciences, Social Informatics and Telecommunications Engineering 2023
Published by Springer Nature Switzerland AG 2023. All Rights Reserved
C. V. Phan and T. D. Nguyen (Eds.): ICTCC 2022, LNICST 473, pp. 136–147, 2023.
https://doi.org/10.1007/978-3-031-28790-9_9

Investment (FDI), and inflation. Therefore, forecasting GDP has a significant contribution to developing the national economy.

It can be seen that GDP is one of the essential indicators in assessing a country's economy. This widely used term in macroeconomics helps readers understand and quickly analyze economic changes.

In recent years, machine learning has been used in many fields, such as recognition, classification, prediction, etc. Applying machine learning techniques to the economic field plays a huge role in predicting the growth or decline of a country. In this way, countries can develop countermeasures to help their economies grow better. Therefore, many studies have been published and contributed significantly to data analysis and warning [1–6].

This study presents the Random Forest (RF) algorithm to forecast countries' GDP. Our contributions include:

- We process and clean the data, then use the Feature importance technique to determine which factors most influence GDP.
- Next, we combine other methods such as PCA and KBest; simultaneously, we tune the hyperparameters for the model to have more optimal results. The highest result is 0.904 with RF KBest.

The rest of the manuscript is organized as follows. We present related work in Sect. 2. Section 3 exhibits the proposed approach for GDP prediction. Results on GDP prediction of different countries will be revealed in Sect. 4, and we conclude some important points of the work in Sect. 5.

2   Related Work

Economic growth is the increase in output an economy produces over time. Since GDP is a composite economic indicator of the economy's overall health, it is used by most countries around the world to gauge economic growth. On that basis, researchers can make development orientations and policies in the next period[1].

The authors in [7] studied the real-time predictive performance of machine learning algorithms estimated on New Zealand data. This study uses a large set of real-time quarterly macroeconomic indicators; they train many popular machine learning algorithms and forecast real GDP growth for each quarter between 2009 and 2018, including GDP data and features, including about 550 domestic and international variables. The results also suggest some benefits to combining the individual ML forecasts. Therefore, the authors recommend using the ML algorithm to supplement the GDP forecasting model. In another study [8], Jaehyun Yoon proposed a method for creating machine learning models, specifically a gradient boosting model and an RF model, to forecast real GDP growth. This study focuses on the real GDP growth of Japan and produces forecasts for the years 2001 to 2018. The forecasts by the International Monetary Fund and the Bank of Japan are benchmarks. This paper shows that for the 2001–2018 period,

---

[1] https://www.imf.org/external/pubs/ft/fandd/basics/gdp.html.

the forecasts by the gradient boosting model and RF model are more accurate than the benchmark forecasts; Between the gradient boosting and RF models, the gradient boosting model turns out to be more accurate. In another paper [9], authors presented an approach to Forecast Economic Recessions. They used Italian data on GDP and a few related variables as a case study. In particular, they evaluated the goodness of fit of the forecasting proposed model in a case study of the Italian GDP. First, the algorithm was trained on Italian macroeconomic variables from 1995 to 2019. Then, they compared the results using the same dataset through Classic Linear Regression Model. As a result, both statistical and ML approaches can predict economic downturns, but higher accuracy was obtained using Nonlinear Autoregressive with exogenous variables (NARX) model.

The authors in [10] deployed micro to macro literature by decomposing earnings into the Research and Development and pre-Research and Development components. Then, they attempted Aggregate accounting Research and Development to forecast real GDP through the personal consumption, business investment, and net export channels of GDP. Another work in [11] evaluated and analyzed the effectiveness of Tencent user density (TUD) data, a typical type of LBSM data in China, in estimating GDP. In addition, the authors in [12] leveraged Matlab2014b software and Excel software to predict GDP on the data from 1980 to 2020. Finally, an analysis was done in [13] with a data-driven GDP-based forecasting model that combined multidimensional data from the aspects of electricity consumption, climate, and human activities and observed that such factors could be related to economic development.

Another study in [14] introduced a new multimodal two-stage approach for regional GDP prediction, which learned the evolution of the GDP with only historical information and tweets. They stated that the method could provide earlier forecasts about the regional GDP. The authors in [15] gave some conclusions in their experiments that The proposed three-stage feature selection method effectively improves the prediction accuracy of TCN by more than 10%. In contrast, the proposed prediction for GDP has reached better forecasting performance than the 14 benchmark models. They also showed that the MAPE values of the models are lower than 5% in all cases. The work in [16] analyzed the relationship between epidemiologic and CHE/GDP data to process ordinary least square multivariate modeling and classify countries into different groups using PC analysis, K-means, and hierarchical clustering. The authors in [17] analyzed the effect of energy and non-energy material productivity on the gross domestic product data covering OECD members from 1990–2020. The work [18] has tried machine learning to predict GDP. An interesting study in [19] predicted GDP extracted from the customized dataset for Gujarat State using ARIMA and RF algorithms.

3   Method

We use the Economic Freedom Index's Predicting GPD dataset[2]. This dataset contains key statistical indicators of the 186 countries collected from 2013 to 2018. We aim to use machine learning to predict each country's GDP growth. The proposed method is shown in Fig. 1.

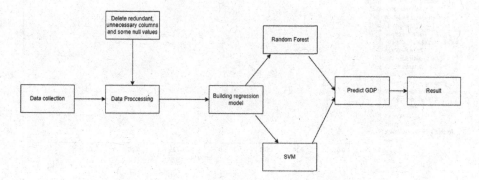

Fig. 1. The proposed flowchart for GDP prediction.

We analyzed the data and found unlabelled characteristics in this dataset, some of which are not as obvious as taxes, government spending, and even significant debt. Therefore, we remove extra columns, some NaN values, and missing/empty entries. We use the Feature importance technique to select the most critical attributes in a data set to determine the factors that most affect GDP using the RF algorithm for Feature importances implemented in scikit-learning. After fitting, the model provides a feature importances attribute that can be accessed to retrieve the relative importance score for each input feature. Figure 2 exhibits the ranking of the importance of the features, while Fig. 3 represents the matrix corresponding to the features. We split the dataset into two parts. The train set is data from 2013 to 2017, and the test set is the 2018 statistical data.

Figures 4, 5, 6, 7, 8 show the GDP growth rates of the regions from 2013 to 2018 (in percent). The growth rates of America and Asia decreased from 2013 to 2018. Europe, the Middle East/North Africa, and Sub-Saharan Africa's growth rates are not stable.

4   Experiments

4.1   Environmental Settings

To evaluate the proposed GDP prediction method, we implement the GDP prediction program, as shown in Fig. 1. We use a computer equipped with a CPU

---

[2] https://www.kaggle.com/datasets/isacscjr/heritage-freedom-index.

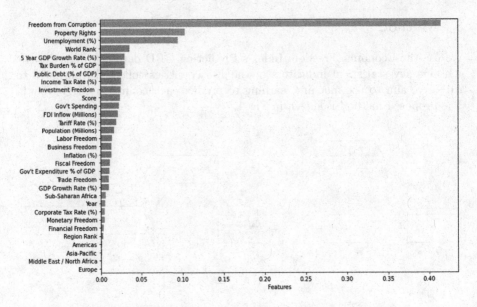

Fig. 2. Feature's importance is affecting the GDP prediction.

Intel core i5 installed an operating system of Windows 10 64 bit, with 1TB HDD memory, and Visual Studio Code software to implement the steps of experiments.

4.2   Performance Evaluation

Evaluating the performance of a model is essential for understanding its accuracy and reliability. In addition, model evaluation techniques can be used to compare the performance of models and decide the best fit for the data. Some metrics for the comparison are presented as follows.

– Mean Absolute Error (MAE): measures errors between paired observations expressing the same phenomenon. The MAE (Eq. 1) measures the quality of an estimator—it is always non-negative, and values closer to zero are good results. Therefore lower the MAE better the model is for the data.

$$MAE = \frac{\sum |f_i - y_i|}{n} \tag{1}$$

– Root Mean Squared Error (RMSE): is the error rate by the square root of MSE (Eq. 2).

$$RMSE = \sqrt{MSE} = \sqrt{\frac{\sum_i^n (f_i - y_i)^2}{n}} \tag{2}$$

– R^2 score (R square), also called the coefficient of determination, represents the coefficient of how well the values fit compared to the original values (Eq. 3).

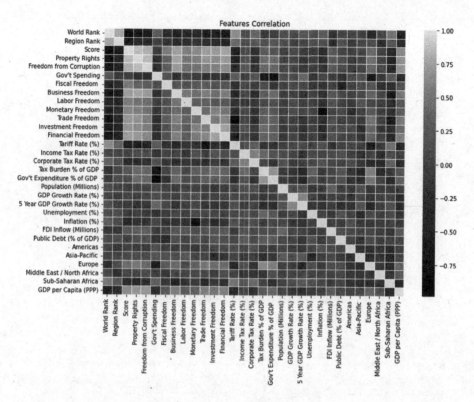

Fig. 3. Features Correlation.

The best possible score is 1.000, which can be negative (because the model can be arbitrarily worse)[3]. The higher the value is, the better the model is.

$$R^2 = 1 - \frac{ESS}{EST} \qquad (3)$$

4.3   GDP Prediction with Various Algorithms

In this study, we compare the results of two algorithms, RF and Support Vector Machines (SVM). The results of the default model are detailed in Table 1. PCA reduces the number of data dimensions by feature extraction to find a new set of attributes from the original set of attributes to improve computational performance and classification accuracy. Meanwhile, KBest uses to extract the best features of a given dataset. The SelectKBest method selects the features according to the highest K scores (in this study, we chose $K = 10$). Table 1 shows that the RF ($R^2 = 0.852$) and KBest RF ($R^2 = 0.857$) models are more efficient than RF PCA ($R^2 = 0.574$).

---

[3] https://scikit-learn.org/stable/modules/generated/sklearn.metrics.r2_score.html.

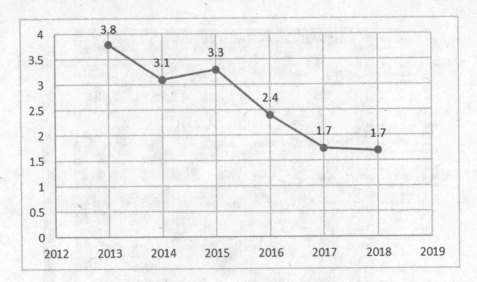

Fig. 4. GDP Growth Rate of Americas.

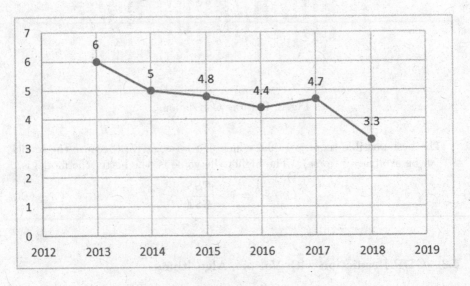

Fig. 5. GDP Growth Rate of Asia.

We found that the results in Table 1 could be improved by tuning the hyperparameters of RF, RF KBest, and SVM algorithms. Therefore, we use GridSearchCV to adjust hyperparameters for the best results automatically. The results show a marked improvement when tuning the hyperparameters after applying GridSearchCV (details in Table 2). Specifically, with RF and RF models KBest, we tune the hyperparameter *n_estimators=500*; with SVM model we use *"C": 10000, "gamma": 0.0001, "kernel": "RBF"*.

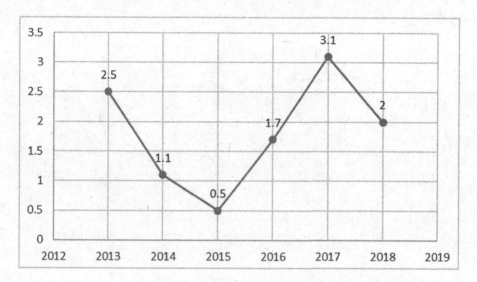

Fig. 6. GDP Growth Rate of Europe.

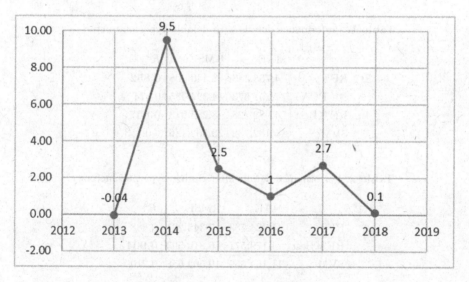

Fig. 7. GDP Growth Rate of the Middle East/North Africa.

Figures 9, 10, 11 show significantly more optimized MAE and RMSE measurements; for example, with RF model KBest, MAE has decreased from 4,982.228 to 4,179.571, RMSE has decreased from 8,283.913 to 6,810.593, and R2 has increased significantly (from 0.857 to 0.904).

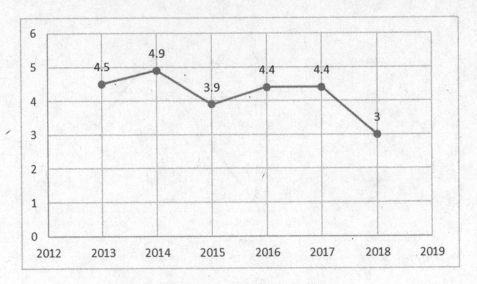

Fig. 8. GDP Growth Rate of Sub-Saharan Africa.

Table 1. Performance details with default hyperparameters.

	MAE	RMSE	R^2
RF	4,768.343	8,440.008	**0.852**
RF PCA	7,251.673	14,324.485	0.574
RF KBest	4,982.228	8,283.913	**0.857**
SVM	15,182.732	23,562.186	−0.153

Table 2. Performance details after tuning hyperparameters.

	MAE	RMSE	R^2
RF	4,234.733	7,345.291	0.888
RF KBest	4,179.571	6,810.593	**0.904**
SVM	11,164.659	19,504.658	0.210

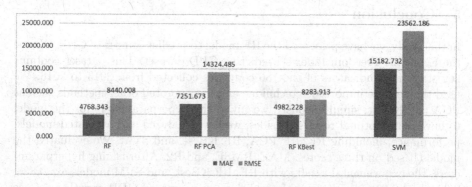

Fig. 9. Experimental results with default hyperparameters.

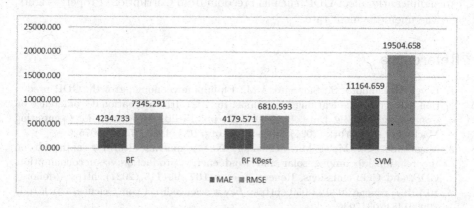

Fig. 10. GDP prediction performance after tuning hyperparameters.

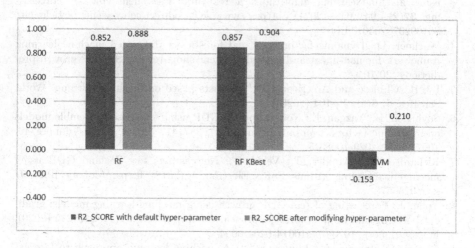

Fig. 11. comparison R^2 Score of GDP prediction before and after tuning hyperparameters.

5   Conclusion

In this study, we have presented the RF model to predict countries' GDP. We use the Economic Freedom Index's Predicting GPD dataset. This dataset contains key statistical indicators of the 186 countries collected from 2013 to 2018. We used the Feature importance technique and incorporated other methods such as PCA and KBest; simultaneously, we tuned the hyperparameters for the model to have more optimal results. Besides, we have analyzed and evaluated models' performance, including RF, RF PCA, RF KBest, and SVM. We evaluated the models based on three scores, MAE, RMSE, and R2. After tuning hyperparameters, the experimental results with RF, RF KBest, and SVM models are 0.888, 0.904, and 0.210, respectively. In addition, we presented GDP growth rates (as a percentage) by region. We also analyzed and found some critical factors that can significantly affect GDP, such as Freedom from Corruption, Property rights, and the unemployment rate.

References

1. Laygo-Matsumoto, S., Samonte, M.J.: Philippine economic growth: GDP prediction using machine learning algorithms. In: 2021 4th International Conference on Computing and Big Data, ICCBD 2021, pp. 15–20. Association for Computing Machinery, New York (2021). https://doi.org/10.1145/3507524.3507526

2. Magazzino, C., Mele, M., Schneider, N.: A machine learning approach on the relationship among solar and wind energy production, coal consumption, GDP, and CO2 emissions. Renew. Energy **167**, 99–115 (2021). https://doi.org/10.1016/j.renene.2020.11.050. https://www.sciencedirect.com/science/article/pii/S0960148120317936

3. Richardson, A., van Florenstein Mulder, T., Vehbi, T.: Nowcasting GDP using machine-learning algorithms: a real-time assessment. Int. J. Forecasting **37**(2), 941–948 (2021). https://www.sciencedirect.com/science/article/pii/S016920702030159X

4. Wochner, D.: Dynamic factor trees and forests - a theory-led machine learning framework for non-linear and state-dependent short-term U.S. GDP growth predictions (2020)

5. Lv, H.: Chinese and American GDP forecasts based on machine learning. World Sci. Res. J. **6**(6), 95–104 (2020)

6. Soybilgen, B., Yazgan, E.: Nowcasting US GDP using tree-based ensemble models and dynamic factors. Comput. Econ. **57**(1), 387–417 (2021). https://doi.org/10.1007/s10614-020-10083-5

7. Richardson, A., Mulder, T., Vehbi, T.: Nowcasting New Zealand GDP using machine learning algorithms. SSRN Electron. J. (2018). https://doi.org/10.2139/ssrn.3256578

8. Yoon, J.: Forecasting of real GDP growth using machine learning models: gradient boosting and random forest approach. Comput. Econ. **57**(1), 247–265 (2020). https://doi.org/10.1007/s10614-020-10054-w

9. Cicceri, G., Inserra, G., Limosani, M.: A machine learning approach to forecast economic recessions—an Italian case study. Mathematics **8**(2), 241 (2020). https://doi.org/10.3390/math8020241

10. Collins, D.W., Nguyen, N.Q.: Aggregate accounting research and development expenditures and the prediction of real gross domestic product. J. Account. Public Policy **41**(1), 106901 (2022). https://doi.org/10.1016%2Fj.jaccpubpol.2021.106901

11. Huang, Z., Li, S., Gao, F., Wang, F., Lin, J., Tan, Z.: Evaluating the performance of LBSM data to estimate the gross domestic product of china at multiple scales: a comparison with NPP-VIIRS nighttime light data. J. Clean. Prod. **328**, 129558 (2021). https://doi.org/10.1016%2Fj.jclepro.2021.129558

12. Wu, J., He, Y.: Prediction of GDP in time series data based on neural network model. In: 2021 IEEE International Conference on Artificial Intelligence and Industrial Design (AIID), pp. 20–23 (2021)

13. Wu, X., Zhang, Z., Chang, H., Huang, Q.: A data-driven gross domestic product forecasting model based on multi-indicator assessment. IEEE Access **9**, 99495–99503 (2021)

14. Ortega-Bastida, J., Gallego, A.J., Rico-Juan, J.R., Albarrán, P.: A multimodal approach for regional GDP prediction using social media activity and historical information. Appl. Soft Comput. **111**, 107693 (2021). https://doi.org/10.1016%2Fj.asoc.2021.107693

15. Li, Q., Yan, G., Yu, C.: A novel multi-factor three-step feature selection and deep learning framework for regional GDP prediction: evidence from China. Sustainability **14**(8), 4408 (2022). https://doi.org/10.3390%2Fsu14084408

16. Oshinubi, K., Rachdi, M., Demongeot, J.: Analysis of reproduction number R0 of COVID-19 using current health expenditure as gross domestic product percentage (CHE/GDP) across countries. Healthcare **9**(10), 1247 (2021). https://doi.org/10.3390%2Fhealthcare9101247

17. Petković, B., et al.: Adaptive neuro fuzzy evaluation of energy and non-energy material productivity impact on sustainable development based on circular economy and gross domestic product. Bus. Strategy Environ. **31**(1), 129–144 (2021). https://doi.org/10.1002%2Fbse.2878

18. Pawar, P., Padmawar, V., Karande, A.: Gross domestic product prediction using machine learning. **08**, 2395-0056 (2021)

19. Vyas, N., Patel, J., Vala, D., Patel, D., Patel, R.: Machine learning based generic GDP analysis and prediction system (2021)

Palmprint Recognition Using Learning Discriminant Line Direction Descriptors

Hoang Van Thien[1]([✉]), Thong Dinh Duy Phan[2], and Thai Hoang Le[3,4]

[1] Faculty of Information Technology, Ho Chi Minh City University of Technology (HUTECH), Ho Chi Minh City, Vietnam
vt.hoang@hutech.edu.vn

[2] University of Information Technology (UIT), Vietnam National University Ho Chi Minh City, Ho Chi Minh City, Vietnam
thongpdd.15@grad.uit.edu.vn

[3] Faculty of Information Technology, University of Sciences, Ho Chi Minh City, Vietnam
lhthai@fit.hcmus.edu.vn

[4] Vietnam National University, Ho Chi Minh City, Ho Chi Minh City, Vietnam

Abstract. Palmprint-based biometrics has received a lot of attention for personal identification. The paper proposes a novel learning discriminant feature technique for palmprint recognition, called the Learning Discriminant Line Direction Descriptor (LDLDD), that learns separately all three kind of directional pattern code. The dominant direction number (DDN) map is calculated first in this method. Then, this technique computes direction pattern maps with three multi-direction encoding methods based on the DDN map, where pixels with the same DDN values will use the same encoding strategy and belong to the same feature map. Finally, $(2D)^2LDA$ is used to train new feature subspaces that project these maps from a high-dimensional space to a discriminant space with lower dimensions. Experiments on Hong Kong Polytechnic University's (PolyU and IITD) public databases show that the proposed method outperforms existing techniques in terms of accuracy.

Keywords: Palmprint recognition · Dominant direction number · Multi direction pattern · Biometrics

1 Introduction

In the past, people utilized identity cards, keys, and passwords for individual recognition. Due to the rapid development of information technology and online financial activities, personal authentication based on biometrics is growing in popularity today. Biometrics based on the physiological and behavioral characteristics of a human offer various advantages including high security, high efficiency, and user friendliness. Biometric features include signatures, gaits, voices, faces, fingerprints, palmprints, etc. The palmprint has some advantages over other biometric features because it contains so much distinguishing information, including principal lines, wrinkles, and texture [1]. Region of

C. V. Phan and T. D. Nguyen (Eds.): ICTCC 2022, LNICST 473, pp. 148–159, 2023.
https://doi.org/10.1007/978-3-031-28790-9_10

interest (ROI) segmentation, feature extraction, and matching are the three main stages of palmprint processing. A sub-region in the palm's center that contains discriminative information is segmented during the ROI segmentation stage and used for feature extraction [2]. A palmprint extraction stage is needed in order to build a description with multiple subject separations [3, 4].The local direction feature is the main attribute used to extract palmprint since it is not changed by fluctuations in illumination [1–3]. Several strategies for constructing palmprint descriptors that take advantage of this local direction feature have been recommended for several decades, and they can be categorized into four general groups: one-direction based approach, local direction statistics-based approach, multiple-directions based approach and fusion discriminant representation approach [1, 3].

The one-direction technique frequently employs a particular type of line shape filter to measure lines in a specific direction and encode the results into a feature code [4–11]. For extracting of palmprint features, a 2D Gabor phase encoding approach with a fixed orientation is proposed [4]. Kong et al. obtained line responses using a Gabor filters and compared the hamming distance between two palmprint images [5]. CompCode is computed using six different Gabor filters with different directions and based on determining the most dominating direction of palm lines using the winner-take-all rule [6]. The Robust Line orientation code (RLOC) methodology employs twelve Radon-based filters to generate the dominant direction features [7].

The multiple-direction based technique makes use of the magnitudes of various direction filters. Sun et al. compute three orthogonal direction codes for palmprint representation using three orthogonal Gaussian filters [8]. Guo et al. [9] develop the binary orientation co-occurrence vector from palmprint images by applying six Gabor filters and concatenating the normalized responses into six directions. BOCV is more resistant to image rotation and accurately describes local direction features. In order to determine the delicate direction points, E-BOCV, acting as the BOCV, created six direction code maps [10]. To encode the results of comparing the six directions, Fei et al. proposed a discriminatory neighboring direction indicator. The indicator is not affected by noise or rotation [11].

The approach based on local direction statistics displays direction features as encoded vectors based on the statistics of one or more direction features. Jia et al. [12] propose the histogram of oriented lines (HOL), which is light-insensitive and forgiving of minor changes. Luo et al. [13] proposed the local line directional patterns (LLDP) technique, which uses palm lines to encode two dominant directions using either the real component of Gabor filters or the modified finite radon transform (MFRAT). Fei et al. propose a local multiple directional pattern (LMDP) [14] to accurately characterize the multiple directions information. Li et al. [15] propose the Local Micro-structure Tetra Pattern (LMTrP) for extracting palmprint features, which captures the local region histograms after effectively removing redundant features and then uses kernel linear discriminant analysis to minimize dimension. Zhang et al. [16] propose collaborative representation (CR)-based method that builds the feature vectors for the palmprint using the competing code's blockwise histograms. Fei et al. [17] present a novel double-layer direction extraction technique that uses latent direction information from the apparent direction's magnitude layer map.

Recently, researchers have been interested in developing several discriminant features learning techniques to learn specific mapping functions that transform raw data in discriminant features subspace. Sub-space learning [18], dictionary learning [19], metric learning [20], and deep learning [22, 23] are examples of these techniques. Principal component analysis (PCA) and linear discriminant analysis (LDA) are the most widely used discriminant feature learning techniques. Ribaric et al. [24] propose a multimodal biometric identification system that uses the PCA to extract the eigenfinger and eigenpalm. Hoang et al. [25] apply 2DLDA to both positive and negative orientations maps to find class separability features for palmprint recognition. Rida et al. [26] present a new ensemble classifier for palmprint recognition based on the Random Subspace Method, which employs 2DPCA to generate nearly incoherent random subspaces. Hoang et al. [27] propose a palmprint recognition method that combines a Local line direction pattern technique with (2D) 2LDA to achieve high discrimination features. Fei et al. [3] propose a palmprint recognition technique that computes the convolution difference between neighboring directions before using the LDA to generate the discriminative code.

In general, some learning discriminating feature-based methods have recently achieved good palmprint recognition accuracy [3, 25]. This paper proposes a novel learning discriminant feature technique for palmprint recognition, called the direction pattern Learning Discriminant Line Direction Descriptor (LDLDD), that learns separately all three kind of directional pattern code. The technique starts by calculating the dominant direction number (DDN) map. Then, based on the DDN map, LDLDD will calculate three direction pattern maps with three multi-direction encoding methods, where pixels with the same DDN values will have the same LLDP encoding strategy and belong to the same feature map. Finally, $(2D)^2LDA$ is utilized to train new feature subspaces that project these maps from a high-dimensional space to a lower-dimensional, discriminant space. Experiments using the public datasets of Hong Kong Polytechnic University (PolyU and IITD) demonstrate that our proposed technique outperforms existing methods in terms of accuracy.

The remaining article is arranged as follows. Section 2 details our proposed the method. Section 3 presents the experimental results. The conclusion is provided in Sect. 4.

2 Our Proposal Method

A pixel in a palmprint image can have one of three scenarios: (1) a ridge runs across it, (2) two intersecting ridges connect at the consideration point, or (3) more than two crossing ridges intersect at that pixel. As a result, a technique for describing the three types of palm line patterns at the pixel is required. Various patterns are represented by distinct maps at the same time to avoid pattern matching ambiguity. Fei et al. [3] proposed the dominant direction number value (DDN), which allows the number of palmlines passing through a point to be determined. Therefore, we propose the Learning Discriminant Line Direction Descriptor (LDLDD) for palmprint recognition that performs the following steps: (1) estimate ridges in various directions using Gabor filters; (2) compute the DDN value of the LDDBP feature at each pixel; (3) compute Multiple line directions descriptors (MLDD) based on DDN map. The results are three direction coding maps without the ambiguity in matching; (4) Finally, apply the $(2D)^2$LDA method for each map in order to learn the feature space with high discriminant in classification and feature size reduction. The results are three feature matrices for each sample type, each with a small number of dimensions for classification using Euclid distance. Figure 1 illustrates the scheme of the proposed algorithm. The following are specific formulas for implementing the proposed method.

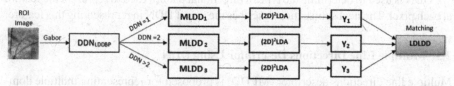

Fig. 1. The scheme of the proposal method

2.1 Gabor Filter for Detecting Line of Palmprint

The proposed method needs measure the appearance of the palm line in different directions. The 2D-Gabor filter is an effective tool for this goal. The 2D-Gabor filter is defined as the followings [4, 13]:

$$G(x, y, \theta, \mu, \sigma) = \frac{1}{2\pi\sigma^2} \exp\left\{-\frac{x^2 + y^2}{2\sigma^2}\right\} \exp\{2\pi i(\mu x \cos\theta + \mu y \sin\theta)\} \quad (1)$$

where $i = \sqrt{-1}, \mu$ denotes the frequency of the sinusoidal wave, θ is used to control the direction, and σ denotes the standard deviation of the Gaussian envelope. Then, the convolution of the Gabor filter is conducted on the palmprint image to obtain line response as follows:

$$r_j = (I * G(\theta_j))_{(x,y)} \quad (2)$$

where I is the palmprint image, $G(\theta)_j$ denotes the real part of the Gabor filter with the orientation of θ_j, '*' is the convolutional operator, r_j is the convolution result, and (x, y) denotes the position of a pixel in I, and the orientation of θ_j is computed as follows:

$$\theta_j = \frac{\pi(j - 1)}{n} j = 1, 2, \dots n \quad (3)$$

2.2 DDN

There are several crossing lines in a palmprint image, therefore, each pixel could has multiple dominant direction. The dominant direction number (DDN) is can be computed as follows [3]:

$$DDN = \frac{1}{2}\sum_{j=1}^{N_\theta} \left| s(r_j - r_{\varphi(j)}) - s(r_{\varphi(j)} - r_{\varphi(\varphi(j))}) \right| \quad (4)$$

where N_θ ($N_\theta = 12$) is the direction number of Gabor functions; j is the corresponding direction index; r_j represents the convolved result on the *jth* direction; $s(x)$ equals to 1 if x > 0 and 0 otherwise; $\varphi(j)$ denotes the adjacent clockwise direction index of j. $\varphi(j)$ equals to N_θ if $j = 1$ and $(j - 1)$ otherwise, and it can be directly calculated as follows:

$$\varphi(j) = mod(j - 2, N_\theta) + 1 \tag{5}$$

DDN is used to determine the type of directional pattern used to represent the feature at each pixel. The next sub-section describes the use of DDN in representing this feature.

2.3 Multiple Line Directions Descriptor Using DDN

Multiple line directions descriptor (MLDD) is proposed for representing multiple dominant directions patterns in which pixels with a DDN value of 1 are represented by respectively the first and last dominant direction indices, pixels with a DDN value of 2 are represented by the first and second dominant direction indices, and pixels with a DDN value more than 2 are represented by DDN dominant direction indices and placed in a separate result maps. MLDD is defined as follows:

$$D^1 = \begin{cases} 0, & \textit{if } DDN \neq 1 \\ m_f \times N_\theta + m_l, & \textit{if } DDN = 1 \end{cases} \tag{6}$$

$$D^2 = \begin{cases} 0, & \textit{if } DDN \neq 2 \\ m_f \times N_\theta + m_s, & \textit{if } DDN = 2 \end{cases} \tag{7}$$

$$D^3 = \begin{cases} 0, & \textit{if } DDN \leq 2 \\ \sum_{i=0}^{N_\theta - 1} s(r_i - r_{DDN})2^i, & \textit{if } DDN > 2 \end{cases} \tag{8}$$

where the index numbers m_f, m_s and m_l are respectively the first, second and last dominant direction indices with the maximum, second maximum and minimum filtering responses; r_k is the k-th minimum directional response (k = DDN).

After applying the MLDD technique to each input image I, the output will be three feature matrices, each of which represents the patterns of pixels with the same characteristic (that have 1 line, 2 lines or more lines at the pixel). These matrices are utilized as features for pattern matching between various objects with no ambiguity. However, because these images are large and include redundant information, the following part will describe how to use (2D)²LDA to extract image features with the goal of reducing the number of dimensions and increasing recognition discrimination (Fig. 2).

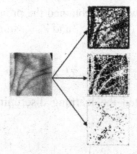

Fig. 2. Three feature matrices of the patterns of pixels.

2.4 2DLDA

Suppose $\{A_k\}, k = 1 \ldots N$ are the MLDD matrices which belong to C classes, and the *ith* class C_i has n_i sample ($\sum_{i=1}^{C} n_i = N$). Let $\overline{A}$ and $\overline{A}_i$ denote the means of *ith* class and the whole training set, respectively. 2DLDA attempts to seek a set of optimal discriminating vectors to form a transform $X = \{x_1, x_2, \ldots, x_d\}$ by maximizing the 2D Fisher criterion denoted as:

$$J(X) = \frac{X^T G_b^X}{X^T G_w^X} \tag{9}$$

where T denotes matrix transpose, G_b and G_w respectively are between-class and within-class scatter matrices:

$$G_b = \frac{1}{N} \sum_{i=1}^{C} n_i (A_i - \overline{A})(A_i - \overline{A})^T \tag{10}$$

$$G_w = \frac{1}{N} \sum_{i=1}^{C} \sum_{j=1}^{n_i} (A_i - \overline{A})(A_i - \overline{A})^T \tag{11}$$

Equation (9) can be obtained by computing orthonormal eigenvectors of $G_w^{-1} G_b$ corresponding to the d largest eigenvalues thereby maximizing function J_x. The value of d can be controlled by setting a threshold as follow:

$$\frac{\sum_{i=1}^{d} \lambda_i}{\sum_{i=1}^{n} \lambda} \geq \theta, \tag{12}$$

where $\lambda_1, \lambda_2, \ldots, \lambda_n$ is the n biggest eigenvalues of $(G_w)^{-1} G_b$ and θ is a pre-defined threshold.

2.5 $(2D)^2$LDA

$(2D)^2$LDA apply 2DLDA on the row-wise direction of MLDD matrices to learn an optimal matrix X and on the column-wise direction of MLDD matrices to learn optimal projection matrix Z. Suppose we have obtained the projection matrices X and Z, projecting the MLDD matrix $D_{m \times n}$ onto $X_{n \times d}$ and $Z_{m \times q}$ simultaneously, yielding a matrix $C_{q \times d}$ [27]:

$$C = Z^T . A . X \tag{13}$$

The matrix C is also called the learning discriminant line direction descriptor (LDLDD) for recognition.

2.6 LDLDD for Palmprint Recognition

The region of interest (ROI) for rotation and translation alignment is initially identified in palmprint images [4]. The ROI images are used as input in our proposed method. The processing steps of the proposed methods for obtaining LDLDD feature are as follows:

- Step 1: Applying Gabor filters to estimate palm lines different directions using formulas (5).
- Step 2: With each image I, computing the DNN value feature at each pixel using formulas (4).
- Step 3: Computing MLDD features: D^1, D^2, D^3 using formulas (6), (7), (8).
- Step 4: Applying $(2D)^2 LDA$ to MLDD feature: D^1, D^2, D^3 using formulas (9)–(11) and obtain the feature matrix: Y^1, Y^2, Y^3 using formulas (13).
- Step 5: The combined feature matrix $\{Y^1, Y^2, Y^3\}$ is LDLDD of input image.

Given a test palmprint image A, use our proposed method to compute LDLDD feature Y: $\{Y^1, Y^2, Y^3\}$, and apply our method to all the training images to get the

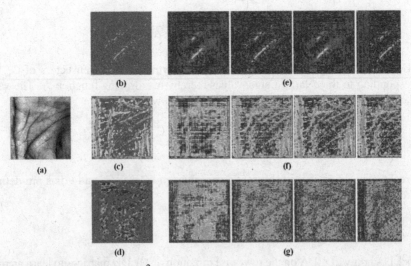

Fig. 3. Results of MLDP and $(2D)^2 LDA$: (a) original palmprint image, (b–d) MLDP image, (e–g) some reconstructed images of the MLDP image of (a–d) with (d, q) = (50, 50), (100, 100), (128, 100), (100, 128), respectively.

LDLDD feature matrix Y_k(k = 1, 2, ..., N). Then, the nearest neighbor classifier is used for classification. Here, the distance between Y and Y_k is defined by: $d(Y, Y_k) = \|Y - Y_k\|$. The distance $d(Y, Y_k)$ is between 0 and 1. The distance of perfect match is 0 (Fig. 3).

3 Experimental Results

All experiments are test on on the commonly used palmprint databases, including Palmprint PolyU and IITD. These methods were conducted using C# on PC with Intel(R) i5 core(TM) i5-4300U CPU @ 1.90 GHz (4 CPUs) ~ 2.5 GHz and Windows 10 Professional operating system. The PolyU palmprint database [28] contains 7,752 images obtained from 386 palms belonging to 193 people. The images are captured over the duration of around 60 days in two sessions. The IITD palmprint database contains 2,601 contactless palmprint images from 460 palms corresponding to 230 persons [29]. For each palm, five to six samples are collected. In our experiments, we use the ROI images with the sizes of 128 × 128 pixels. The parameters of the IITD and PolyU datasets in our experiments are listed in Table 1. Palmprint identification is a one-to-many matching process for determining the class label of a query palmprint image. The rank-1 identification rate, which compares a query sample to all of the training samples and uses the label of the most similar sample as the query sample's class label, is used to calculate identification accuracy. Verification is a one-to-one comparison that determines whether the person is who he claims to be. To generate incorrect and correct distances, each palmprint image in the testing set is compared to all palmprint images in the training set. Because a training palmprint has some templates in the training set, a palmprint query in testing set is matched with its templates in the training set to produce correct distances. The minimum of these distances is taken as correct distance. Similarly, a query in testing set is compared all templates of the other palms in training set to produce incorrect distances. We take the minimum of these distances as the incorrect distances. If the matching distance between two images from the same palm is less than the threshold, the match is genuine acceptance. Similarly, if the matching distance between two images from different palms is less than the threshold, the match is a false acceptance. EER (Equal Error Rate) was calculated using the statistical pairs of False Reject Rate (FRR) and False Accept Rate (FAR). Tables 2 and 3 show the average rank-1 identification rates and EERs of our proposed method in comparison with the state of art methods with the PolyU database and the IITD (Figs. 4 and 5).

Table 1. Parameters of the PolyU and IITD Datasets.

Dataset	Each class			All class		Number of scores	
	Training set	Testing set	Training set	Training set	Testing set		
		Registration set	Unregistration set			Correct distance	Incorrect distance
IITD	3	3	3	450(3 × 150)	450(3 × 150) + 150 (3 × 50) = 600	450	600
PolyU	5	5	5	1000(5 × 200)	1000(5 × 200) + 500(5 × 100) = 1500	1000	1500

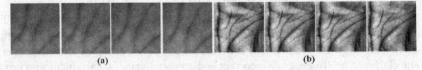

Fig. 4. Palmprint ROI samples from (a) PolyU, and (b) IITD databases.

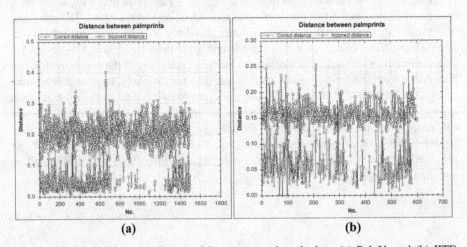

Fig. 5. Correct and incorrect distances of our proposed method on (a) PolyU, and (b) IITD datasets, respectively.

Table 2. Average performance with POLYU Dataset.

Matcher	EER (%)	Recognition rate (%)	Time of feature extraction (s)
HOL [12]	2.73	97.9	0.020
LLDP [13]	1.27	99.1	0.074
PalmNet [21]	3.87	91.2	1.610
LDDBP [4]	1.06	99.4	0.075
Our proposed method	0.87	99.8	0.350

Table 3. Average performance with IITD Dataset.

Matcher	EER (%)	Recognition rate (%)	Time of feature extraction (s)
HOL [12]	7.33	83.33	0.016
LLDP [13]	5.11	86.45	1.287
Palmnet [21]	7.78	77.56	1.710
LDDBP [4]	5.56	88.45	0.076
Our proposed method	4.45	91.22	0.431

4   Conclusion

Direction feature and the discriminability of multiple direction patterns are important in palmprint recognition. In this paper, the Learning Discriminant Line Direction Descriptor (LDLDD) is proposed for palmprint recognition that learns separately all three kind of directional pattern code. The dominant direction number (DDN) map is calculated first in this method. LDLDD will then create three MLDD maps with three multi-direction encoding methods based on the DDN map, where pixels with the same DDN values will use the same encoding strategy and belong to the same feature map. Finally, $(2D)^2LDA$ is used to train new feature subspaces that project LLDP maps from a high-dimensional space to a discriminant space with lower dimensions. The promising effectiveness of the proposed method has been validated using Hong Kong Polytechnic University's (PolyU and IITD) public databases. In the future, we will expand the current approach to other biometric recognition applications.

References

1. Kong, A., Zhang, D., Kamel, M.: A survey of palmprint recognition. Pattern Recognit. **42**(7), 1408–1418 (2009)
2. Xiao, Q., Lu, J., Jia, W., Liu, X.: Extracting palmprint ROI from whole hand image using straight line clusters. IEEE Access **7**, 74327–74339 (2019)
3. Fei, L., Zhang, B., Xu, Y., Guo, Z., Wen, J., Jia, W.: Learning discriminant direction binary palmprint descriptor. IEEE Trans. Image Process. **28**(8), 3808–3820 (2019)

4. Fei, L., Zhang, B., Xu, Y., Huang, D., Jia, W., Wen, J.: Local discriminant direction binary pattern for palmprint representation and recognition. IEEE Trans. Circuits Syst. Video Technol. **30**(2), 468–481 (2020)
5. Kong, W.K., Zhang, D., Li, W.: Palmprint feature extraction using 2-D Gabor filters. Pattern Recognit. **36**(10), 2339–2347 (2003)
6. Kong, A.W.-K., Zhang, D.: Competitive coding scheme for palmprint verification. In: Proceedings of the 17th International Conference on Pattern Recognition (ICPR), Cambridge, UK, vol. 1, pp. 520–523 (2004)
7. Jia, W., Huang, D., Zhang, D.: Palmprint verification based on robust line orientation code. Pattern Recognit. **41**(5), 1504–1513 (2008)
8. Sun, Z., Tan, T., Wang, Y., Li, S.Z.: Ordinal palmprint representation for personal identification. In: Proceedings of the IEEE Computer Society Conference on Computer Vision and Pattern Recognition (CVPR), vol. 1, pp. 279–284 (2005)
9. Guo, Z., Zhang, D., Zhang, L., Zuo, W.: Palmprint verification using binary orientation co-occurrence vector. Pattern Recognit. Lett. **30**(13), 1219–1227 (2009)
10. Zhang, L., Li, H., Niu, J.: Fragile bits in palmprint recognition. IEEE Signal Process. Lett. **19**(10), 663–666 (2012)
11. Fei, L., Zhang, B., Xu, Y., Yan, L.: Palmprint recognition using neighboring direction indicator. IEEE Trans. Human-Mach. Syst. **46**(6), 787–798 (2016)
12. Jia, W., Hu, R.-X., Lei, Y.-K., Zhao, Y., Gui, J.: Histogram of oriented lines for palmprint recognition. IEEE Trans. Syst. Man, Cybern. Syst. **44**(3), 385–395 (2014)
13. Luo, Y.-T., et al.: Local line directional pattern for palmprint recognition. Pattern Recognit. **50**, 26–44 (2016)
14. Fei, L., Wen, J., Zhang, Z., Yan, K., Zhong, Z.: Local multiple directional pattern of palmprint image. In: 23rd International Conference on Pattern Recognition (ICPR), pp. 3013–3018 (2016)
15. Li, G., Kim, J.: Palmprint recognition with Local Micro-structure Tetra Pattern. Pattern Recognit. **61**, 29–46 (2017)
16. Zhang, L., Li, L., Yang, A., Shen, Y., Yang, M.: Towards contactless palmprint recognition: a novel device, a new benchmark, and a collaborative representation based identification approach. Pattern Recognit. **69**, 199–212 (2017)
17. Fei, L., Zhang, B., Teng, S., Zhang, W.: Local apparent and latent direction extraction for palmprint recognition. Inf. Sci. **473**, 59–72 (2019)
18. Wen, J., et al.: Robust sparse linear discriminant analysis. IEEE Trans. Circuits Syst. Video Technol. 1-13 (2018). https://doi.org/10.1109/TCSVT.2018.2799214
19. Ivana, T., Frossard, P.: Dictionary learning. IEEE Signal Process. Mag. **28**(2), 27–38 (2011)
20. Lu, J., Liong, V.E., Zhou, X., Zhou, J.: Learning compact binary face descriptor for face recognition. IEEE Trans. Pattern Anal. Mach. Intell. **37**(10), 2041–2056 (2015)
21. Genovese, A., Piuri, V., Plataniotis, K.N., Scotti, F.: PalmNet: GaborPCA convolutional networks for touchless palmprint recognition. IEEE Trans. Inf. Forensics Security **14**(12), 3160–3174 (2019)
22. Svoboda, J., Masci, J., Bronstein, M.M.: Palmprint recognition via discriminative index learning. In: Proceeding of International Conference on Pattern Recognition, pp. 4232–4237 (2016)
23. Minaee, S., Wang, Y.: Palmprint Recognition Using Deep Scattering Convolutional Network, pp. 1–13. arXiv preprint arXiv:1603.09027 (2016)
24. Ribaric, S., Fratric, I.: A biometric identification system based on eigenpalm and eigenfinger features. IEEE Trans. Pattern Anal. Mach. Intell. **27**(11), 1698–1709 (2005)
25. Hoang, V.T., Thai, L.H.: On Discriminant Orientation Extraction Using GridLDA of Line Orientation Maps for Palmprint Identification (2014). https://doi.org/10.1007/978-3-319-02741-8_21

26. Rida, I., Herault, R., Marcialis, G., Gasso, G.: Palmprint recognition with an efficient data driven ensemble classifier. Pattern Recogn. Lett. (2018). https://doi.org/10.1016/j.patrec.2018.04.033,pp.1-7

27. Van, H.T., Hung, K.D., Van, G.V., Thi, Q.P., Le, T.H.: Palmprint recognition using discriminant local line directional representation. In: Le Thi, H.A., Le, H.M., Pham Dinh, T., Nguyen, N.T. (eds.) ICCSAMA 2019. AISC, vol. 1121, pp. 208–217. Springer, Cham (2020). https://doi.org/10.1007/978-3-030-38364-0_19

28. PolyU Palmprint Database. http://www.comp.polyu.edu.hk/~biometrics/. Accessed 1 Jan 2004

29. IITD Touchless Palmprint Database. Accessed 10 June 2008. https://www4.comp.polyu.edu.hk/~csajaykr/IITD/Database_Palm.htm

Layering Images with Convolution Neural Networks on Cloud Computing

Tam Van Nguyen[1], Luan Khanh Tran[2] (ID), Tu Cam Thi Tran[3] (ID), and Hiep Xuan Huynh[4(✉)] (ID)

[1] Department of Mechanical Weakness - Information Technology, Office of Hau Giang Provincial Party Committee, Vi Thanh, Hau Giang Province, Vietnam
tamnv.vptu@haugiang.gov.vn
[2] Bac Lieu University, Bac Lieu, Vietnam
tkluan@blu.edu.vn
[3] Vinh Long University of Technology Education, Vinh Long, Vinh Long Province, Vietnam
tuttc@vlute.edu.vn
[4] Can Tho University, Can Tho, Vietnam
hxhiep@ctu.edu.vn

Abstract. Artificial neural networks combined with deep learning (DL) techniques are becoming a very powerful tool that gives the best performance for many difficult problems such as: the speech recognition, the image recognition, etc. the language processing. The training of the neural network models takes place in many different languages, different techniques, different sizes of organizations. However, previous studies only focused on the model training techniques, the datasets, currently there is no research that fully introduces running artificial neural network models, the network models are run in the cloud connecting directly from RStudio. In this article, we focus on creating models and applying deep learning models of the artificial neural networks based on the cloud computing, in order to create a separate research direction. The results of this study open up a new approach to cloud-based deep learning programming, providing an additional choice of the deep learning approaches for those wishing to enter the field.

Keywords: Deep learning · Cloud computing · Keras · AWS cloud · Convolution Neural Networks · Image

1 Introduction

In neural networks, convolutional neural networks [1] (ConvNets or CNNs, Convolutional Neural Networks) is one of the main methods to perform image recognition and image classification. CNN is widely used in a number of fields such as object detection, face recognition... Artificial Neural Network (ANN) is a programming model, it describes the operation of the neural network [2]. Artificial neural network combined with deep learning techniques (Deep Learning - DL) is becoming a very powerful tool

C. V. Phan and T. D. Nguyen (Eds.): ICTCC 2022, LNICST 473, pp. 160–171, 2023.
https://doi.org/10.1007/978-3-031-28790-9_11

that gives the best performance for many difficult problems such as: the image recognition, the speech recognition or the natural language processing [3, 4]. That has spurred the discovery of the network by both new and professional researchers in many other fields. There are a lot of the previous studies in the implementation of image classification with convolutional neural networks but mainly revolve around understanding neural networks, analysis techniques, studying practical applications from neural networks. Artificial neural networks such as: Conceptual understanding of convolutional neural network a deep learning approach [5], Deep Learning Approach for Automatic Classification of X-Ray Images using Convolutional Neural Network [6], etc.

However, there is no research that fully introduces running neural network model on cloud computing platform directly from RStudio. The problem is how to directly interact with the structure of the cloud computing from RStudio, using cloud storage services to store data to run for the models, run experiments for some neural network model to represent the possible results of the proposed model.

In this article, we present a practical direction of deep learning convolutional neural network on cloud computing. This approach is carried out on the basis of studying the literature and choosing the simplest method to conduct the experiment. Using the Rstudio to connect with a cloud server has the benefits: (1). The works will be more proactive. (2). When starting the server, we only need to interact with Rstudio without having to log in to the cloud server. (3). The execution log is recorded directly on the Rstudio session.

The structure of the article is presented as follows: In Sect. 2, we present the understanding of AWS cloud computing, the connection technique from RStudio to AWS. Section 3 presents an overview of CNN, introduces 3 basic models of CNN. Section 4 presents an experimental presentation of the image classification model on the AWS cloud. Finally, the conclusion is shown in Sect. 6, this part presents the results, the comments and the evaluations of the proposed model.

2 AWS Cloud and Interactive Engineering in RStudio

2.1 AWS Cloud

AWS (Amazon Web Services) is a cloud computing services platform that provides compute, database storage, distribution, and other functions [7]. In this article, AWS is used to create a server from RStudio, and AWS is used to create the S3 storage service for the article's experiments.

2.2 Interactive Engineering with AWS in RStudio

To interact with AWS in RStudio, an AWS account needs to be created by the user, once successfully registered, the system needs to be logged in with the newly created account, to the IAM management console, the key pair is generated for access to AWS from RStudio. Note that since the newly generated key pair information is only seen once, this key pair information should be stored in a secure place with secret mode [8].

On RStudio, the aws.ec2 library is installed to perform interactions with AWS. This package is not available on CRAN yet. To install the latest development version, it can be installed from the cloud drat repository:

```
# latest stable version
install.packages("aws.ec2", repos = c(getOption("repos"),
 "http://cloudyr.github.io/drat"))
```

The example below demonstrates interactions from RStudio to the AWS cloud, launching an RStudio server instance, and launching an Amazon Machine Image (AMI), environment variables containing the credentials that need to be reset.

```
library(aws.ec2)
Sys.setenv(
  "AWS_ACCESS_KEY_ID" = "mykey",
  "AWS_SECRET_ACCESS_KEY"="mysecretkey",
  "AWS_DEFAULT_REGION" = "us-west-1"
)
```

The code below will create an RStudio server and set up the ports to connect from R, and launch the newly created server.

```
# Describe the AMI (from: http://www.louisaslett.com/RStu-
dio_AMI/)
image <- "ami-3b0c205e" # us-east-1
#image <- "ami-93805fea" # eu-west-1
describe_images(image)

# Check your VPC and Security Group settings
## subnet
subnets <- describe_subnets()
## security group
my_sg <- create_sgroup("r-ec2-sg", "Allow my IP", vpc = sub-
nets[[1L]])
## use existing ip address or create a new one
ips <- describe_ips()
if (!length(ips)) {
    ips[[1L]] <- allocate_ip("vpc")
}

# create an SSH keypair
my_keypair <- create_keypair("r-ec2-example")
pem_file <- tempfile(fileext = ".pem")
cat(my_keypair$keyMaterial, file = pem_file)

# Launch the instance using appropriate settings
i <- run_instances(image = image,
                   type = "t2.micro", # <- you might want to
change this
                   subnet = subnets[[1L]],
                   sgroup = my_sg,
                   keypair = my_keypair)
Sys.sleep(5L) # wait for instance to boot

# associate IP address with instance
instance_ip <- get_instance_public_ip(i)
if (is.na(instance_ip)) {
    instance_ip <- associate_ip(i, ips[[1L]])$publicIp
}
# authorize access from this IP
try(authorize_ingress(my_sg))
try(authorize_egress(my_sg))
```

The code below shows the steps to create the direct connections to SSH through RStudio using the "ssh" package. Successful connection, we perform some basic commands such as creating an R file with name is "helloworld.R", inserting commands into this file and uploading this file to the server to run it.

```
# log in to instance
library("ssh")
session <- ssh::ssh_connect(paste0("ubuntu@", instance_ip),
 keyfile = pem_file, passwd = "rstudio")
# write a quick little R script to execute
cat("'hello world!'\nsprintf('2+2 is %d', 2+2)\n", file =
 "helloworld.R")
# upload it to instance
invisible(ssh::scp_upload(session, "helloworld.R"))
# execute script on instance
x <- ssh::ssh_exec_wait(session, "Rscript helloworld.R")
## disconnect from instance
ssh_disconnect(session)
```

After the job is done, we must make sure to turn off it and to clean up it.

```
## stop and terminate the instance
stop_instances(i[[1L]])
terminate_instances(i[[1L]])

## revoke access from this IP to security group
try(revoke_ingress(my_sg))
try(revoke_egress(my_sg))

## delete keypair
delete_keypair(my_keypair)

## release IP address
release_ip(ips[[1L]])
```

2.3 Organize Data on AWS

We use the simple storage service on the AWS cloud (S3) to store the data for the deep learning models in this article. Creating a Simple Storage group of Amazon for the data with the default name: sagemaker-<aws-region-name>-<aws account number>.

```
session <- sagemaker$Session()
bucket <- session$default_bucket()
prefix <- 'r-batch-transform'
```

After running the above statements, we have the data stack on the AWS cloud. Specifically, in the S3 service, the default name for my account is: "sagemaker-us-east-1-575208616377". We will use this account to run experimental models.

3 Convolutional Neural Network Learning

Convolutional Neural Networks (CNNs) are one of the advanced Deep Learning models. It helps us to build the intelligent systems with high accuracy. CNN is widely used in the problem of the recognizing objects in the images [9]. The image classification models: VGG-19, ResNet50 and Incep-tionV3 in this study are commonly models in the practice.

3.1 VGG-19

VGG – 19 is a convolutional neural network, it is trained on more than a million images from the ImageNet database (this is an image base consisting of 14 million images, it is organized according to wordnet hierarchy), VGG – 19 is the visual network, it supports the study of the images and the sights. (See Fig. 1).

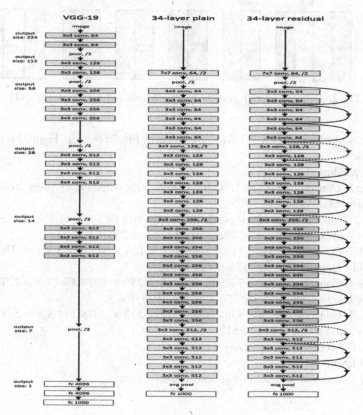

Fig. 1. Description of the model VGG-19.

This network consists of 19 layers deep and can classify images into thousands of types of objects like animals or objects. A fixed size of (224 * 224) RGB image was given as input to this network which means that the matrix was of shape (224,224.3). Each pixel is subtracted the mean RGB value, this work computed over the whole training set in data. Using kernels of (3 * 3) size with a stride size of 1 pixel. Spatial padding was used to preserve the spatial resolution of the image. Max pooling was performed over a 2 * 2-pixel windows with stride 2. Using Rectified linear unit (ReLu) to make the model classify better and to improve computational time because the "tanh" functions or "sigmoid" functions are used in the previous models. Implemented three fully connected layers from which first two were of size 4096 and after that a layer with 1000 channels for 1000-way ILSVRC classification and the final layer is a SoftMax function.

3.2 ResNet50

The overall model of ResNet is shown in Fig. 2.

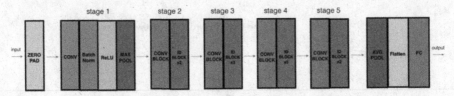

Fig. 2. Detailed description of the neural network architecture ResNet [11].

Identity block - ID BLOCK ×3 means 3 Identity blocks overlap. Figure 2 is depicted as follows:

Zero-padding: Input with (3, 3).

Stage 1: Convolution (Conv1) with 64 filters with shape (7, 7), using stride (2, 2). BatchNorm, MaxPooling (3, 3).

Stag 2: Convolutional block use 3 filters with size $64 \times 64 \times 256$, f = 3, s = 1. There are 2 Identity blocks with filter size $64 \times 64 \times 256$, f = 3.

Stage 3: Convolutional use 3 filter sizes $128 \times 128 \times 512$, f = 3, s = 2. There are 3 Identity blocks with filter size $128 \times 128 \times 512$, f = 3.

Stage 4: Convolutional use 3 filters size $256 \times 256 \times 1024$, f = 3, s = 2. There are 5 Identity blocks with filter size $256 \times 256 \times 1024$, f = 3.

Stage 5: Convolutional use 3 filters size $512 \times 512 \times 2048$, f = 3, s = 2. There are 2 Identity blocks with filter size $512 \times 512 \times 2048$, f = 3.

The 2D Average Pooling: using with size (2, 2).

The Flatten.

Fully Connected (Dense): using SoftMax activation.

3.3 InceptionV3

Inception v3 was originally released in 2015 [12–14]. Inception v3 has a total of 42 layers and low error rate. The design of Inceptionv3 was intended to allow deeper networks while also keeping the number of parameters from growing too large: it has "under 25 million parameters". The model of InceptionV3 is shown in Fig. 3.

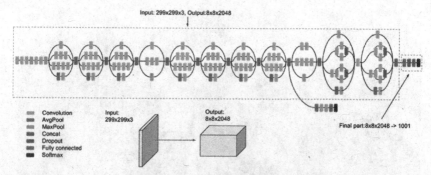

Fig. 3. The model of InceptionV3.

Table 1. Describes the outline of the V3 model at startup. Here, the output size of each module is the input size of the next module.

Type	Patch/stride	Input size
Conv	3 × 3/2	299 × 299 × 3
Conv	3 × 3/1	149 × 149/32
Conv padded	3 × 3/1	147 × 147/32
Pool	3 × 3/2	147 × 147/64
Conv	3 × 3/1	73 × 73/64
Conv	3 × 3/2	71 × 71/80
Conv	3 × 3/1	35 × 35 × 192
3 x Inception	Module 1	35 × 35 × 288
5 x Inception	Module 2	17 × 17 × 768
2 x Inception	Module 3	8 × 8 × 1280
Pool	8 × 8	8 × 8 × 2048
Linear	Logits	1 × 1 × 2048
SoftMax	Classifier	1 × 1 × 1000

When the Inception V3 kicks in, it's made up of 42 layers, which is higher than the previous V1 and V2 models.

4 Experiment

4.1 Data

In this article, Fig. 4 was selected for the experiment with the image of an elephant, it is walking in the woods, the format of this image has an extension, that is ".jpg", the size of this image is 224 × 224 pixels, that is the input matrix for the proposed model,

Fig. 4. Image of an elephant, it is walking in the woods.

4.2 Tool

As introduced above, in this experiment we will use the R Programming Language in RStudio, and an AWS cloud account to be able to provide an R server and a hosting service. The image classification models include VGG-19, ResNet50, and InceptionV3. Finally, we use the corresponding support library packages including: aws.ec2, keras, TensorFlow.

4.3 Scenario

The image of the elephant is prepared with size 224 × 224 to match the model. Then we save the image in the AWS cloud S3 service. From R make the connection to the server on AWS. Finally, we will run the models: VGG-19, ResNet50, and InceptionV3.

Classifying ImageNet's layers with ResNet50, Fig. 5:

```
  class_name class_description      score
1  n02504013   Indian_elephant 0.79484349
2  n01871265            tusker 0.11192206
3  n02504458  African_elephant 0.08656283
```

Fig. 5. The experimental results with ResNet50.

Figure 5 presents the classification results with ResNet50 model. The results show that trust level of class "n02504013 Indian_elephant" is 0.79484349. This trust level is higher than the trust level of class n01871265 and the trust level of class n02504458.

Extracted features from an arbitrary intermediate layer with VGG19 in Fig. 6:

⊙ layer	list	[(..), (..), (..)]
layers	int	3
load	method	<bound method ImageFile.load of <PIL.JpegImagePlugin.JpegImageFile image mode=RG ...
load_djpeg	method	<bound method JpegImageFile.load_djpeg of <PIL.JpegImagePlugin.JpegImageFile ima ...
load_end	method	<bound method ImageFile.load_end of <PIL.JpegImagePlugin.JpegImageFile image mod ...
load_prepare	method	<bound method ImageFile.load_prepare of <PIL.JpegImagePlugin.JpegImageFile image ...
load_read	method	<bound method JpegImageFile.load_read of <PIL.JpegImagePlugin.JpegImageFile imag ...
map	NoneType	None
mode	str	'RGB'
palette	NoneType	None
paste	method	<bound method Image.paste of <PIL.JpegImagePlugin.JpegImageFile image mode=RGB s ...
point	method	<bound method Image.point of <PIL.JpegImagePlugin.JpegImageFile image mode=RGB s ...
putalpha	method	<bound method Image.putalpha of <PIL.JpegImagePlugin.JpegImageFile image mode=RG ...
putdata	method	<bound method Image.putdata of <PIL.JpegImagePlugin.JpegImageFile image mode=RGB ...
putpalette	method	<bound method Image.putpalette of <PIL.JpegImagePlugin.JpegImageFile image mode= ...
putpixel	method	<bound method Image.putpixel of <PIL.JpegImagePlugin.JpegImageFile image mode=RG ...
pyaccess	NoneType	None

Fig. 6. Feature extraction results from a layer.

The result of the extracted features from an arbitrary intermediate layer at class 0 × 000001835CE73910 have 150528 extracted elements.

Tweaking InceptionV3 on a new layer group in Fig. 7:

```
1  input_2
2  conv2d
3  batch_normalization
4  activation
5  conv2d_1
6  batch_normalization_1
7  activation_1
8  conv2d_2
9  batch_normalization_2
10 activation_2
11 max_pooling2d
12 conv2d_3
13 batch_normalization_3
14 activation_3
15 conv2d_4
16 batch_normalization_4
17 activation_4
18 max_pooling2d_1
19 conv2d_8
20 batch_normalization_8
21 activation_8
22 conv2d_6
23 conv2d_9
24 batch_normalization_6
25 batch_normalization_9
26 activation_6
27 activation_9
28 average_pooling2d
29 conv2d_5
30 conv2d_10
31 conv2d_10
32 conv2d_11
33 batch_normalization_5
34 batch_normalization_7
35 batch_normalization_10
36 batch_normalization_11
37 activation_5
38 activation_7
39 activation_10
40 activation_11
41 mixed0
42 conv2d_15
43 batch_normalization_15
44 activation_15
45 conv2d_13
46 conv2d_16
47 batch_normalization_13
48 batch_normalization_16
49 activation_13
50 activation_16
51 average_pooling2d_1
52 conv2d_12
```

Fig. 7. The results of tweaking InceptionV3 on a new layer group.

Input_tensor: The Keras tensor option (i.e. the output of layers.Input()) is used as input to the model. Input_shape: shaper option, this option is specified if include_top is false or the input shape should be (299, 299, 3) (with the channels_last is the data format) or (3, 299, 299) (with the channels_first is the data format). It must have three input channels and the width and height cannot be less than 139. For example (150, 150, 3) is valid. Optional number of classes to classify images into, only to be specified if "in-clude_top" is True, and if no "weights" argument is specified.

With the accuracy of VGG-19 = 90.0, Restnet 50 = 92.1 and Inception V3 = 93.7, respectively. The results show that the accuracy of all three models is very high. However, the accuracy of Incemtion V3 is the highest.

5   Discussion

To do well with deep learning on the AWS cloud, we need to have an understanding about their activities, understanding about deep learning algorithms, understanding about the field of research in practice, and creativity. All must be harmoniously combined to create a complete deep learning model. In this study, we only use some deep learning models from the convolutional neural networks. But in reality, there are many types of the deep learning models, so for a more comprehensive look we can apply this approach to other types of the deep learning models.

6   Conclusion

In this work, we have presented a deep learning approach by a simple process, specifically, three techniques: VGG-19, ResNet50, and InceptionV3 are used in the experimental model. The experimental results show that products created from deep learning model are feasible, it provides a new view of the system for the users who want to learn about the field of deep learning. Although incomplete, it has created the first steps for in-depth research on the convolutional neural networks learning on the AWS cloud in the future.

References

1. Dogaru, R., Chua, L.O.: Universal CNN cells. Int. J. Bifurcation Chaos – IJBC **9**, 1–48 (1999)
2. Awodele, O., Jegede, O.: Neural networks and its application in engineering. In: Proceedings of Informing Science & IT Education Conference (InSITE) (2009)
3. Samek, W., Binder, A., Montavon, G., Lapuschkin, S., Müller, R.K.: Evaluating the visualization of what a deep neural network has learned. IEEE Trans. Neural Netw. Learn. Syst. **28**(11), 2660–2673 (2016)
4. Abiodun, I.O., Jantan, A., Omolara, E.A., Dada, V.K., Mohamed, A.N., Arshad, H.: State-of-the-art in artificial neural network applications: a survey. Heliyon **4**(11), e00938 (2018). PMCID: PMC6260436
5. Schmidhuber, J.: Deep learning in neural networks: an overview. Neural Netw. **61**, 85–117 (2014). PMID: 25462637
6. Indolia, S., Goswani, K.A., Mishra, S.P., Asopa, P.: Conceptual understanding of convolutional neural network- a deep learning approach. Procedia Comput. Sci. **132**, 679–688 (2018)

7. Mondal, S., Agarwal, K., Rashid, M.: Deep learning approach for automatic classification of X-ray images using convolutional neural network. In: 2019 Fifth International Conference on Image Information Processing (ICIIP), vol. 9, pp. 326–331 (2019)
8. AWS Homepage. http://www.aws.amazon.com/vi/. Accessed 30 June 2022
9. Wäldchen, J., Mäder, P.: Machine learning for image-based species identification. Methods Ecol. Evol. **9** (2018)
10. Wen, L.; Li, X., Gao, L.: A new transfer learning based on VGG-19 network for fault diagnosis. In: 2019 IEEE 23rd International Conference on Computer Supported Cooperative Work in Design (CSCWD), pp. 205–209 (2019)
11. https://viblo.asia/p/gioi-thieu-mang-resnet-vyDZOa7R5wj (2020)
12. iq.opengenus.org. https://iq.opengenus.org/inception-v3-model-architecture/. Accessed 20 June 2022
13. Xia, X., Xu, C., Nan B.: Inception-v3 for flower classification. In: 2017 2nd International Conference on Image, Vision and Computing (ICIVC), pp. 783–787 (2017)
14. Wang, C., et al.: Pulmonary image classification based on inception-v3 transfer learning model. IEEE Access **7**, 146533–146541 (2019)

Author Index

C

Cuu, Ho Van   61

D

Dinh-Thanh, Nguyen   123
Do Van, Thanh   43
Do, Nam Hoang   88
Duc, Le Anh   79

G

Giao, Bui Cong   61

H

Horalek, Josef   9, 23
Huynh, Hiep Xuan   160

L

Le, Thai Hoang   148

M

Minh, Hai Nguyen   43

N

Nguyen, Hai Thanh   136

P

Pham, Dang Van   88
Phan, Thong Dinh Duy   148
Phan, Trang Huyen   136
Phan, Vinh Cong   88

S

Sobeslav, Vladimir   9, 23
Svoboda, Tomas   9

T

Thi-Ngoc-Diem, Pham   123, 136
Tran, Chi Le Hoang   136
Tran, Luan Khanh   160
Tran, Tu Cam Thi   160
Tung, Nguyen Thanh   79

U

Urbanik, Patrik   9, 23

V

Van Han, Nguyen   3
Van Nguyen, Tam   160
Van Thien, Hoang   148
Vinh, Phan Cong   3

C. V. Phan and T. D. Nguyen (Eds.): ICTCC 2022, LNICST 473, p. 173, 2023.
https://doi.org/10.1007/978-3-031-28790-9

Printed in the United States
by Baker & Taylor Publisher Services

Printed in the United States
by Baker & Taylor Publisher Services